When Words Fail

Sept. 2000
ELUL 5760

TO SANDY,

with warmest wishes,

Sholom

When Words Fail

A Religious Response to Undeserved Hurt

Rabbi Sholom Stern

JASON ARONSON INC.
Northvale, New Jersey
Jerusalem

This book was set in 12 pt. Granjon by Alabama Book Composition of Deatsville, AL and printed and bound by Book-mart Press, Inc. of North Bergen, NJ.

Library of Congress Cataloging-in-Publication Data

Stern, Sholom.
    When words fail : a religious response to undeserved hurt / by
Sholom Stern.
        p. cm.
    Includes bibliographical references and index.
    ISBN 0-7657-6093-2
    1. Stern Sholom. 2. Pastoral counseling (Judaism)
    3. Loneliness—Religious aspects—Judaism. 4. Consolation (Judaism)
    5. Suffering—Religious aspects—Judaism. I. Title.
    BM652.5.S74 1999
    296.6'1—dc21   99-19291

Printed in the United States of America on acid–free paper. For information and catalog write to Jason Aronson Inc., 230 Livingston Street, Northvale, NJ 07647-1726, or visit our website: www.aronson.com

In loving memory of my parents
Nahum Zalmon and Anna Stern, *z"l*

Tiferet Banim Avotam
"The glory of children are their parents"
(Pirkei Avot 6:8)

CONTENTS

INTRODUCTION

When telling people that I was writing a book dealing with themes like illness, pain, loneliness, death, and suffering from the perspective of classical Jewish texts, the question to follow was, why? The assumption by many was that the book was written in response to a friend's triumph over illness, or to an agonizing death of a loved one, or to my own brush with illness and death.

As if to apologize for not having a heartrending story to tell them, I would say, "I'm sorry to disappoint you, but there has been no earth-shattering experience in my life that propelled me to write this book. Essentially, I wrote this book so that I could share with the reader the insights of our tradition on themes that are close to all of our hearts."

As one who has served in the rabbinate for well over three decades, I was all too familiar with serious illness and death. Inexplicable deaths of healthy robust people, toddlers, young college students, recently wed people, and suicides are not strange to a rabbi in a synagogue. They are all within the orbit of what a rabbi and his congregation must face together.

There were those phone calls like the one when I learned that someone whom I had seen the day before was now in the hospital wavering between life and death after being injured in an automobile accident. The rabbi is expected to introduce a note of order out of chaos, some meaning out of the absurd and painful realities of life. With tragedy so often occurring, I always pray that I will never be so callous as to adjust to the suffering of others. Yet, however difficult bearing the aforementioned kind of tragedies was, they were happening to other individuals.

As for me, life was beautiful. I have always had a very high energy level and almost fancied myself to be immortal. With pride I would like to tell people of my late maternal grandfather, a renowned rabbi in Williamsburg, Brooklyn, who upon retiring from the rabbinate at age ninety-two, moved to Israel and lived in Jerusalem until his death seventeen years later. At the time of his death he was the oldest man living in Israel. He had been lucid until his very last hour on this earth. From his deathbed, twenty minutes before he expired, while reflecting on his life, he told my mother that he came into this world without any understanding and he was now leaving without any understanding. He then asked my mother to listen to him as he recited the *Shema*. How patriarchal, I thought, was it to meet his mortality with a trenchant observation and with the hallowed words of our tradition on his lips.

Both of my parents were granted longevity, each dying at the age of ninety. I recall once that in a seminar in graduate school a teacher asked her students how long they expected to live. I answered, "till ninety-nine." Perplexed, she inquired why I selected ninety-nine. I told her that in the Talmud it is recorded that one who reaches the century mark is as though he was dead. What was fascinating about my truthful response, said in jest, was that I deemed myself to be in control of my own destiny. I was the one imagining termination of my life just at the right time. Mine was the hubris of one who at that stage of his life thought that if he ran fast enough the angel of death would not catch up with him. I acted as if illness was something that would elude me, at least for many years to come.

Then one day after I submitted this book to the publisher for editing my paradise world began to unravel. In a routine medical checkup it was discovered that I had a tumor in my bladder. The doctor reassured me that there was no need to be alarmed and that generally such tumors were benign. Surgery took place on a Friday morning and six hours later I was discharged from the hospital. In order to convince myself that everything was in order I returned to work two days later on a Sunday morning to officiate at a funeral.

A couple of days later my wife asked me if the biopsy report came back. I was embarrassed to tell her that I had forgotten all about it. After all, if I had a benign tumor, why bother to check. Moments later, just as I was ready to call the doctor, I received a call from his office asking me to come in the next day to speak to him. At that point I felt like the first rumblings of trouble had descended upon me. Immediately I knew that if the pathologist's report was that the tumor removed was benign, the doctor would not be asking to see me. The next morning, filled with anxiety and fears, I saw the doctor. When my wife insisted on coming I did not protest. I was embarrassed to admit to her that I really needed her support.

As soon as the doctor started to speak and tell me how, theoretically, the tumor was fully removed I became very suspicious. I interjected, "What's the force of the word *theoretically?*" He went on to explain that he could not be one hundred percent certain that all of the tumor had been removed. He then showed me the report of the pathologist, which indicated that I had urothelial carcinoma with a high grade tumor and suspected invasion into the vascular system. In other words, the cancerous cells were malignant. "Fortunately," he said, "there has been no invasion of these cells in the muscle area of the bladder." He then drew diagrams of the bladder and gave my wife and me a crash course on all of its intricacies. "Where do we go from here?" I asked. "Your best bet is Memorial Sloan Kettering Hospital. They will know how to deal with it," he calmly and caringly responded.

As he was speaking, the word *cancer* kept darting through my mind. The thought of me being a patient at Sloan Kettering, a cancer research center, was terrifying: "This was the place for sick people, not healthy people like me." I still found comfort in denying that there was anything wrong with me. Three months later, after undergoing two more surgeries, or what are euphemistically and therapeutically referred to as "procedures," my worst fears were not realized. The biopsy from each of the procedures indicated no cancerous cells in the bladder.

"So what did you learn after subjecting yourself to three procedures in a span of three months?" a friend asked me. "I don't want to sound pedestrian," I answered, "but there is no way to feel the preciousness of life without undergoing some experience in which your life is threatened." My illness startled me and made me realize the truth of the cliché of life being a gift that can never be taken for granted.

What I had known cognitively and intellectually, I now knew emotionally and personally. For example, when visiting ill people in the hospital I often would present to them a booklet containing prayers and inspirational thoughts that hopefully provided a measure of support and healing. I had read the entire booklet carefully before deciding to distribute it to those confined to hospitals or their homes because of illness. When I took ill I opened up the booklet and started to read a paragraph that spoke of how the coming days may hold danger for the one who is ill. It continued by speaking of the need for strength that has its source in God. I immediately burst into tears, identifying completely with those words asking God to give me the strength that I desperately needed to cope with my situation. The words now had penetrated right through my gut.

In one of the chapters of this book, "Give Me Friendship or Death," I cited a number of biblical and rabbinic sources dealing with the blessings of friendships. In reflecting on those three terrifying months of illness, I concluded that most of us underestimate the role that family and friends play in the healing process.

I'm reminded of the anecdote told of a fundraiser for a hospital that was on the cutting edge of medicine. The fundraiser always praised the hospital to the hilt speaking of it as a caring institution pioneering and trailblazing new approaches in medicine. One day he decided to take an in-depth tour of the hospital. After spending a week visiting every department of the hospital he confided in a friend the following, "You know all the lies that I have been telling about this hospital over the years? Well, they are all true." When I revisited Jewish sources that speak of how indispensable friendships and acts of empathy and kindness are in the healing process, the first thought that came to my mind was that all the "lies" of the talmudic sages that I have shared with others were all true. Today many may feel bolstered by the weight of modern medical technology. I felt even more bolstered by the love and care of family and friends. The all consuming attention lavished on me by my wife, Batya, and my children, Eliyahu and Danya, who guarded and carefully monitored every step I made, particularly when I discouraged them with one of my favorite refrains, "Everything is alright," made me feel very protected and secure.

Other family members and friends whose comforting, reassuring, and empathic words, daily inquiries, prayers, and humorous quips made me feel that in the battle for survival I had the best supporting cast.

I am indebted and grateful to the doctors who in addition to healing me treated me as a person and not simply as another bladder case.

Ralph Waldo Emerson once said that, "He has seen but half the universe who has never been shown the house of pain." I write these words in a state of good health and guarded optimism. I'm grateful that the pain incurred by three procedures is now only a memory and not something that I must endure.

Now let me tell you something about this book.

I have written this book for the pastoral counselor and for all

those who accept the teachings of their respective religious traditions and the insights of the behavioral sciences as being indispensable tools in the healing process. The truth of the matter is
that anyone who brings with him the spiritual or sacramental
teachings of his faith combined with an orientation employed by
counselors, psychologists or psychotherapists is functioning as a
pastoral counselor.

Often in conversing with others we find ourselves saying
something like, "I don't want to sound like a psychologist, but
from the way I see it, she is depressed." In accounting for the
behavior of others we are apt to speak of their unconscious moti-
vations. Or in accounting for the forgetfulness of a friend we find
ourselves saying, "You must have suppressed it." We use the term
inferiority complex, as popularized by the psychologist Alfred
Adler, even though we may never have read anything he wrote.
To a certain degree we all function as psychologists. Similarly,
many of us who are not pastoral counselors function as pastoral
counselors.

It is widely accepted that pastoral counseling considers the
tripartite nature of man—his body, mind, and spirit—when
attempting to help others. It may safely be said that all pastoral
counselors view God as an important component in the healing
process of man. Anytime we pray on behalf of someone, we have
acted in a certain sense as a pastoral counselor. Anytime we enter
a Jewish home to visit the bereaved sitting *shivah* and we recite the
traditional formula, *HaMaḳom Yenachem Etchem B'Toch Shaar
Aveilei Tziyon V'Rushalayim*, "May God comfort you together
with all the mourners of Zion and Jerusalem," we assume the role
of the pastoral counselor. We function as pastoral counselors simply by inviting a friend to a synagogue, church, or mosque, or to
seek guidance and strength from his or her religion in trying
moments.

All clergymen have been confronted with situations in which
people turn to them for counseling. As a rabbi many times I have

been consulted as one would consult a psychologist. The most common reason for people consulting me is that they have a relationship in need of repair with a loved one, be it a spouse, a child, or a parent. There have been many instances in which advice has been given independent of encouraging the person to develop a relationship with God.

At the same time it is important to bear in mind that pastoral counseling accepts the spiritual reality of God. In one form or another every clergyman in his or her own way attempts to bring God into the lives of others. Healing has at its base a spiritual reality that reaches to some sort of belief. As one raised in the Jewish faith, in which studying sacred texts like the Torah and Talmud has been elevated to an act of worship, I continue to struggle with the challenge of how these sacred texts, which purport to represent the word of God, impact the lives of people who live in a predominantly secular world. My understanding of man has been largely shaped and influenced by the reading of those sacred texts along with insights gleaned from the behavioral sciences. This work is rooted in the conviction that synthesizing Jewish tradition with the behavioral sciences enables one to gain a deeper and more mature understanding of how to cope with existential issues that confront us.

What I have attempted to do in this book is to take themes such as loneliness, companionship, comfort, listening, silence, nonverbal communication, responding to tragedy, and reconciling ourselves with a God who appears at times to be silent to our cries, and share with the reader interpretations of some of the biblical and rabbinic sources on these issues. I have also chosen to include perspectives from the behavioral sciences on the aforementioned issues.

I know that some may argue that this book is laced with a feeling of "me, too." That is, it contains an outlook that wants to demonstrate the similarities between Judaism and the behavioral sciences. I have wrestled with the thought of compiling and interpreting only sources from biblical and rabbinic literature on topics related to pastoral counseling and letting them speak for themselves without citing sources from the behavioral sciences. However, my mind is not compartmentalized and I choose to study sacred texts with the benefit of insights from a variety of disciplines, including sociology, psychology, psychiatry, psychotherapy, and so forth.

The religion that I represent claims to express eternal verities. Other religions make similar claims. Ultimately the eternal verities of any religion are tested in the laboratories of daily life where men and women are challenged to treat others with decency and kindness. Similarly, the effectiveness of any pastoral counselor will be determined by his ability to act kindly and empathetically, and his ability to accept all human shortcomings. The pastoral counselor must be trained to accept the social failures of others as readily as he or she accepts social successes.

It is important that we be honest with ourselves and admit that all too often religion has chosen to speak in the name of authority rather than with the voice of compassion. Thinkers throughout the ages have engaged in metaphysical speculation about God and have claimed to be the possessors of true opinions concerning Divine matters.

As a Jew who believes that the Torah was revealed by God at Mount Sinai, it remains my unshakable conviction that ultimately the truths of Judaism as well as the truths of other religions are not determined by metaphysical speculations. Rather, the truths of religion are determined by acts of kindness, righteousness, and justice.

During the medieval period it was common for people to speculate as to which religion was the "true religion." Philosophers attempted to demonstrate the superiority of one religion over others. For example, Yehudah HaLevi, who lived during the latter part of the eleventh century and early part of the twelfth century, wrote the *Kuzari,* a treatise that attempts to show how

Judaism was superior to both Christianity and Islam. Maimonides, who is considered the greatest of all Jewish philosophers, and whose life was marked by an intellectual pursuit of God and an absorption in the contemplation of God, recognized that the truths of Judaism will, ultimately, not be reached by articulating opinions concerning Divine matters. In his magnum opus, the Mishnah Torah, a code of Jewish law, in the section dealing with the laws of charity, he writes that *Dat HaEmet*, "the true religion," is established only through acts of charity. He speaks of cruelty and a lack of compassion as characteristics of pagans. In the same section he makes the bold claim that if a Jew acts cruelly and mercilessly, one can question his Jewish lineage. It is ironic that in a legal code Maimonides would offer a non-legal definition of what it means to be a Jew. As such, Maimonides did not seek to change the legal definition of who is a Jew. Yet, it was unthinkable to him that a life bereft of moral virtue could in any way be classified as a Jewish life.

Over the course of the years, I have come to appreciate the observation made by my teacher, the late Abraham Joshua Heschel. He once said, "When I was young I was impressed with people who possessed superior intelligence. When I grew older and a little wiser, I was far more impressed with those who were kind."

This study has been inspired by the responses of those whom I have tried to help during periods of illness or during and after the loss of loved ones. In the thirty-three years I have spent in the American rabbinate, I never cease to be amazed how kind and sensitive remarks to the emotionally distressed have the capacity to touch people's souls and provide a measure of healing. There have been times when a gentle touch of another person's hand or a hug has been more efficacious in raising one's spirits than the most eloquent words one can articulate.

The rabbi historically has first and foremost been given the privilege of teaching Torah to his people. The American rabbin-

ate has also required rabbis to hone their skills in pastoral counseling and to pay attention to injury, sickness, and affliction, as
well as anguish. I was fortunate to be introduced to the field of
pastoral counseling in rabbinical school at the Jewish Theological
Seminary in New York, and later in postgraduate studies at
Hebrew Theological College in Skokie, Illinois, which has established the first full-time Jewish program in pastoral counseling.

Living in an age in which psychology is such a dominant field
of study and whose influence permeates through all sectors of
society, the clergy is tempted to internalize feelings of inferiority
toward his rich religious legacy in comparison to the superiority of
the behavioral sciences and the teachings of the mental health
movements. The findings of psychology in many cases become the
ultimate arbiter of right and wrong.

In this book I will attempt to demonstrate that the Jewish
tradition and the classical teachings of Judaism, as reflected in
biblical and rabbinic literature, as well as in the codes and in
hasidic literature, contain insights into the nature of man and
anticipate those insights popularized by today's behavioral scien-
tists.

The focus of my study will be on the roles of the comforter and
comfort in the Jewish tradition.

One writer has pointed out that the twin functions of religion
are to afflict the comfortable and to comfort the afflicted. The
latter will occupy our attention. We will examine the way that
tradition provides solace, comfort, inspiration, and hope to those
broken in spirit and wounded by the pain and tragedies that afflict
people.

Over the course of the years this writer, as a rabbi confronting
a number of pastoral situations, has come to the realization that
the emotionally distressed are also apt to be emotionally sensitive.
They often have a way of knowing whether or not a person is
sincere. They intuitively know whether a rabbi's words represent
deep-seated convictions or mere pious platitudes bereft of mean-

ing. When a rabbi radiates love and concern they have a way of knowing it, and in turn they will respond positively it.

In the opening section of the sixth chapter of *Pirke Avot*, the text says in regard to those entrusted with the task of teaching Torah: "Praised be he who favored them and their teachings." The teachers of Torah cannot guide others unless they themselves embody the teachings of the Torah they purport to uphold. Therefore, the text speaks of God favoring them before lavishing praise upon their erudition of the tradition. If the rabbi is able to manage his own personal life well it will inevitably have a bearing on how people respond to him. If he has strength of character and projects an image of piety, compassion, and understanding, he may lead others to affirm the conviction expressed by the psalmist: "I have set the Lord always before me, because he is at my right hand, I shall not fall apart."

I am indebted to Rabbis Reuven Bulka and Elysha Sandler who brought to bear on this volume their superb critical acumen. I am also indebted to my dear friends and colleagues, Rabbi Yaacov Haber, Rabbi Barry Dov Schwartz, and Rabbi Jerry Zelizer for encouraging me to organize the different themes of this volume and present them in a reasonably coherent structure. I am grateful to Professor Burton Visotsky of the Jewish Theological Seminary for his insights into midrashic sources.

It has been my pleasure to work together with two consummate professionals at Jason Aronson, editor-in-chief Arthur Kurzweil and production editor Hope Breeman, both of whom offered invaluable assistance in bringing this book to fruition. My warm thanks are extended to my devoted secretary, Bernice Parks, for preparing this manuscript with dedication and skill.

I would also like to express my gratitude to the members of Temple Beth El of Cedarhurst, New York, who valued the research I conducted and who were supportive of having this research reach a wider audience.

Beyond all words, I owe my boundless appreciation to my

dear wife Batya whose extraordinary and caring devotion to her
parents during a sixteen year period when they were seriously
ill, as well as to me during my brief period of illness, taught me
that God sends angels who bring light to those who are ill. Her
deeds have demonstrated the validity of the thesis of this book,
namely that the glory of God is revealed in the majesty of human
kindness.

1

THE PASTOR IN JUDAISM

The title of this chapter, "The Pastor in Judaism," impinges strangely on Jewish eardrums. Rabbis see themselves as teachers of Torah, as those entrusted with the responsibility of interpreting our sacred texts to our correligionists. For a good portion of our history, our identity as Jews has been shaped by our ancient texts. We are often referred to as the people of the book. Rabbis see themselves as guardians of many sacred books.

The truth of the matter, however, is that the term "pastor," as I shall attempt to demonstrate, is at the very heart of the Jewish tradition. Spending over three decades in the rabbinate has led me to conclude that one's success as a rabbi is largely determined by one's ability to be an effective pastor. Whatever erudition and knowledge of our sacred texts the rabbi has, his greatest impact on the lives of the men, women, and children that he serves comes from what others see in him in his role as pastor.

SPEAKING AUTHORITATIVELY, BUT WITH A COMPASSIONATE VOICE

The term pastoral counseling has been applied to the clergy, who are called upon to tend to the needs of those who suffer in body, mind, and spirit. Because religion speaks in the name of authority, as well as with the voice of compassion, the rabbi, priest, or minister who lives close to his people, observing them in a variety of settings, and often over a span of many years, is potentially able to provide for them a very effective form of therapeutic help. If he can draw from what is perceived to be the eternal verities of his time-honored faith, which has had a salutary effect on the lives of countless individuals, and at the same time draw from the insights of the behavioral sciences and the various health movements, he will be in a position to make a unique contribution in helping his people grow spiritually and emotionally.

Edgar Jackson, a noted interpreter of pastoral psychology, has pointed out that the major interest in pastoral psychology and its application in parish counseling emerged from the Protestant tradition. The need for pastoral care on an individualized basis was one of the conditions that led to the Protestant Reformation. Also, the exploration of pastoral psychology gave another opportunity to Protestant ministers to continue their endless and elusive quest for identity.[1]

The term pastor has taken on a Christian connotation because it is used often as a euphemism for a Protestant minister. The American College Dictionary defines pastoral as: "of or pertaining to shepherds." The minister–parishioner relationship therefore is defined in terms of a relationship analogous to a shepherd and his flock. The flock requires the tender loving and individual care of the shepherd. Similarly, there are special skills to the highly refined form of pastoral care which utilizes the insights of religion combined with the best that the mental health movement has provided. Together, these disciplines address themselves to the emotional, psychological, and religious needs of the individual.

Actually, the concept of a religious leader as a pastor is at the very heart of the Jewish tradition. It is not necessary to substitute, as did one writer, the concept of rabbinic counseling to give this

---

1. Edgar Jackson, *Parish Counseling,* (New York: Jason Aronson Inc., 1975), p. 4.

specialized area a Jewish basis. The classical Jewish leader, the rabbi, is also a pastor. The tradition speaks of Moses as "Moshe Rabenu," Moses our Teacher, and he is considered the first rabbi of Israel. Today, every rabbi views himself as a link in a long chain which emanates from Moses. The Midrash, that body of literature which adds richness to the biblical text by its imaginative elaboration, also portrays Moses as a pastor. It is only after he proves himself to be a consummate shepherd who cares deeply for his flock that Moses merits the privilege of becoming the leader of the Jewish people.

The Midrash relates how he leads the young animals to pasture first, that they might have the tender, juicy grass for their food. The older animals he brings to graze off herbs which are suitable for them, and the sturdy ones he brings to a place where there is hard grass which others cannot eat but which afforded good food for them. In other words, Moses is depicted as caring for the individual needs of each of his flock. Then God spoke to him, saying, "he that understands how to pasture sheep providing for each what is good for it, he shall pasture my people." The Midrash continues and tells the tale of how once a kid escaped from the flock and Moses followed it, determined to bring it back to the flock. Moses saw that the kid stopped at every place where water was to be found.

Upon seeing this, Moses said, "Poor kid, I did not know you were thirsty and running after water. You must be tired." Moses then lifts up the kid and carries it back to the herd on his shoulders. Then God said, "You had compassion with a flock belonging to a man of flesh and blood. You shall now be the pastor of my flock."[2]

The kid that leaves the fold can symbolize for our purposes those who are alienated and cut off from others. Often, they are

2. Midrash *Shmot Rabbah* 2:2.

the wounded in body and spirit who feel alone, isolated, and abandoned. Moses does not neglect them. Just as he cared for the straying kid by carrying it on his shoulders, likewise he will watch over every one of his people, willing to carry all their burdens and worries on his shoulders.

After Moses serves the Jewish people and the time comes to think in terms of a successor to replace him, the Bible records the following: "And Moses spoke unto the Lord saying, Let the Lord, the God of the spirits of all flesh set a man over the congregation, which may go out before them and which may go in before them, and which may lead them out and which may bring them in, that the congregation of the Lord will not be sheep which has no shepherd." (Numbers 27:16–17)

The pastoral imagery is also present in another Midrash which shows Moses examining and probing God before he accepts the responsibility of being the emancipator of the Jewish people from Egyptian bondage. The Midrash records that when the Holy One, blessed be, commanded Moses, "Come now and I will send you unto Pharaoh," the latter replied, "Who am I that I should go unto Pharaoh?" Moses further said to the Eternal: "You said to me, 'Bring forth my people out of Egypt!' How shall I protect them from the burning heat of the summer and the cold of the winter? How shall I provide them food and drink? How many animals, how many pregnant women, how many children, how many old people are found among them? Have you prepared fodder for their beasts, soft food for those bearing a child, parched corn and nuts for the children? Do you have the answer to these questions?"[3]

Then the Midrash has Moses speaking to the greatest of all pastors, God, the words taken from the Song of Songs, "Tell me O You whom my soul loves, where do you feed, where do you make

---

3. *Shmot Rabbah* 3:4.

the flock to rest?" (Song 1:7) And God responds by saying the following: "From the cake which will go forth with them from Egypt and which will be enough to satisfy them for thirty days, you will know how I will care for them and provide their necessities."[4]

Here Moses is depicted as cross-examining God to make certain that all the fundamental needs of the Jewish people will be provided. God is put in a position of having to justify his credentials before Moses. God tries to convince Moses that He will not abandon the Israelites. After all, when they emerged from serfdom in Egypt, He sustained them for thirty days with unleavened bread.

The pastoral life also prepared David to become king over Israel. He was a shepherd passing his days like Moses in the wilderness, pasturing sheep. The Midrash relates how he as the supposed son of a slave was not educated with his father, Jesse's other sons. Instead, he becomes a shepherd, and with gentle consideration he leads the flocks entrusted to him. The young lambs he guided to pastures of tender grass; the patches of less juicy herbs he reserved for the sheep; and the full-grown sturdy rams were given the tough weeds for food. Then God said: "David knows how to tend sheep, therefore he shall be shepherd of my flock Israel."[5]

His skills as a pastoral counselor are put to practice immediately, for when Saul fell into an incurable melancholy, David was summoned to the court to cheer up the despondent and depressed king by playing upon the harp.

Later in Jewish history, the Messiah is depicted as being a descendant of David. He is referred to as Ben David, the son of David. It is interesting to note that one of the names associated

4. *Shmot Rabbah* 3:4
5. Midrash *Tehilim* 78:70.

with the Messiah according to the Talmud is "Menachem," the comforter.[6] And bringing comfort assumes a paramount role by the pastor.

It is no accident that one of the most towering figures of rabbinic literature is Akibah, a man whose early years were spent as a shepherd. Springing from the ranks of the "plain people," he was beloved by his people. His humble origins as a pastor paves the way for him becoming a leader of the Jewish nation who will be the supreme comforter of his people providing solace for them at critical periods of Jewish life.[7]

CHIEF ACTOR IN THE HEALING DRAMA

The celebrated chapter from the Book of Psalms Chapter 23 presents imagery from pastoral life. It opens with the words "The Lord is my shepherd." God is the Pastor who will help me find tranquillity and serenity.

A way of dramatizing God's nearness to man is reflected in the psalmist speaking of God in the third person in the beginning of the psalm and then switching to the second person when man is depicted as languishing in the valley of the shadow of death. The psalmist writes "*He* permits me to lie down in green fields. *He* leads me beside quiet waters. *He* guides me on paths of righteousness. *He* refreshes my soul for the sake of his glory." He then suddenly switches to the second person: "Even when I walk in the valley of the shadow of death, I shall fear no evil because *you* are with me. *Your* rod and staff comfort me. *You* prepare a table for me

---

6. *Sanhedrin* 98b.

7. See *Makkot* 24b. Akibah's colleagues say to him, "Akibah, you have comforted us, Akibah, you have comforted us."

before my enemies. *You* anoint my head with oil, my cup over-flows." In other words, in the face of adversity, God and man are bonded to each other. God will restore man's sense of self-esteem and confidence. Once man lifts himself out of the valley of the shadow of death and the danger point has passed, God is then referred to again in the third person. The psalmist declares, "Surely goodness and mercy shall follow me all the days of my life and I shall dwell in the house of the Lord forever." However, whether God is referred to in the second or third person the psalmist reassures man that God will never permit him to be cut off. Man may linger in the valley of the shadow of death for a while, but man will be sustained by God during these lonely moments. God will restore man's sense of self esteem and confidence.

The image of God as a pastor was destined to become the imagery associated with the most popular of all *Piyutim* (poems) of the High Holiday liturgy the *Netaneh Tokef*. The author of this poem depicts a heavenly scene on the Day of Judgment. The *shofar* is sounded; there is heard but a still small voice to herald the appearance of the Divine Judge. One by one, as sheep are counted by the shepherd, each life passes in review before him, and its fate is inscribed in a book of records which contains the seal of every person's hand. When the poet sought to project an image of a God who cares for each individual, the image used was God as the pastor.

As is evident from the aforementioned, pastoral counseling is not alien to the Jewish tradition. On the contrary, it is deeply rooted in it. While it has become one of the major functions of many Protestant clergymen, and while some Protestant seminaries have established full-time departments of pastoral psychiatry or pastoral counseling, the pastor has an impressive role in Jewish history tracing himself back to Moses, who was called the "Pastor of Israel."

Today's rabbi has become the guide for the perplexed and agitated in spirit. He will become a more effective Pastor of Israel provided he draws his inspiration from the greatest of all pastors, God who "heals the broken hearted and binds up their wounds."

2

GIVE ME FRIENDSHIP OR DEATH

I recall in my senior year of rabbinical school at the Jewish Theological Seminary a visiting rabbi participating in a course entitled "Practical Theology," which was designed to initiate students into the daily struggle of the rabbinate. He said the following words: "Gentlemen, you are about to enter the loneliest profession of the world." He proceeded to speak of the dissonance he experienced between the public image he projected as a rabbi imbued with an unflinching faith in God and his real self, which was a man wracked with doubt and skepticism.

I have reflected on my colleague's statement many times but have arrived at an entirely different conclusion. The truth of the matter is that all of us in one form or another have in common a terrifying loneliness. Every profession has moments when its practitioners are seized with it. The doctor who has a reputation for saving the lives of many people has probably taken serious risks. In some instances, there may have been a patient or two, or more, who has died as a result of his daring efforts. With whom can he share his information? A lawyer may have decided during a case she argued on behalf of a client who was subsequently acquitted that the client had lied to her and was really guilty. Revealing this information is not an easy thing to do and results in increasing her loneliness.

I once read a sermon of a colleague of mine who was asked by a congregant the following question: "Rabbi, when I have a problem, I speak to you. When you have a problem, to whom do you speak?" The rabbi answered, "I speak to God." That

*response may be apocryphal, but one thing is certain: When we
are gripped with the hopelessness of living without God, it
often paves the way of living with God.*

*We have all accepted as a self-evident truth that wellness is
never promoted when man lives as an island all by himself.
The Jewish tradition captures man's condition in the pithy
maxim, the theme of this chapter, "O Chavruta O Mituta"
(Either Friendship or Death). The Hebrew word for friend,*
Chaver, *has the same letters as the Hebrew word* chibur,
*meaning connected. The goal of any pastoral counselor is to
have people see their lives as being connected with God, man,
and their respective religious traditions. At all times the goal is
also to have the person connect with the healing forces that
God has placed within himself. As Albert Schweitzer once
said, "Every patient carries a doctor as a healer within himself."*

HEALTH AND HUMAN COMPANIONSHIP

Today, it is common for us to hear that one has died because of
a broken heart. A broken heart is often used as a poetic image
for loneliness and despair. In actuality, it is a medical reality.[1]
In our fragmented society, the lack of human companionship,
chronic loneliness, and social isolation as well as the sudden loss of
loved ones is one of the leading causes of premature death.[2] And
while lack of human companionship is related to virtually every

---

1. James J. Lynch, in his volume *The Broken Heart, The Medical
Consequences of Loneliness*, documents that loneliness and lack of personal fulfillment represent a major health hazard (New York: Basic
Books, Inc., 1977), p. 3.
   2. Ibid., p. 3.

major disease from cancer and tuberculosis to mental illness, the link is particularly marked in the case of heart disease, the nation's leading killer. Every year, millions die, quite literally of a broken or lonely heart.[3]

That health and human companionship go together is a point which is well borne out in both biblical and talmudic literature. The following illustrations from these strands of literature are meant to be illustrative of the aforementioned point and not exhaustive.

I have shunned going in a chronological order primarily because illustrations in rabbinic literature are more complete in their reportage than those in biblical literature. The rabbis of the Talmud reveal to us much more of human emotions and feelings than the writers of the Bible. Therefore, I choose to first select illustrations from the Talmud.

The Talmud records in *Baba Metziah* 84a how one talmudic scholar, Rabbi Johanan, who lived during the third century, once was involved in a dispute with his brother-in-law, another talmudic scholar whose name was Rish Lakish. The disputation centered around at what stage of their manufacture does a sword, knife, dagger, spear, handsaw, and scythe become impure and subjected to the laws of impurity. Rabbi Johanan ruled when they are tempered in a furnace. Rish Lakish maintained when they had been furbished in water. Rabbi Johanan, seeing that Rish Lakish, his pupil and brother-in-law, did not agree with him, became irritated and said to him: "A robber understands his trade," a reference to Rish Lakishe's alleged background as a thief.[4]

---

3. Ibid., p. 4.

4. Henrich Graetz, *History of Jews*, vol. 2 (Philadelphia: Jewish Publication Society, 1893), p. 496; and Isaac Hirsh Weiss, *Dor Dor V'Dorshav*, vol. 3 (Berlin, 1924), p. 81, see also *Gittin* 47a; Talmud also records how he worked and watched a garden protecting it against infiltration of thieves. *Moed Katan* 17a. See also footnote in "Dor Dor

As a result of being insulted, Rish Lakish was deeply hurt, became ill, and shortly afterwards passed away. Rabbi Johanan was then plunged into deep grief and depression. His colleagues selected Rabbi Eleazar ben Pedat to go and try to raise his spirits. When he came to Rabbi Johanan, he attempted to be very supportive by agreeing with Rabbi Johanan's analysis of difficult points of Jewish law. Whenever a controversial area of Jewish law was discussed, Eleazar ben Pedat observed: "There is a Baraitha which supports you." Rabbi Johanan was unimpressed by Eleazar ben Pedat's support and said to him: "Are you the son of Lakisha?[5] When I would make a statement of law the son of Lakish would counter with twenty-four objections. In return I would respond with twenty-four answers. As a result my thinking was crystallized and became sharper, and I would understand the law better. In contrast you R. Eleazer b. Pedat say 'A Baraitha has been taught which supports you.' Don't I know myself that my position is valid?" Rabbi Johanan continued to tear his garments and weep, saying "Where are you O son of Lakisha, where are you son of Lakisha?" He continued to cry until his mind was turned. Thereupon, the rabbis prayed for him, and he died.[6]

It appears that the illness which caused him, as the rabbis of the Talmud say, to have his "mind turned" was a profound sense of loneliness. Being bereft of his friend, and not having an intellectual equal who would challenge him, pushed his physical health to the breaking point. He missed the give and take with his

---

V'Dorshav," pp. 83–84. Both Graetz and Weiss contend that Rish Lakish was a circus attendant driven to this work because of economic hardships.

5. Weiss, Ibid., p. 80. The full name of Rish Lakish was Rabbi Shimon Ben Lakish. Lakisha is not the name of his father but the name of a town. *Bar*, meaning a citizen of, that is, R. Shimon, a citizen of Lakish.

6. *Baba Metziah* 84a.

colleague. Eleazar ben Pedat's obeisance and deferential tone of finding a source which corroborated Rabbi Johanan's position proved to be woefully inadequate to compensate for the loss of Rabbi Johanan's companionship with Rish Lakish.

When one is cut off from human companionship, one discovers a deep reverence for friendship, as did Rabbi Johanan.

Undoubtedly, a contributing factor to Rabbi Johanan's death was the tremendous sense of guilt which overcame him following the death of Rish Lakish. The feeling of guilt in having done something to bring about the death of another is a very natural occurrence among those who sustain the loss of a very dear one.[7]

GUILT AND MOURNING

I recall once visiting with a congregant whose husband underwent what was considered to be minor surgery. The worst occurred, and the man did not survive the surgery. Upon learning of his death, I immediately rushed to the hospital to be with the bereaved wife. When I saw her, she was crying profusely and was inconsolable, repeating over and over again, "It was my fault. I never should have permitted him to have surgery. Honey, please forgive me for killing you."

In *Psychology of Melancholy*, Mortimer Ostow writes:

Guilt often appears during mourning. Its severity then usually bears no relation to any actual negligence or responsibility for the misfortune. The most dutiful may feel

---

7. Arthur C. Carr, "Bereavement as a Relative Experience," in *Bereavement: Its Psychological Aspects*. Edited by Schoenberg, Gerber, Weiner, Kutscher, Peretz and Carr (New York and London: Columbia University Press, 1975), p. 7.

the most guilt, and perhaps the most negligent the least. Here the guilt expresses the wish for a reunion with the lost parent even if it is not the parent who has died, but rather for example, a child. The mourner sees himself abandoned by his parent, just as we all ordinarily go about our business expecting unconsciously the magical protection of our parents and being disappointed when misfortune indicates that this expectation was unrealistic. We ask ourselves, "Why did it happen to me? What did I do to deserve this?" We seem to imply that if we behave ourselves properly, and do what our parents taught us to do, then we have a right to expect immunity and protection against misfortune.[8]

Guilt is always less likely when there has been free expression of feelings between the dying person and the bereaved to be. Since the death of the man in this case (of the woman whose husband was expected to pull through surgery without any difficulty) was so sudden, her guilt feelings were more intense. I later learned that she neither encouraged nor discouraged him from having the surgery. It took her many months to overcome the guilt feeling that she had for not dissuading him from having surgery.

In the aforementioned story from the Talmud, however, Rabbi Johanan's guilt feeling over the death of Rish Lakish is only an ancillary factor in contributing to his losing his mind and dying. The main factor is the unbearable loss of a friend, which makes it difficult for him to function.

Another illustration of loneliness contributing directly to death is to be found in the talmudic legend which tells of one Honi HaMaagal, a circle drawer, who once had a hearty meal and then fell into a deep slumber which lasted for seventy years. When he

8. Mortimer Ostow, *Psychology of Melancholy* (New York: Harper & Row Publishers, 1970), p. 36.

awakened, he saw a man gathering the fruit of a carob tree and he asked him: "Are you the man who planted the tree?" (This was a reference to an earlier story juxtaposed to this section of the Talmud which tells of a man who was planting a tree and who told Honi that his fruit would grow seventy years later.) The man replied, "I am his grandson." Thereupon, Honi exclaimed: "It is clear that I slept for seventy years." He returned home and inquired, "Is the son of Honi the circle-drawer still alive?" The people answered him, "His son is no more, but his grandson is still living." Thereupon, he revealed to them that he was Honi the circle-drawer, but no one believed him. He then went to the *Beth HaMidrash* (The House of Study) and there he overheard the scholars say, "the law is as clear to us as in the days of Honi the circle drawer for whenever he came to the *Beth HaMidrash* he would arbitrate any difficulties that the scholars had." He then called out, "I am he," but the scholars would not believe him nor did they give him the honor due to him. This hurt him greatly, and he prayed for death and he died. Raba said: "Hence the saying, 'Either companionship or Death.' "[9]

In this talmudic tale, Honi's loneliness not only stemmed from no one recognizing him but also from the lack of respect that was shown to him by those who should have known better, namely the scholars. It was humiliating for Honi to be ignored by his colleagues. As a noted scholar himself, he was used to having others defer to his judgment. The biblical injunction to show deference to the *zaken* (old) was understood by the rabbis as an acronym for *"zo shekanah hochmah,"* the one who acquired wisdom. Honi's opinions in the past were valued. Now, they were totally ignored. Where could he turn for companionship if scholars who in the past eagerly sought his opinions now treated him as if he was non existent?

---

9. *Taanit* 23a.

Today, diet, smoking, lack of exercise, and faulty living habits have all been identified by the experts as risk factors that affect the incidence of coronary heart disease in various countries. The aforementioned story adds another cause of death, for implicit in it is the idea that life may be shortened by lack of human companionship. Dr. James Lynch cites careful scientific studies which clearly demonstrate that the mortality statistics for heart disease among those adult Americans who are not married are striking— a death rate from heart disease that is as much as two to five times higher for nonmarried individuals, including those who are divorced, widowed, or single than for married Americans.[10]

CASE STUDY OF A SELF-INDULGENT LIFE

The Talmud relates another fascinating episode of a man named Eleazar ben Dordia, who had led a very promiscuous life, having relations with many harlots. Once, upon hearing that there was a certain harlot in one of the towns by the sea who accepted a purse of denarim for her hire, he took a purse of denarim and crossed seven rivers for her sake. As he was with her, she blew a deep breath and said: "As this blown breath will not return to its place, so will Eleazar ben Dordia never be received in repentance." He thereupon went and sat between two hills and mountains and exclaimed: "O ye, hills and mountains, plead for mercy for me!" They replied: "How shall we pray for you? We stand in need of it ourselves, for it is said, For the mountains shall depart and the hills be removed!" (Isaiah 54:10) So he exclaimed: "Heaven and earth, you plead for mercy for me!" They too replied: "How shall we pray for you? We stand in need of it ourselves, for it is said, for the

10. Lynch, p. 35

heavens shall vanish away like smoke, and the earth shall wax old like a garment." (Isaiah 51:6) He then exclaimed: "Sun and moon, you plead for mercy for me." They said: "How shall we pray for you? We stand in need of it ourselves, for it is said, there the moon shall be confounded and the sun ashamed." (Isaiah 24:23) He then said, "Stars and constellations, you plead for mercy for me!" They said: "How shall we pray for you? We stand in need of it ourselves, for it is said, and all the hosts of heaven shall dissolve away." (Isaiah 34:4) Said he: "The matter then depends upon me alone!" Having placed his head between his knees, he wept aloud until his soul departed.[11]

In these fantasies and imagined dialogues between Eleazar and different parts of the heavens and earth, one is left with the impression that they symbolize a support system that fails him. He needed empathy and understanding of his plight. He wanted his pain to be assuaged. He was crushed in spirit and totally humiliated. His life had passed before his eyes and he realized that he had veered from a righteous path. He needed friends to bolster his sense of self-esteem. He felt the pangs of remorse deeply. He craved attention and awaited some kind of response and love which would show concern. None was forthcoming, as every part of the natural world was indifferent to his pain. The natural world represented his friends who had abandoned him. Finally, in a state of deep depression, he sat down all by himself, placed his head between his knees, and wept.

In this context, the placing of his head between his knees and weeping conjures up an image of a typical depressive reaction. Depression is an exaggeration of the mood that all of us experience for brief periods of time. "The person sinking into a deepening depression begins to be preoccupied with feelings of failure, sinfulness, worthlessness, and despair. He cannot be reasoned with or

11. *Avodah Zarah* 17a.

told to cheer up, for his woe is an internal event that does not correspond to reality as others see it. Overcome with his personal hopelessness, the depressive individual cuts off communication with the outside world, abandons active attempts to help himself, and usually begins to contemplate ending it all by suicide."[12]

While Eleazar Ben Dordia does not commit suicide, it is apparent from the story that he loses his will to live as a result of being abandoned by everyone. The emotional changes associated with a deep-seated depression were evident in this episode.

In reviewing the story, one can feel his sadness, his lowered self-regard, his failure, and a feeling of hopelessness which cannot be alleviated.

EXCOMMUNICATION AND MOURNING

It is noteworthy that in Jewish law when *niddui* (excommunication) was imposed upon an individual, which meant a practical prohibition of all social intercourse with society, the individual who was placed under the ban was to conduct himself as one who was in mourning.[13] *Niddui*, as employed by the rabbis during talmudic times and the Middle Ages, was a rabbinic institution. Its object was to preserve a solidarity of the nation and strengthen the authority of the synagogue by enforcing obedience to its mandates. It became chiefly a legal measure resorted to by a judicial court for certain prescribed offenses.

During the period of *niddui*, no one except the members of the immediate family was permitted to associated with the offender,

---

12. *Psychology Today* (Del-Mar, California: CRM Books, 1972), p. 602.

13. Yoreh Deah 334.2. See also gloss by Isserles: *Jewish Encyclopedia*, vol. 5, "Excommunication," 1904, pp. 285–287.

to sit within four cubits of him, or to eat in his company. He was expected to go into mourning, to refrain from bathing, cutting his hair, and wearing shoes, and he had to observe all the laws that pertained to a mourner.[14]

Niddui meant social isolation generally for a period of seven days, or in Palestine for thirty days and a period of mourning to be assumed by the one upon whom it was imposed. It graphically conveys the correlation between loneliness and death. In this instance, the man under the ban of excommunication was to respond as if there had been a death in the family. It represents another concretization of the talmudic epigram "Either Friendship or Death."

The Talmud records the poignant story of how Eliezer ben Hyrcanus, one of the most prominent rabbis of the first and second centuries, was excommunicated by his colleagues and how the bitterness of isolation eventually resulted in his death. The rupture between Rabbi Eliezer and his colleagues came when the Sanhedrin deliberated on the susceptibility to Levitical uncleanness of an aknai-oven.[15]

The majority decided that such an oven was capable of becoming unclean but Eliezer dissented. As he thus acted in direct opposition to the decision of the majority, it was deemed necessary to make an example of him, and he was excommunicated. Still, even under these circumstances, great respect was manifested toward him in a very sensitive manner.

The Talmud in *Baba Metziah* 59b relates how upon excommunicating him, the Rabbis said, "Who shall go and inform him?" Rabbi Akibah volunteered to go, for he feared that if Rabbi Eliezer was informed in a tactless and brutal way that he was to

---

14. Yoreh Deah, ibid.

15. *Baba Metziah* 59b. An aknai oven consisted of tiles separated from one another by sand, but externally plastered over with cement.

become socially ostracized, it would have an even more devastating effect on him. Akibah equated a tactless way of informing Rabbi Eliezer with the destruction of the whole world. Akibah then donned black garments, the clothing associated with mourning and the clothing which one under the ban had to wear. He sat at a distance of four cubits from Rabbi Eliezer, which as indicated above was required in Jewish law when meeting one who had been excommunicated.

After Rabbi Eliezer asked him, "What particular thing happened today?"—which is another way of saying, how is this day different from yesterday—Akibah discreetly and gently broke the news that Rabbi Eliezer was excommunicated. He said "My master it appears to me that your colleagues keep aloof from you." It was at that point that Rabbi Eliezer tore his garments, took off his shoes, removed his seat and sat on the earth while tears streamed from his eyes. These were all mourning practices which symbolically conveyed to the one under the *herem* (excommunication) that his friends were now dead to him and that he was forbidden to contact them. Separated from his colleagues and excluded from the deliberations of the Sanhedrin, Eliezer passed his last years of life unnoticed and in comparative solitude.

When his former colleagues heard that he was near death, the most prominent of them hastened to his bedside at Caesarea. When they appeared before him, he began to complain about his long period of social isolation. They tried to mollify him by professing great and unabated respect for him and by claiming that it was only the lack of opportunity that had kept them away.

He felt that they might have profited by his teachings. Thereupon, they asked him to communicate to them traditions concerning moot points, particularly Levitical purity and impurity. He consented and answered question after question until he expired. The last word he uttered was *tahor* (pure), and this was considered as an auspicious omen of his purity; whereupon, they all rent their garments in token of mourning and Rabbi Joshua revoked the sentence of excommunication.[16]

Perhaps the Rabbis held themselves partially to blame for the death of Rabbi Eliezer. In one Baraita found in *Sanhedrin* 68a, when they came to visit him while he was ill, Rabbi Eliezer rebukes them for waiting so long to come. They offer the lame excuse that they were too busy. He then, in a characteristic direct manner, chides them by saying, "I will be astonished if you will die a natural death." In other words, you will suffer because of what you did to me. Akibah then turns to Eliezer and says, "And what about me?" (How shall I die?) Eliezer says, "Your death will be more severe." Eliezer was bitterly disappointed with Akibah, for he felt Akibah should not have collaborated with the others in excommunicating him. In effect, he was telling Akibah that he was not impressed with the delicate way in which Akibah broke to him the news that he was excommunicated.

Man has a horror of aloneness. And of all kinds of aloneness, moral aloneness is the most terrible.[17]

Rabbi Eliezer never was able to recover from the ban of excommunication leveled against him. He understood the pain of isolation. It was probably during his latter days when he underwent profound melancholy that one of his favorite aphorisms was composed: "Warm thyself by the fire of the wise men, but be cautious of their burning coals that you will not be burned, for their bite is the bite of a jackal, their sting is that of a scorpion, their hissing is that of a snake and all their words are fiery coals."[18]

When one is cut off from human companionship, one discovers a deep reverence for friendship, which Rabbi Eliezer tragically did not have following his excommunication.

In another section of the Talmud, we learn that there are four

---

16. *Sanhedrin* 101a, *Berachot* 28b, *Sanhedrin* 68a.
17. Clark E. Moustakas, *Loneliness (New York: Prentice Hall, 1961)*.
18. *Avot* 2:10.

individuals who are considered dead: the poor man, the *metzorah* ("leper"), the blind man, and one who has no children.[19] "Why should the *metzorah* be considered as if he was dead?" asked the late Rabbi Hayim Levi Shmulavich of the Mir Yeshivah. He dismisses the point that the *metzorah* is deemed as being dead because of his unbearable pain. After all, the gift of life has not been denied to him. The reason for equating his lot with that of a dead man is rather due to the isolation from the rest of the community which the *metzorah* must endure. The biblical text records, "Alone he shall dwell, outside the camp shall be his habitation." (Leviticus 13:46)[20] Similarly, the blind man, by virtue of being sightless, much of the world is cut off from him, and he too must live a good portion of his life in a state of loneliness. The poor man is also socially isolated, for often it is the rich man whom everyone seeks to befriend. And the one who has no children is denied the most tangible way of expressing immortality, for man lives on through his children. The thought that for many of us, years after we expire no one will ever know whether or not we have lived is a depressing one which is capable of driving a sensitive person into a deep seated melancholy. Through our children, we are able to save ourselves from anonymity that death eventually brings in its wake. The thought that there are children and in many instances grandchildren and even great-grandchildren who will remember and talk about us from time to time is a comforting one. Contemplating our own death makes us feel very lonely, but a measure of solace comes to us with the recognition that our offspring will perpetuate our memories.

From its very inception, we find in biblical literature the theme that for man to be fully man he needs companionship. In the story of creation, God declares it is not good that man shall be

---

19. *Nedarim* 64b.

20. Shichot Musar, Hayim Levi Shmulavich, 1980, p. 113, second section.

alone. (Genesis 2:18) Man cannot attain fulfillment unless his life is shared with another human being. It is only through Eve sharing her life alongside of her husband that Adam becomes a complete human being. The Rabbis underscore this point when they say that one who is without a woman finds himself without joy, without a blessing, and without good.[21] In the same section of the Talmud, the rabbis teach us that only through his wife does a man become a "man," for only husband and wife together are Adam.[22]

In commenting on the passage "it is not good that man shall be alone," Samson Raphael Hirsch writes: "As long as men stand alone it is altogether not yet good, the goal of perfection which the world is to attain through him, will never be reached as long as he stands alone."[23]

Umberto Cossuto, in his commentary on the Book of Genesis, draws attention to the fact that the Hebrew words *lo tov*, which are ordinarily translated as "it is not good," represent an absolute negative. The Torah deliberately does not use the words Ein Tov, which would also have been translated as It is not good. But the word *ein* does not negate the possibility that it can be good or that it is better than bad. When the biblical text uses the word *lo*, it establishes categorically that a life alone without a woman is not good. It thus emphatically forecloses the possibility that it may ever be good for man to live alone without a wife.[24]

---

21. *Yevamot* 64b.

22. The Talmud states that a man who has no wife is not a man. This is based on the biblical verse "Male and female created he them and blessed them and called their name Adam in the day they were created." (Genesis 5:2) See *Yavamot* 63a.

23. Samson Raphael Hirsch, *The Pentateuch*, translated by Isaac Levy, vol. 1 *Genesis* (New York: Judaic Press Inc., 1971), pp. 18–19.

24. Umberto Cossuto, *A Commentary on the Book of Genesis*, Jerusalem: Magness Press, 1969), p. 83.

Although it is true that in order to grasp the meaning of being human we analyze the human individual rather than the human species, an analysis that disregards social involvement, man's interdependence, and correlatively will miss the heart of being human.[25]

In addition, biblical literature offers several illustrations of how lack of human companionship and death are interrelated.

ALONE WITH GOD

In the first Book of Kings, we read of the confrontation between the prophet Elijah and the false prophets of Baal. After Elijah taunts, mocks, and humiliates the four hundred and fifty prophets of Baal, he is able to demonstrate the supremacy of the Lord. The people at the behest of Elijah slay those false prophets who led them astray in committing idolatrous practices.[26] In the next chapter, we learn that Elijah is forced to flee to the desert because Queen Jezebel, who is a devotee of Baal, is threatening to have him killed. There, in the desert, God reveals himself to Elijah and asks Elijah, "What are you doing here (in the desert)." (1 Kings 19:9) The Malbim, Rabbi Meir Leibush of Koenigsburg, understands the question to mean that the prophet is not supposed to be isolated in the desert from the masses. He is supposed to be involved in their lives.[27]

To the question, What are you doing in the desert, Elijah responds, "I have been very jealous for the Lord God of hosts: For the children of Israel have forsaken thy covenant, thrown down

25. Abraham Joshua Heschel, "Who Is Man?" (Stanford, CA: Stanford University Press, 1965), p. 45.

26. 1 Kings, chapter 18.

27. Malbim 1 Kings 19:9.

thine altars and slain thy prophets with the sword, and I have been left alone and they seek to take my life." (1 Kings 19:10)

Earlier in the same chapter, we read: "He (Elijah) went a day's journey into the wilderness and came and sat down under a juniper tree; and he requested for himself that he might die; and said, 'It is enough; now O Lord, take away my life; for I am not better than my fathers.'" (1 Kings 19:4) Thus again, we see the correlation between loneliness and death.

Elijah learns that the price of asserting the supremacy of the Lord and maintaining unswerving allegiance to the covenant is loneliness. Elijah learns that the person who expresses strong convictions in everyday life often stands alone.

Even after the Lord reveals himself to Elijah a second time (1 Kings 19:11–13), he again tells God that he is alone. It is an almost exact repetition of 19:10 when he speaks of his determination to abide by the covenant even when God's people have forsaken it.

Elijah, who will not tolerate any compromise, must stand alone. And in a moment of weakness, he falters and doesn't want to live anymore.

The prophet Jeremiah is also no stranger to loneliness. He laments his fate of being singled out to deliver God's message to his people. "I sat not in the assembly of the mockers nor rejoiced; I sat alone because of your hand; for you have filled me with indignation." (Jeremiah 15:17) He curses the day that he was born, which marked his entrance into the land of the living. It would have been better if he had never been conceived or, failing that, he wishes that he would have died in his mother's womb or would have perished at the moment of birth.[28]

No loneliness is greater than the messenger of God who is unable to transmit the message. No one is so alone as the prophet whom God chooses to isolate from those he is sent to warn and

---

28. See Jeremiah 20:14–15; 20:17–18.

save. No one is so alone as the man who must speak and is not heard. Jeremiah cries out, "My heart is broken within me. I am like a drunken man. . . . I have become a laughing stock all these days everyone mocks me; for as often as I speak I have to cry out and complain of violence and abuse." (Jeremiah 23:9; 20:8–9)

Still another illustration of the correlation between loneliness and death can be found in the third chapter of Job. There, Job breaks his silence with a lament of his cruel fate and gives vent to the same aforementioned feelings that Jeremiah the prophet expressed. Job is alone without his property, his children, afflicted with physical illnesses, and estranged from God, whom he perceives as hunting him without any valid reason. In such a despondent condition, alone from all these treasures, he gives vent to the feeling that death would be better than the fate meted out to him.

The noted psychologist Bruno Bettelheim, in discussing the meaning and importance of fairy tales, noted, "There is no greater threat in life than that we will be deserted, left all alone."[29] "When we are young," he explained, "this fright is more pronounced, but it is not limited to childhood and youth. In the unconscious it can occur at all ages."[30] Because this apprehension of being left totally alone is so embedded in the individual for whatever mysterious reasons, its antidote consists primarily in being reassured of continuing love and closeness. Such assurance must be constantly reinforced for "the ultimate consolation," Bettleheim succinctly says, "is that we shall never be deserted."

One of the most enigmatic chapters in the Bible is the fourth and last chapter of the book of Jonah. Jonah the prophet was called upon to go to the people of Nineveh (the capital city of Assyria) and warn them that unless they repented, Nineveh would be

---

29. Bruno Bettelheim, *The Uses of Enchantment* (New York: Alfred A. Knopf, 1976), p. 145.

30. Ibid., p. 15.

destroyed. Jonah does not accept his calling, and rather than traveling eastward to Nineveh he heads in the opposite direction, going westward to Tarshish in Spain. Eventually, he resumes his assignment and calls upon the people of Nineveh to perform *teshuvah* (repentance). The people of Nineveh rise to the challenge and repent of their ways. At that point, we find that Jonah, rather than being elated, is despondent and depressed. On two occasions, he expresses the wish that he die.[31] Why should the prophet become dispirited and depressed when the people of Nineveh perform *teshuvah*? Jonah preferred to serve as God's instrument of castigation as His "angry man" rather than as the messenger of His mercy and forgiveness.

He would have preferred that the residents of Nineveh not perform *teshuvah*. After all, the residents of Nineveh are heathens. Jonah was not interested in any form of social interaction with the residents of Nineveh. As a result, it would appear that when his mission was completed and they repented, he was stricken again with a sense of loneliness. And loneliness in its acute form as we repeatedly have sought to establish brings in its wake a death wish.

When a prophet predicts the disastrous consequences that will occur to the sinner, he demonstrates and proves his prophetic foresight. Thus, his prestige is enhanced. But when he prevents a disaster by persuading a sinful people, he is at a disadvantage. What one has prevented from happening is not subject to evidential confirmation. The rabbis of the Midrash tell us that Jonah was a disciple of Elijah. He had previously been charged with the task of proclaiming the destruction of Jerusalem. The people repented and as his prediction was not fulfilled, he became known as a "false prophet." He was therefore afraid to go to Nineveh, because he said, "I am certain that the heathens will repent and so the punishment with which I shall threaten them will not be ex-

---

31. Jonah 4:3; 4:8.

ecuted, I shall then be known as a false prophet among the heathens.[32]

SITTING *SHIVA* WITHOUT ANY VISITORS

Probably the most graphic and striking expression of desolation, loneliness, and desertion is to be found in the first chapter of the Book of Lamentations. In it, the author describes how Jerusalem, the capital city, which was once crowded, is now desolate and empty. The image that is used is that of a widow in mourning. And four times do we have the pathetic image of a person mourning with no one to comfort her.[33]

"Bitterly she weeps in the night, her cheek wet with tears; there is none to comfort her of all her friends." (Lamentations 1:2) The image conjured up here is of a mourner sitting *shivah* (the seven-day period at home following a death) with no one coming to visit. If we live, we all must face death. What makes us be able to sustain the death of our loved ones is the presence of some kind of support system. What gives Job the strength to constantly demand from God an explanation as to why, he who views himself as being an innocent man, should undergo excruciating suffering? It is the presence of his friends, Eliphaz, Bildad, and Zophar, that provide the support system which enables Job to endure.

Certainly, later in Jewish history, homilists had to come to grips with the questions which agonized the Jewish people: Had

---

32. Pirke R. Eliezer, ch. 10. The translations are adapted here from Louis Ginzberg's *The Legends of the Jew* (Philadelphia: Jewish Publication Society of America, 1954), vol. 4, p. 246.

33. See Lamentations 1:2; 1:9; 1:16; 1:21.

they been deserted by God in wake of the destruction of both temples? Melvin Jay Glatt writes: Linked to an overall mood of despair there would be one basic question gnawing at Jews. It would be a concern more inwardly felt, perhaps than openly expressed; more unconscious than overt but nevertheless real. This would be the haunting query as to whether the physical destruction of State, sanctuary, and community with its resultant Diaspora was perhaps evidence of God's abandonment of his people. . . . Was it possible that the love between God the parent, and Israel the child, had come to an end?[34]

BEYOND THE DESTROYED TEMPLE

The midrashic homilists were convinced that God did not abandon his people. They constantly made statements which illustrated the continued close relationship that God maintained with the Jewish people.

The homilists, by constantly citing the kind acts of God, were offering a way of avoiding having the people sink into a deeper state of depression. For if the people would have ever come to the conclusion that as a result of the destruction of the temple, and the collapse of the revolution launched against the Romans during the period of Bar Kochba, that God had abandoned his people, the recuperative potential of our ancestors would have suffered a mortal blow.

Such an apprehension and fear is mirrored in the following Midrashic comment on a verse in Psalms, which reads: "The Lord raises those who are bowed down." (Psalms 146:8) The homilist adds, "Who are those bowed down? They are the children of

---

34. Melvin J. Glatt, *A Study in Midrashic Responses to Group Trauma* (New York: Jewish Theological Seminary of America, 1979), pp. 17–18.

Israel exiled from their land. Since the day that they were exiled from Jerusalem they had not been able to stand up straight, but are bowed down so low before their enemies that their adversaries trample all over them."[35]

One can discern a skeptical attitude as to the efficacy of the Jewish people to maintain the resilience to regain the necessary self-esteem to survive creatively.

The Midrash homilists answered these skeptical thoughts by making it crystal clear that God had not abandoned his people. The Temple might be in ruins, but still God has not departed from the site of the sacred house.[36] Despite the destruction of his holy habitation, Israel could and did hear the prayers of his people.[37] Even when the children of Israel are most degraded, God continues to call them his brother and companion.[38]

In another Midrash, the prophet Jeremiah, who was an eyewitness to the destruction of the first temple, is depicted as engaging God in a dialogue. He asks, virtually demands, to know whether the catastrophe means that God has rejected his people. "Master of the Universe," Jeremiah says, "could you possibly be forsaking us outright?" God responds, "Go to Moses who was the mentor of all teachers and the instructor of all prophets. Address your question to him and learn from his response. He will tell you that already in his time, I said I never would reject Israel. Even if their waywardness would make me angry at them still I would never detest them."[39]

All extreme suffering evokes the experience of being forsaken

---

35. Midrash Tehillim 146:6.
36. Shmot Rabbah 2:2; Midrash Tehillim 11:3.
37. Midrash Tehillim 4:1.
38. Ibid., 4:3.
39. Pesikta Rabbati 31:3. For a fuller treatment of midrashim offering a form of group therapy to a people who feared they had been abandoned by God after the destruction of the second temple and the

by God. "My God, My God, why has thou forsaken me?" (Psalms 22:2) is a cry that has been heard repeatedly.

In the depths of suffering, people see themselves as abandoned and forsaken by everyone. Therefore, the Midrash expositors, in the spirit of the talmudic and biblical traditions, forever sought to impress upon the people that God would never forsake them. On a basic level, the most fundamental way to indicate that we have not been forsaken is when another engages us in a dialogue. There are literally thousands of statements in both the Talmud and the late Midrashim in which the dialogue is maintained between God and the Jewish people. Both speak to each other. A figure of speech which appears countless times is *Knesset Yisrael*, "the people of Israel speak before God."[40] As in biblical literature, talmudic and midrashic literature are replete with God speaking with all kinds of people.[41]

LIFE AND DIALOGUE

Dialogue is the essential element of every social interaction. It is the elixir of life. The broken hearts of adults, the proportionally higher death rates of single, widowed, and divorced individuals common to all these situations is a breakdown in dialogue. The elixir of life somehow dries up, and without it people begin to

---

unsuccessful *bar kocha* revolution, see *A Study of Midrashic Responses to Group Trauma* by Melvin Jay Glatt.

40. *Menachot* 53a, *Eruvin* 21:2, Shmot Rabah 45b, Midrash Tehillim 13:1.

41. Shir Hashirim Rabah 3:1; Midrash Tehillim 22:10; Shir Hashirim 1:43; *Avodah Zarah* 35a, *Pesachim* 118b; *Hulin* 20b. See Machlool HaMaamarim V'Hapitgamim (Jerusalem: Mosad HaRav Kook, 1961), vol. 1, pp. 201–215.

wither away and die. Those who lack the dialogue early in life can
perish quickly, while those who lose it as children, adolescents, or
adults feel acutely what they have lost and struggle to get it back.[42]

In its most general meaning, dialogue involves the sharing of
thoughts, physical sensations, ideas, ideals, hopes, and feelings. An
individual may lack a dialogue of love and still remain relatively
healthy as long as other forms of human dialogue are maintained
and the individual does not become socially isolated.[43] For example, in the book of Job, which is treated elsewhere in this book,
there are many instances where the dialogue between Job and his
friends is heated full of anger, acrimony, and bitter satire. But it
still is healthier for some kind of dialogue to be maintained than
none. In what may be perhaps an extreme extension of this position, James Lynch suggests that married couples who live together in "bonds of hatred" may be physically healthier than those
who live together as surrogate monkeys without any dialogue.
The total lack of dialogue between a couple "living together" may
be the ultimate form of hatred.[44]

There is a whole genre of Midrashim in which the people
remonstrate God for his ways which appear to be unjust. One may
see expressed in them a feeling of outrage and anger against God,
but its salutary effect is to be understood in the context of an
ongoing dialogue which will have its ups and downs.

In one of them, the midrashic expositor places the following
words in the mouth of the Jewish people as they speak to God:
"You don't work miracles for us as you did for our forefathers! Is
there no merit to us? Is that what we are to think." "Our ancestors
in Egypt performed only one mitzvah—they offered up the
paschal lamb—and they were helped. We obey so much and yet
there is no salvation for us?" "I will say to God my Rock: Why

42. Lynch, p. 215.
43. Ibid., p. 217.
44. Ibid., p. 217.

have you forgotten me? Why do I mourn under the oppression of the enemy?" (Psalms 42:10)[45]

In the Book of Job, there are many illustrations of Job in the depths of despair attempting to reach out to God and viewing Him as an adversary. "In his wrath he has torn me apart for he hates me; He has gnashed his teeth at me; my foe sharpens his eyes against me." (Job 16:9)

In projecting his anger onto God, Job feels further alienation from God, for the anger that rages within Job brings in its wake a greater sense of isolation and loneliness. Harriet Lerner points out that an angry confrontation is a statement of differences between people which elicits a heightened sense of standing on one's own two feet separate and apart from a relational context. In anger, the person establishes an automatic aloneness and makes himself temporarily separate from the object of the anger.[46]

The connection between anger and aloneness is reflected in Job's outburst in Chapter 19, where he says,

> He (God) has kindled his anger against me and treats me
> as a foe. . . . My brethren are distant from me and my
> friends are wholly estranged. My kinsfolk and intimates
> no longer know me; the guests in my own house have
> forgotten me. My maidservants count me as a stranger, an
> alien have I become in their sights. I call to my servant, but
> he does not answer. In words I must plead with him. I am
> repulsive to my wife and loathsome to my own children.
> Even youngsters despise me; when I rise they talk against
> me. All my intimate friends abhor me, and those I love
> have turned against me. My bones cling to my skin and my
> flesh, and I have escaped only with the skin of my teeth.

---

45. Midrash Tehillim 42:6.

46. Harriet Lerner, *American Journal of Psychoanalysis*, vol. 40, No. 2, 1980, p. 140.

Have pity on me. O my friends, have pity for the hand of
God has struck me. Why do you persecute me like God
and are not satisfied with my flesh. (Job 19:11–22)

Here Job has projected the anger that he feels towards God by
speaking of God as being angry at him. The anger felt by Job only
increases his sense of isolation as all those he comes in contact with
are perceived as being distant, remote, and inaccessible. As long as
Job is enraged, his sense of isolation will not subside. He desperately wants a caring response from his friends as he beseeches
them, "Have pity on me, O my friends have pity." (Job 19:21)
However, while such an explosive rage and anger is present, he
remains unreceptive to those expressions of support which they
attempt to give to him.

But to his credit, Job ventilates his feelings and each complaint
becomes in a certain sense a stepping stone towards ultimate
reconciliation with God.

It has been said that one may be with God, or against God, but
not without God. Job's desperate cries of anguish against God lay
the groundwork for the reestablishment of a more mature relationship with God. He ultimately, as will be shown elsewhere in
this book, is restored to a spiritual fellowship with God. In all
friendships, there are moments of acute disappointment and dis-
illusionment. There are always breaches even to the most harmo-
nious and peaceful relationships. The classical Jewish sources
cited in this chapter have lent credence to the finding of medical
science that there are health implications for human companionship. These sources have sought to show that there is a correlation
between loneliness, isolation, and death. Once again, the choice is
ours to make. We must either live together or face the possibility of
prematurely dying alone. In the words of the Talmud, "Either
Friendship or Death"—life and dialogue are the same.

3

ENTER THE COMFORTER

Once, in my earlier years in the rabbinate, I was sitting in my office deeply engrossed in the writing of a sermon. My secretary called and informed me that the mother of one of our members was critically ill in the hospital and the family was anxious to have the rabbi come and visit as soon as possible. The secretary's message registered on my ears, but not on my heart. At that moment, I was determined to finish writing the sermon, which weighed heavily upon me.

About an hour and a half later, having completed the sermon, I got into my car and rushed over to the hospital. By the time I arrived, the elderly lady had passed away and the family was emotionally very distraught. The first words to greet me were, "We called the synagogue office nearly two hours ago. Where were you when we needed you?" I then tried everything within my power to help the family, but my efforts were to no avail since, from their vantage point, I wasn't around when needed. Sure, ninety-five percent of the time, arriving at the hospital an hour or two later wouldn't make a difference, but it did then. I learned a lesson that I never forgot. Being there when needed is the greatest comfort that one can provide.

In this chapter, we shall take a look at the friends of Job who sought to provide comfort for Job after he experienced a series of crushing losses. By today's standards, Job's friends violated every basic lesson as to how to deal with the bereaved. But they were there. That is the greatest comfort to any mourner.

THE NONPROFESSIONAL
IN THE HEALING PROCESS

The supreme comforter of the Jewish tradition is God Himself. The Torah records that Abraham died, and God visited
his son Isaac; "And it came to pass after the death of Abraham that
God blessed Isaac his son." (Genesis 25:11) The Talmud offers the
following commentary on the passage: "Just as God comforts the
bereaved so are you to comfort the bereaved."[1] We mortals are
called upon to imitate the ways of God and to bring comfort and
solace to the bereaved.

The best known comforters in biblical literature are the three
friends of Job: Eliphaz, Bildad, and Zofar. Readers throughout
the ages have different impressions of the personalities of the three
friends. Every student of the Bible knows that ultimately their
assistance was limited and that God, near the conclusion of the
book, tells Eliphaz that both he and his two friends have been
guilty of untruths in their attempted defense of God and that they
would be forgiven only if Job interceded on their behalf.[2]

But at the same time it would be wrong to dismiss the effectiveness of the friends in offering solace and comfort in a very
critical situation. What will be done in this section is to focus on
one of the friends and evaluate the techniques used by him which
enabled Job to come to grips with his losses and pain.

Although the friends of Job are not presented to the readers as
therapists or counselors, nevertheless they utilize various forms of
psychotherapy, some of which are still in the vogue today.

Today, we are often prone to seek out the professional to help
us deal with emotional and psychological problems that beset us.

---

1. *Sotah* 14a.
2. Job 42: 7–8

What the book of Job reminds us is that the nonprofessional can also make a significant contribution to the field of mental health.

A valuable part of the biblical and talmudic legacy is the non-ecclesiastical character of traditional Judaism. It was the prophet, the nonpaid professional like Amos, Elijah, and Jeremiah, who all denounce the royal ruler and priests as well as the masses of the people for being derelict in their allegiance to the only true government, the Kingdom of God.

Robert Gordis points out that this tendency was intensified by the historic role of Ezra at the reconstitution of the Second Commonwealth of the Babylonian exile. In entrusting spiritual leadership to the scribes or scholars in the synagogue and schoolhouses rather than to the priests in the Temple, he strengthened the nonecclesiastical character of traditional Judaism.[3] The Bible is essentially the creation of the amateurs in both senses of the term, the nonprofessional devotee and the lover of God who seeks to obey His will.

THE THERAPIST AS A FRIEND

In keeping with the spirit of recognizing the role of the nonprofessional, it is not the *kohen*, (the priest), or the *b'nai neviim*, (members of the prophetic guild), or the *hacham*, (the sage) who comes to provide a proper support system during Job's moment of travail. Rather, it is three people who are described simply *Reei Iyyob*, "as friends of Job" who will serve the function of professional therapists. Actually, the greatest compliment that can be paid to any therapist is for the patient to refer to him or her as "my friend." Job's friends plan an interpersonal interaction with Job in

---

3. Robert Gordis, *The Root and The Branch* (Chicago: University of Chicago Press, 1962), p. 74.

a nonmedical setting for the purpose of modifying and improving his moral conduct.[4]

The value of the comfort which Job's three friends gave to him was consistently underestimated by Job and indeed by most Bible commentators. But there can be no doubt that the presence of the comforters created a situation for Job pregnant with therapeutic and pathogenic possibilities. Together they form a group. Their common religious and ideological heritage is the basis for cohesion.[5]

I recognize that there are those who read the book of Job purely as an imaginative theological treatise. In this approach, the sole purpose of the dialogue is to give the author the opportunity of repudiating the conventional theology which is articulated by Job's friends. According to this view, Job is not a historical figure. Rather, he becomes the vehicle for the author articulating a new understanding of the problem of evil. Rish Lakish declares in the Talmud that Job never was created, nor did he exist, but rather Job is a parable. (Baba Bathra 15a)

In the same section, the Talmud, while discussing the historicity of the Book of Job, asks, if the Book of Job was a parable, why is Job's name cited together with Uz, the land from which he came. There is validity to an approach operating on the assumption that there was a historical figure named Job who became the nucleus of a folk tradition used by the author. The author could have conceivably thought of the kind of debates that ensued between friends when confronting the reality of coming to grips with a sudden inexplicable loss of a loved one. While the book may

---

4. S.L. Garfield, "Clinic Psychology," p. 219, quoted in Israel J. Gerber's *Job on Trial* (Gastonia, North Carolina: E.P. Press, Inc., 1982), p. 33.

5. J.H. Kahn, *Job's Illness, Loss, Grief & Integration* (Oxford, England: Pergamon Press, 1975), p. 62.

very well be the work of creative imagination, I shall treat the debate between Job and his friends as a live debate between real people. By doing so, the full richness of the dialogue is enhanced.

I will examine Eliphaz, who is the oldest and most urbane of the three friends, and attempt to analyze his approach in aiding Job.

Before proceeding, it is noteworthy to point out that Jewish law views Eliphaz and Job's two other friends as prototypes as to how one should conduct himself upon entering the house of a mourner. When they arrived at his home, the biblical text records: "For seven days and seven nights they sat beside him on the ground and none of them said a word to him for they saw that his suffering was great." (Job 2:13) It was only after Job spoke in Chapter 3 that Eliphaz responded in Chapter 4. Based upon the aforementioned passage, the Talmud states that one is not permitted to speak in a house of mourning until the mourner himself speaks.[6] This teaching was codified later in Jewish law.[7]

All of us have had the experience of conversing and then finding a lull in the conversation. Often, there is a frantic effort to say something so as to avoid the silence. A title of a book of Hebrew poems, *LaSheket Yesh Kol, Silence Has Its Voice Too*, conveys the thought that there can be a powerful form of communication without words being spoken.[8]

As stated earlier, it is only after Job breaks the silence that Eliphaz responds. Job laments his cruel fate, cursing the day he was born. How much better it would have been if he had never been conceived, or, failing that, had died in his mother's womb or had perished at the moment of birth. Were he dead, he would be in

---

6. *Moed Katan* 28b

7. *Shulhan Aruch*, Yoreh Deah 376.1.

8. Zeira Mordecai, (Tel Aviv: Education & Culture Centre of the General Federation of Labor Histadruth, 1966).

Sheol, the land of shadows where kings and princes fare no better than slaves and where the oppressor and his victim are equally at rest. (Job 3)

What is often overlooked is that the aforementioned expressions of one wishing to escape from life with its unending successions of terror is a very healthy response to what Job has experienced. The silence of the comforters matching the silence of Job released the anger which had been concealed in Job's depression. Up to the breaking of the silence, Job "did not utter one sinful word." Neither did the comforters utter a word of reproach to Job.

In this way, they differed from his wife, who had challenged the whole basis of Job's faith and way of life. Job's wife had reproached him for maintaining his perfection, granting him that perfection existed and merely questioning its worth on a scale of everyday values.[9] After he sustains losses of property and children and is stricken with a loathsome skin disease, she bitterly says, "Do you still hold fast to your piety? Curse God and die." The Midrash projects Job's wife as seeking to protect him. Fearful that he would not bear his horrible suffering with steadfastness, she pleads with him to pray to God for death that he might leave this world as an upright man.[10]

Using Freudian psychoanalytical theory, we may say anxiety is a product of the inevitable clash between the id and superego. The superego is the representative of the traditional values and ideals of society. The superego is composed of the conscience and the ego ideal. The conscience punishes behavior it considers immoral and the ego ideal rewards self-enhancing behavior. The id, on the other hand, is the original system of the personality. It is the reservoir of instinctual psychic energy (the libido), and it is com-

---

9. Kahn, p. 63.

10. Louis Ginzberg, *The Legends of the Jews* (Philadelphia: 1969), vol. 1, p. 235.

pletely unconscious. The id cannot tolerate tension, so it tries to discharge any tension that arises in it.[11]

In the case of Job, he wishes to retain a public posture of being a man who is pious and devout, who will not permit the adversity which he has encountered to change him. Initially, he inhibits his impulse to let down his guard and reveal to the community that he is "human" by challenging God for afflicting a man like him who is "pious." At the beginning of the book, he inhibits his aggressive impulse because he understands that society condemns it. Initially, we encounter a man who projects an image of being a paragon of virtue. But inside him there is seething repressed anger which eventually will be released. The biblical text itself may suggest that this anxiety, stemming from the tension between the superego and id, was already brewing before Job vented his anger at his cruel fate.

After Job rejects his wife's counsel to curse God, Job utters what is perhaps the most pious statement in the entire book: "Shall we accept good from God and not accept evil?" (Job 2:10)[12]

Immediately afterwards, the text records: "Yet even in all this Job committed no sin with his lips." (Job 2:10) Rashi, the medieval exegete, comments, "but he sinned in his heart." In other words, Rashi understood that there was already a conflict between Job's need to reduce uncomfortable tension by ventilating his feelings, and the ideals of society which Job adhered to, and which in this context meant stifling and repressing negative feelings towards God.

---

11. *Psychology Today*, ibid., p. 416.

12. Later the idea of this statement by Job became codified as a point of Jewish Law; the Mishnah in *Berachot* 9:1 states: It is obligatory to bless God for the evil as one is required to bless him for the good. The fact that this kind of aggadic statement becomes part of the Mishnah, a legal code, reflects how piety in face of tragedy became part of Jewish ideals.

SILENCE, A PRELUDE TO VENTING ANGER

The silence of the friends who came and sat for seven days together with Job without uttering a word has its value because of an insight that is often overlooked. In descriptions of psychotherapy, it is often taken for granted that the therapeutic medium is verbal communication. But the silences are as important as the spoken messages, and it is the sympathetic and accepting silence of the therapist which frequently aids the patient in constructing his cure.[13]

As stated earlier, the silence of the friends makes it easier for Job to vent his anger. Anger is a regular accompaniment of the normal mourning process and it is much like the temper tantrum of a frustrated child who loses self-control in the face of an unendurable hurt. The most important fact about this anger is that it enables the sufferer to turn his misery outward and so experience it in a more bearable form. Hence, the importance of the scapegoat.[14]

When anger is turned upon another, a scapegoat is sought. It may be someone within the family, a business partner, the attending physician, or religious leader. In the case of Job, it is upon God Himself, the supreme religious leader.

One may question the wisdom of Eliphaz, the eldest of the three friends, in speaking when he does. Perhaps just as the friends of Job sat and were silent with him for a period of seven days and seven nights, Eliphaz and Job's other two friends should have resumed their silence once again.

To answer this question properly, one must evaluate what Job

---

13. Kahn, p. 63.

14. Louis Linn and Leo Schwartz, *Psychiatry and Religious Experience* (New York: Random House, 1958), p. 182.

said in order to determine whether or not any kind of response should have been forthcoming. Obviously, such an analysis has its limitations. The task of offering a psychological analysis of those who are no longer living is fraught with many difficulties. We do not have any idea of their body language. We have no way of measuring the intensity of emotion and feeling with which the recorded words have been said. The text probably only capsulates a fuller dialogue between Job and his friends and thus we miss much valuable information. The real setting of the dialogue is not known to us. What kind of house did Job live in? What was his relationship with his children? What was his life like up to this point? One can add literally hundreds of points missing from the text that would shed light for anyone wishing to offer a diagnosis of Job. But, despite these glaring shortcomings, the text does yield for us important information.

In Chapter 3, when Job laments his cruel fate, he uses the imagery of his mother's womb. He says of the day of his birth, "Let the stars of its dawn be dark, may it hope for light, but have none, nor see the eyelids of the morning, because it did not shut the doors of my mother's womb or hide misery from my eyes. Why did I not die in the womb? Or perish as I came from it?" "Why were there knees to receive me and why breasts for me to suck? Or even if I had been an aborted birth like the stillborn infants who never see the light. There the victims are at rest. All the prisoners are at ease. They hear the taskmaster's shouts no more. There the small and great are equal and the slave is free from his master." (Job 3:9–12; 16–19) Similarly, the Talmud in *Nidah* 30b depicts the days that the embryo is in the mother's womb as the best days of his life. All of his physical needs are provided and the Talmud also speaks of these days as days in which the embryo learns the entire Torah. In other words, the world inside the mother's womb represents the ideal perfect world.

Otto Rank describes what he calls the "birth trauma," the theory of the cry for the return to the womb. When life gets hard and reality brutal, when the world rebuffs us and our spirits are bruised, we psychically remember that there was a time in our experience when everything was perfect. Profoundly and unconsciously, we do remember the womb. It was the one time when there was no pain, no anxiety, no fright[15]; all was filled with security with no trouble.

Advanced psychosis such as schizophrenia is an example of trying to return to the womb. In mental hospitals, we often find people who are in a fetal position lying down with knees drawn up and their heads down.[16] Perhaps when Eliphaz heard Job using this kind of imagery, he feared that Job had undergone significant changes and diagnosed Job as having proclivities to schizophrenia, and thus he feels compelled to say something to avoid having Job sink further into this infantile stage.

DOES JOB EXPRESS A DEATH WISH?

Furthermore, there are some who read Chapter 3 as Job expressing a wish for death. Other passages, such as 6:8–10, 7:15, and 10:18–19 all express a possible wish for death. Ultimately, Job does not attempt suicide because, despite all the anger and indignation leveled against God, he knows that his God will vindicate him. His God is more interested in hearing Job reveal his innermost thoughts even when they appear to the simple to be blasphemous. Job's God is not interested in hearing from him pious platitudes. "Indeed he will surely be my salvation for it is no flatterer coming before him." (Job 13:16) A flatterer expresses the

---

15. Otto Rank, *The Trauma of Birth* (New York: Harcourt Brace & Company, 1929).

16. Wesley C. Baker, *More Than A Man Can Take: A Study in Job* (Westminster Press, 1946).

words that he expects the other will want to hear. From the vantage point of the author of Job, God will not turn back the tormented soul even when to others his words may appear to be heretical. Possibly some of the verses cited below indicate a preference for death over life which is not the same as contemplating suicide.

The question remains unresolved. But a sensitive friend like Eliphaz, hearing the cry of a wretched and tormented soul who says, "Why did I not die in the womb or perish as I came forth from it?" and who will later say, "O that I might have my petition and God would grant my hope that it would please God to crush me to loose his hand and cut me off! For this would be my consolation as I trembled in pitiless agony" (Job 3:11; 6:8–10) or "so that I prefer strangling death rather than this existence. I loathe my life I shall not live forever. Let me alone, for my days are as breath" (7:15–16), might have deduced that Job does not want to live. Given the limitations of being able to probe another person's psyche, Eliphaz may have interpreted the aforementioned words as suicidal wishes. And if he (Eliphaz) was to err, it would be better to err on the side of being overalarmed rather than treating lightly what may have been a desperate call for help.

And what is this death wish if not a desperate cry for help to be able to continue living? The response that Job tries to evoke is the restoration of meaning to his existence. "Suicide attempts," writes Bruno Bettleheim, "are generally attempts which are expected to be aborted but unfortunately are not."[17]

Conversely, one can argue that any attempt to see Chapter 3 as expressing a death wish fails to take into consideration that his bitter lament about being better off not having been born is reflective of a mind set which became normative in Jewish theology. Perhaps its clearest expression is to be found in the Talmud,

17. Bruno Bettelheim, *Surviving and Other Essays* (New York: Alfred A. Knopf, 1979), p.4.

where there is recorded an issue debated for two and one half years between the House of Hillel and the House of Shamma. The House of Hillel maintained better was it for man to have been created than not to have been created, while the House of Shamma maintained, "Better would it have been for man not to have been created than to have been created." The issue was called to a decision and it was concluded that "better would it have been for man not to have been created, but now that he has been created, let him examine his behavior."[18] Or what shall we say about the editor of the Mishnah, Rabbi Judah, the Prince, who at his death called upon heaven as a witness that he did not enjoy this world even to the extent of his small finger.[19]

In an article entitled "Is Judaism An Optimistic Religion?" Shubert Spero writes, "Any attempt to take God and Judaism seriously must involve profound life-long anxieties and not peace of mind in any usual sense of that term; that metaphysical optimism notwithstanding, the more accurate description of the Jewish religion temperament is probably pessimism; that in spite of the fact that the Torah does not forbid us to enjoy life, it does not follow that the thinking Jew therefore necessarily does enjoy it."[20] While Spero's attempt to portray Judaism as a pessimistic religion is rejected by virtually all scholars, the problem of theodicy, that is, the existence of both physical and moral evil, remains the Achilles' heal of religion. In moments when we anguish over the inability to reconcile the presence of evil with a compassionate and loving God, it's easy to empathize with Job's pessimistic assessment of the predicament of life.

So one could conclude that Job's statements are in keeping

---

18. *Eruvin* 13b.

19. *Ketubot* 104a.

20. Shubert Spero, "Is Judaism An Optimistic Religion?" in *A Treasury of Tradition*, edited by Norman Lamm and Walter S. Wurzburger (New York: Hebrew Publishing Company, 1967), pp. 204–205.

with the spirit to be found in the aforementioned statements from the Talmud, which reveal a pessimistic or realistic assessment of the predicament of life.

Job's statements of despair and depression are not to be taken as abstract intellectual expressions of the absurdity of the human predicament but rather as statements reflecting the mental set of one who has sustained losses which are appalling, shocking, and distressing. Job is now afflicted with a variety of personal illnesses, such as *shehin* (Job 2:7), an eruption of loathsome sores that cover his own body. He also suffers from depression as a result of his loss of livestock, that is, all of his property and wealth and his most precious possessions, his seven sons and three daughters. As such, after he speaks in Chapter 3, bitterly crying out hopelessly and in tremendous pain, it is understandable why Eliphaz decides to step forward and speak rather than continuing to be silent.

He is cautious and hesitant, first securing permission to share a thought with Job: "If one tried a word with you, would you be offended, yet who can refrain from speaking?" (Job 4:2) Just as Job had initially suppressed venting his anger and then released it, likewise Eliphaz informs Job that there are thoughts within him that have been bottled up which he can no longer suppress.[21]

Recognizing that any word said to Job may not mollify him and soothe his anguish and pain, he couches his words in a delicate manner in which it sounds like a third person is speaking. "If one tried a word with you, would you be offended?" (Job 4:2) The sensitive way he begins to speak is followed up almost apologetically with the words, "Yet who can refrain from speaking?" Something must be said. He reminds Job that he (Job) was the one who strengthened others during their moment of travail. "Behold you have encouraged many and strengthened weak hands. Your

---

21. For a parallel verse describing pent-up thoughts bottled up inside a person which await a release see Jer. 20:9.

words have upheld the stumbling and you have strengthened the weak-kneed. But now that it has come to you, you cannot bear it, it touches you, and you are dismayed." (Job 4:3–4)

Perhaps Eliphaz correctly diagnosed one of the symptoms of grief, which is loss of muscular strength. One grieving individual told his doctor, "My legs just don't seem to be able to hold me up."[22]

Eliphaz, as one of Job's three friends, looks at Job and sees an entirely new man. "Now when they caught sight of him from afar they could not recognize him." (Job 2:12) His shoulders were probably sagging, as is a common occurrence with grieving people. The eruption of shehin (a skin disease) covers his body. He is probably slumping forward and sighing very deeply. In Job 3:24 he complains, "Indeed my sighing comes like my daily bread, my groans are poured out like water." Thus, when Eliphaz sees his friend in such a pathetic position, he draws upon the imagery which suggests an ability to walk erect without stumbling and slumping. "Your words have upheld the stumbling and you have strengthened the weak-kneed." (Job 4:4)

In a Greek apocryphal book containing an aggadic story of Job, we find the author embellishing the description of the radical changes that Job had undergone as a result of his misfortunes. It is told that when the four friends arrived in the city in which Job lived, the inhabitants took them outside the gates and, pointing to a figure reclining upon an ash-heap at some distance off, they said, "Yonder is Job." At first, the friends would not believe them and they decided to look more closely at the man to make sure of his identity. But the foul smell emanating from Job was so strong that they could not come near to him. They ordered their armies to scatter perfumes and aromatic substances all around. Only after

---

22. Arthur Freese, *Help For Your Grief* (New York: Schocken Books, 1977), p. 33.

this had been done for hours, they could approach the outcast close enough to recognize him.[23]

It was Thomas Mann who once said, "A man's dying is more the survivors' affair than his own." Job is a crushed man. We often hear about the identity problems as the survivor has to redefine who he is and what he wants when his habitual moorings are gone.[24]

Job's identity problem is compounded by virtue of the fact that he physically is now a different looking man.

Eliphaz is calling upon Job to regain inner strength by reminding him that Job was the one who used to console sufferers. He is thus challenging Job to put into practice those teachings which have governed his life. He in effect is saying that Job always advised others to be steeled through adversity, now it is the hour that he must practice what he preached.

Israel Gerber speaks of Eliphaz as employing authoritarian firmness.[25] Underlying this approach is the supposition that people in extreme situations need to be controlled and need to be told what to do, otherwise they will sink into further depression and inactivity, which is reflected in Job's outcry in Chapter 3. Then, Eliphaz reminds Job of one of the great truths of religion, that the righteous are never destroyed. "Think now, what innocent man was ever destroyed; where was the upright cut off? (Job 4:7) At the same time, Eliphaz reminds Job that the wicked will be punished either in their own persons or that of their children.

"Whenever I have seen those who plow iniquity and sow trouble they reap it! By the breath of God they are destroyed. . . .

---

23. Testament of Job (7–9), See Ginzberg, vol 2, p. 237 and vol. 5, p. 387.

24. Martin Shepard, *Someone You Love Is Dying* (New York: Harmony Books, 1975), p. 159.

25. Gerber, p. 35.

The mighty lion wanders about without prey, and the young of the lioness are scattered." (Job 4:8–11)

Eliphaz here is appealing to Job's intelligence and ability to reason, explaining to him the cause of his affliction. He assumes that if Job comprehends the situation, he will repent and modify his behavior.

Perhaps Job himself is more receptive to an intellectual interpretation, as indicated elsewhere in the book, where he says, "Teach me and I shall be silent, and where I have erred make me understand." (Job 6:24)

SHATTERING OF ETERNAL VERITIES

It is here that Eliphaz touches upon a point that will be difficult for Job to accept. For herein lies the dilemma of the book itself. The reality of Job's experience shatters the so-called eternal verities of his faith. He presumes righteousness. He is totally, unequivocally, and unambiguously convinced of his moral rectitude and piety.

He takes a passionate oath insisting that he will never concede that he is guilty, and by that token, deserving of the agony that he has suffered. "As God lives, who has robbed me of my right and by the Almighty who has embittered my soul." (Job 27:2) This is an oath which is not couched in words like, I think, I assume I claim, but rather "As God lives," which is his way of saying, "I believe with every fiber of my being."[26]

However, there is no indication that this position of Job,

---

26. Rashi states that from this verse Rabbi Joshua derived the fact that Job worshipped God out of love because man does not make a promise in the name of the King unless he loves the King. Mishnah *Sotah* 5:5.

namely, that one can be righteous and still suffer, is ever considered to be valid by Job's friends. Throughout the book, they maintain a theological viewpoint which states that Job suffers because he has sinned. It is interesting to note that in a formulation that in some respects is similar to equity theory, the social psychologist Melvin Lerner has proposed the existence of a justice motive. Basically, this construct assumes the belief in a just world— a belief that there is an appropriate fit between what people do and what happens to them. By blaming the victim, we can maintain our belief that people get what they deserve. In interviews with hundreds of victims of rapes, assaults, and kidnappings, we find that many of these victims receive, instead of sympathy, inquisitions and censure from their family and friends. When a person has been mugged, for example, a frequent response of friends, family, and police is to interrogate the person relentlessly about why he or she got into such an unfortunate situation. "Why were you walking in the neighborhood alone?" "Why didn't you scream?" "Why were you carrying so much money?" Such reactions reflect our need to find rational causes for apparently senseless events.[27] In April 1968, right after Martin Luther King's assassination, a representative sampling of 1,337 American adults was asked: "When you heard the news of the assassination, which of these things was your strongest reaction: 1) anger, 2) sadness, 3) shame, 4) fear, 5) he brought it on himself?" About one-third (426) of the respondents chose the response "he brought it on himself" (Rokeach, 1970). For these respondents, Lerner's "just world" hypothesis applies: Since Dr. King was killed, he must have deserved to be killed.[28]

It is tempting at one level to believe that bad things happen to

---

27. Lawrence S. Wrightsman and Kay Deaux, *Social Psychology in the 80's* (Monterey, Cal.: Brooks/Cole Publishing, 1977), pp. 229–230.
   28. Ibid., p. 231.

people (especially other people) and that people get exactly what they deserve. By believing that, we keep the world orderly and understandable.[29]

Eliphaz could easily identify with the following point of view expressed by the prophet Isaiah: "Tell the righteous it shall be well with them for they shall eat the fruit of their deeds. Woe to the wicked, it shall be ill with him, for what his hands have done shall be done to him." (Isaiah 3:10–11) Or the sentiment expressed by the author of Proverbs would also be one with which he could identify: "No ill befalls the righteous, but the wicked are filled with trouble." (Proverbs 12:21)

It would be hundreds of years later before the third century Sage Jannai would express in an abstract and unemotional form the truth which the author of the book of Job had discovered through bitter experience: "It is not in our power to understand either the suffering of the righteous or the prosperity of the wicked."[30]

Eliphaz hammers across to Job the "eternal verities" of a comfortable religious outlook which explains everything in a lucid manner: "Think now, what innocent man was ever destroyed; where was the upright cut off?" (Job 4:7) God is just, and therefore Job is getting what he deserves.

Eliphaz operates on the premise that first you diagnose a problem, explain it to the bereaved, and then the bereaved will realize his erring ways and repent. When that takes place, Job's pain and agony will subside.

The force of the word *zachor* in Job 4:7, which literally means "remember," but which we have translated as "think," is used by Eliphaz so that the historical experiences of the past and countless

---

29. Harold J. Kushner, *When Bad Things Happen to Good People* (New York: Schocken Book, 1981), p. 9.

30. M. *Avot* 4:15.

of other situations in which the "truths" of religion were operative
will hopefully bring Job to his senses and help him realize that he
has sinned.

Perhaps the use of the word *zachor* is in response to a common
phenomenon in the grieving process, the difficulty of remember-
ing. As one psychiatrist put it, "The bereaved don't learn as
readily. They get preoccupied with their own problems, rather
than absorbing new ideas. In short, the grieving person may not be
able to remember how much he or she paid for something just
bought or what a friend's new telephone number is, where ordinarily it would be easy to do so."[31]

Eliphaz, as stated earlier, begins his address in a conciliatory
and not an accusatory tone. However, as he continues, his tone of
speaking becomes less and less pleasant. The approach of Eliphaz
is based on the recognition that there are instances when the
counselor should keep the patient at a certain level of anxiety by
presenting to him stimuli that will not be pleasant for him to
assimilate. You don't keep a patient calm, but rather through
providing information that will anger the patient, the patient will
then ventilate and eventually relax. When a patient is relaxed you
present to him stimuli that are a little harsher and by then, the
patient will be able to handle it a little better. What Job is accused
of in Chapter 4 is milder than what Eliphaz accuses him of in
Chapter 15. In the third cycle, Chapter 22, Job is accused by
Eliphaz of violating virtually every moral sin under the sun.

It is wholly impossible to engage in psychotherapy or in psychoanalysis without confronting the patient once, twice, or many
times. Confrontation cannot be avoided, nor should it be avoided.[32]

In Chapter 22, Eliphaz confronts Job with the hope that Job

---

31. Freese, p. 66.
32. James Mann, *Confrontation in Psychotherapy*, edited by Gerald
Adler and Paul Myerson (New York: Science House, p.41).

will feel the need to change. The purpose of confrontation is to show the patient what he or she is resistant to talk and feel about.[33] In a confrontation setting, the more the therapist dislikes the patient's behavior, the more driven he may feel to have the patient change it, and his anger conveys with force this expectation to the patient.[34]

BITTUSH—A HASIDIC APPROACH TO RECOVERY

Centuries after Job was written, some hasidic rebbes would use a highly controversial method of counseling which bears some affinities to the method employed by Eliphaz. This approach was known as *bittush*, (shattering). It was predicated upon the belief that chronic depression can best be broken by heightening the condition to a piercingly acute state. "Interpreting the story of Exodus on this level, they taught that the hasid must sacrifice his 'animal soul' in order to liberate his imprisoned yearnings for renewed life."

How was this "death" to be accomplished? Sometimes the hasid's discipline was intensified through fasting and enforced solitude. But above all, rebbes strove to induce the hasid to cry— not with fleeting tears, but with wracking, soul-wrenching sobs, weeping that welled up from one's entire being. Feelings of aching dullness had to give way to release. The hasid's inner resignation was transformed first to the wordless scream "Help me Father!"; then to a long wail like a *shofar* blast; then to a broken weeping; and finally to a shattering whimpering. Only after utter despair could some laughter and joy be heard, the hasidic leaders

---

33. Arvidson, p. 166.
34. Welpton, p. 254.

stressed. The hopelessness that had characterized the inescapability of death had become the impetus for a flight to life.

Of course, not every person was strong enough to withstand such a crisis; but the rebbes regarded palliatives and easy assurances as serving ultimately only to prolong a serious depression. As long as one appeared able to withstand the *bittush*, no one could spare him the ordeal. It was deemed the surest and quickest way to mental recovery.[35]

A hasidic rebbe, Rabbi Nachman of Bratslav, once put it this way: "In working with people to bring them to themselves, one must work at great depth, a depth scarcely imaginable."

The method of *bittush* employed by some hasidic rebbes in Poland in the nineteenth century may not be in the vogue today, just as the methods employed by friends of Job would generally not win sympathetic support today. But what is most crucial is whether or not the suffering person is able to have his pain alleviated and once again be able to function and deal with the exigencies of daily life.

Eliphaz and Job's other friends sought to overcome Job's elaborate defenses and have him come to grips with the truth, even though what they said was very unpleasant. They shook Job into a realistic self-appraisal. Rabbi Isaac Meir of Ger once said, "I need a rebbe who will flay the living skin from my flesh, not one who will flatter me." Ecclesiastics similarly reminded his readers, "It is better to hear the rebuke of the wise, than for a man to hear the song of fools" (Ecclesiastics 7:5)

Job's friends used a directive method in which they sought to uncover the mistaken idea and harmful attitudes which they felt were responsible for the suffering endured by Job. Today it is far

---

35. Zalman M. Schachter and Edward Hoffman, *Sparks of Light*, Counseling to the Hasidic Tradition, (Shambhala, Boulder-Longdon 1983), pp. 152–153.

more in vogue for a therapist to develop a relationship whereby the patient is able to gain understanding of himself so that he can take positive steps to effectuate changes. The judgmental approach employed by the friends of Job is currently not riding on a wave of popularity. The friends of Job who appear to speak in the name of authority rather than at times with the voice of compassion cannot be dismissed as ineffective or insensitive friends simply because they don't comport to a modality in style today.

Actually, Job's friends are in one significant respect similar to clergymen. For clergymen more than psychiatrists are authority figures and they are in a particularly strong position to enforce normal behavior and reality based reactions on those who temporarily lose control.

Thus, one minister pulled one of his parishioners out of an acute anxiety state by saying firmly, "Now Judy, buck up." He later told me with some awe, "You know, she did."

Eliphaz also tries to have Job gain insight into his predicament by bringing to his attention some kind of communication that he received from God. "Now to me a word came stealthily, and my ear caught an echo of it amid thoughts and visions of the night when deep sleep falls upon men." (Job 4:12–13) The thoughts and visions of the night represent a form of revelation. They represent the voice of authority, of God himself. The thoughts and vision of the night offer cogent and irrefutable evidence that Job's disclaim of any guilt is not valid. Again, Eliphaz couches his remarks indirectly. He does not accuse Job of being a sinner. He simply reminds him that all men are imperfect: "Can a human being be righteous before God? Can a mortal be pure before his maker?" (Job 4:17) Again, there is no direct mention of Job sinning.

Eliphaz, after picturing the punishment that will eventually overtake the sinner, proceeds to remind Job that the anger that Job feels is hardly helpful now. Job should call out to God and admit that he is in error and not carry on in a state of rage: "Call out—who is there to answer you? To whom can you turn other than to God? Anger surely lulls the fool and impatience slays the simpleton." (Job 5:1–2) Eliphaz is here trying to get Job to calm down.

Eliphaz reminds Job of another basic teaching, namely that evil is a human invention: "indeed, misfortune does not come forth from the ground, nor does evil sprout from the earth. It is man who gives birth to evil as surely as the sparks fly upward." (Job 5:6–7) Here Eliphaz is trying to appeal to Job to take control over his predicament. Job perceives of himself as being a helpless victim. Eliphaz gently reminds him that just as he (Job) brought the evil upon himself, likewise he will learn to cope much better with his losses after he admits that he has sinned.

Later in Chapter 5, Eliphaz introduces the idea that suffering serves a noble purpose. Victor Frankl, a Viennese psychiatrist who escaped the concentration camps, developed a new approach to psychology called logotherapy. According to logotherapy, the striving to find meaning in one's life is the primary motivational force in man.[36]

Unlike psychoanalysis, which focuses on the patient's past, logotherapy focuses on the patient's future. In logotherapy, the patient is confronted with and reoriented toward the meaning of life.[37]

Therefore, suffering may well be a human achievement, especially if the suffering grows out of existential frustration. According to Frankl, there is much wisdom to the words of Nietzsche: "He who has a why to live for, can bear almost any how."[38] Traditional psychotherapy has aimed at restoring one's capacity to work and to enjoy life: logotherapy includes these, yet

36. Victor Frankl, *Man's Search for Meaning: An Introduction to Logotherapy* (New York: Washington Square Press Inc., 1963), p. 154.
37. Ibid., p. 153.
38. Ibid., p. 164.

goes further by having the patient regain his capacity to suffer, if need be, thereby finding meaning in suffering.[39]

Eliphaz exhorts Job to be proud of his suffering and to consider it ennobling rather than degrading. He says: "Happy is the man whom God reproves, do not despise chastisements of the Almighty." (Job 5:17) He continues by reassuring him that ultimately Job will find relief from his suffering, " For he makes sore and binds one up. He wounds and his hands bring healing." (Job 5:18)

Job is now called upon to recognize that the vast majority of those who suffer grief and go through bereavement recover. Eliphaz tries to impress upon Job that if one takes advantage of the opportunity for growth and change, which grief often brings in its wake, one can emerge as a stronger, more mature and happier person. The tremendous emotional upheaval, the death of someone close, virtually forces us to reassess our entire life from a wholly new perspective, producing a change we can turn into growth if we wish it. Perhaps in the aforementioned light, we can best understand the following rabbinic statements:

> *Havivin Yesurin*, "Beloved is pain";[40] *Yehay Adam Sameach B'Yesurin Yoter Min Hatovah*, "A man should be happier with pain than good"; *Im Hayim Atah Mevakesh Tzapeh L'Yesurin*, "If thou desirest Life hope for pain"[41]; *Kol HaSameach B'Yesurin Shebain Alav Mevee Yeshuah L'Olam*, "He who rejoices over the pains with which he is afflicted, brings salvation to the world."[42]

---

39. Ibid., p. 180.

40. *Taanit* 21:1. Later the term *Havinin Yesurin* (Beloved is pain) became a popular expression denoting a certain theological orientation (See *Berachot* 5b).

41. Psikta Drav Kahana 179B, Midrash Tehillim 16:12.

42. *Taanit* 8a, See Torah *Min Hashamayim B'Aspiklaria Shel*

The aforementioned should not be viewed only as statements reflecting individuals with extraordinary spiritual power, but also as mirroring a law of life. There is no growth without grief and no gain without loss. Eliphaz expresses confidence that there is a road back from suffering. He continues by saying that, "At the devastation of famine you will laugh and the beasts of the earth you will not fear." (Job 5:22) The laughter here is one of defiance, a laughter which symbolizes a determination not to be vanquished by the tragedies of life.

Eliphaz tried to lift Job's spirits up by telling him that Job will be imbued with this ability to laugh defiantly at attempts to destroy him. Eliphaz nears the conclusion of his first speech by painting a picture in which Job would live to a ripe old age in serenity and peace. He has not only presented to him the "distilled wisdom" of the ages but also one which has been subjected to sound critical investigation: "Behold, this we have searched out—it is true We have heard it, now take it to heart." (Job 5:27)

In the second cycle of speeches, Eliphaz is not as patient. He attempts to discredit Job by psychoanalyzing him. He suggests that Job's protestations are prompted by feelings of guilt. "It is your guilt that teaches your mouth and makes you choose crafty speech." (Job 15:5) Perhaps the motivation of Eliphaz for making such an interpretation was because he could not tolerate Job's angry feelings. He obviously also felt that there was a defensive self-justifying element to his explanation.

Again, there is an appeal to authority: "Both the gray beard and the aged are among us, older in years than your father." (Job 15:10)

Hadorot, A.J. Heschel, 1962, pp. 93–110 for an overview of how rabbis dealt with suffering. Also see "The Meaning of Suffering, a Talmudic Response to Theodicy," Matthew B. Schwartz, *Judaism*, Fall 1983, pp. 441–451, and *Chazal*, Ephrayim E. Urbach, Jerusalem: Magness Press, 1975. The latter work also has been translated into English. See *Sages Their Concepts & Beliefs* (Jerusalem: Magness Press, 1979).

Again, Eliphaz resorts to one of the oldest of all psychothera-
peutic techniques, authoritarian firmness. It is designed to frighten
Job into altering his alleged wicked behavior.[43]

At this point, a new teaching is introduced here. "Do not envy
the wicked," says Eliphaz, "for he will live with constant fear. All
his days, the wicked will tremble throughout the few years stored
up for the oppressor. The sound of terror is always in his ears; even
while at peace he fears the despoiler coming upon him." (Job
15:20–21)

NEVER LETTING GO OF GUILT FEELINGS

One of the classic biblical illustrations of being overcome with a
profound sense of guilt after committing a sin is revealed in the
saga of Joseph and his brothers. When Joseph rose to the rank of
Grand Vizier in Egypt, his brothers were forced to come down to
Egypt during a famine that seems to have spread over many parts
of the Ancient Near East. The brothers now stand before Joseph,
who is in charge of distributing food supplies. He recognizes
them, but they do not recognize him. At least twenty years have
elapsed from the time they shamefully and pitilessly sold him into
slavery. He tests them to see if they truly honor their father, love
their brother Benjamin, and are contrite over the heinous crime
they had committed over twenty years earlier. Joseph accuses
them of being spies and incarcerates them for a three-day period.
He retains one of them as a hostage on the condition that they
return to Canaan and bring back with them their brother Benjamin. Upon hearing the condition of the release, the brothers
turn to each other and say, "Alas we are being punished on

---

43. Gerber, *Job On Trial*, ibid., p. 35.

account of our brother because we looked on his anguish, yet we paid no heed as he pleaded with us. That is why this distress has come upon us." (Genesis 42:21) No one else had raised the issue of Joseph being sold into slavery. Over twenty years have passed since that shameful day. However, the guilt feeling still gnaws away at them, and immediately they correlate their punishment now with what had taken place much earlier. There are values they lived by, and now they expect to be punished for their failure to live up to those values.

After they bring Benjamin back with them, Joseph orders a goblet to be placed in the sack of Benjamin, unbeknownst to Benjamin or any of the other brothers. After the brothers depart from Egypt to return home, they are stopped by a messenger of Joseph and accused of stealing a goblet. They are convinced of their innocence. They propose that the death penalty be meted out to the thief, and if any of them are found guilty, then they should all be held as slaves. The steward, however, says that only the guilty party will be held as Joseph's slave. When the investigation results in the goblet being discovered in the sack of Benjamin, Judah, speaking on behalf of all of his brothers, says, "What shall we say unto my lord, what shall we speak? Or how shall we clear ourselves. God has uncovered the crime of your servants." (Genesis 44:16) Judah knows that the accusation leveled against them has no foundation. He knows there are trumped up charges against them. The sin that Judah is referring to is the sin that they had concealed all those years, namely the sale of their brother Joseph into slavery. The crime committed against their brother weighed heavily on them. Their consciences could not make peace with it. Wherever they turned, the sin of twenty years earlier loomed large in front of them.

King David expresses a similar kind of sentiment as does Judah when he says, "For I acknowledge my transgressions; and my sin is ever before me." (Psalms 51:4) The reference in the

Psalm is to David's illicit relationship with Bat Sheva.[44] As Eliphaz reminds Job, the "sound of terror" is always in the ear of those that do evil.

In Dostoyevski's *Crime and Punishment*, Raskolnikof anguishes over the murder that he has committed. It does not permit him to have one moment of peace.

Job earlier has contended, "The tent of the robbers are at peace." (Job 12:6) Eliphaz takes issue with that and says: "All the days, the wicked is trembling. The sound of terror is always in his ears; even while at peace he fears the despoiler coming upon him. He does not escape from the darkness, but can look forward only to the sword. He wanders about for bread asking, 'Where is it?' knowing that the day of darkness awaits him." (Job 15:20–23)

"The sound of terror is always in his ears" would seem to indicate that he has hallucinations. The darkness that he cannot escape from appears to be depressions. Hallucinations and delusions always tied to guilt frequently accompany severe depression.[45] The robber overloaded with feelings of guilt also becomes seriously depressed, according to Eliphaz. Again, by indirection, he doesn't accuse Job of rebelling and repudiating the teachings of God, but simply says that the wicked will suffer because he is rebelling against God. "He stretches out his hand against God and played the hero against the Almighty." (Job 15:25)

Eliphaz has not as yet confronted Job directly and said outright that "you, Job, are a sinner." That takes place as indicated earlier in Chapter 22. At this stage, accusing him directly would be much too threatening to Job. No matter how cautious are the interpretations of Eliphaz, resistance develops in Job like it does as

---

44. For a full discussion of Joseph's brothers' guilty feelings, see *Iyunim B'Sefer Bereshit*, Nechama Leibowitz, Jerusalem: Jewish Agency, 1970; pp. 329–333.

45. Peter E. Nathan and Sandra L. Harris, *Psychopathology and Society* (New York: McGraw Hill Inc., 1975), p. 226.

often by any patient in response to insights offered by the therapist. Immediately after Chapter 15, we find Job in Chapter 16
maintaining complete innocence. He knows there is a witness in
heaven who will ultimately vindicate him: "Behold even now, my
witness is in heaven and he who vouches for me is on high." (Job
16:19) The ability to handle this resistance is an important part of
the analyst's skill. Resistance is the form repression takes in the
psychoanalytic situation. Thus, the analyst's task is to weaken it.[46]

However, in the case of Eliphaz and his friends, there is a
misdiagnosis. Job's resistance to admission of his guilt will not be
diminished. The purpose of the book of Job is to teach us that man
can suffer without sinning. Job's position is vindicated, as indicated in the last chapter, and Eliphaz and his friends are found
guilty of speaking falsely in their defense of God: "The Lord said
to Eliphaz the Temanite, 'My anger is kindled against you and
your two friends for you have not spoken the truth about me as my
servant Job.'" (Job 42:7)

In the third cycle of speeches, Chapter 22, Eliphaz moves from
the third person to second person, and he offers a catalogue of all
the sins committed by Job: "Your wickedness is immense and
there is no end to your iniquities. For you have taken pledges even
from your kinsmen for no reason and stripped the naked of their
clothing. No water have you given to the weary, and from the
hungry you have withheld bread. For you believe the man of
violence owns the land and he who is powerful lives upon it.
Widows you have sent away empty-handed and the arms of the
fatherless are crushed." (Job 22:5–9) In other words, you, Job,
have operated on the principle that might makes right.[47] You have
violated every law of human decency. Neither Job nor Eliphaz

---

46. Norman D. Sundberg, Leona E. Tyler, *Clinical Psychology*
(New York: Appleton Century Crofts, 1962), p. 378.
47. In the Talmud Rabbi Elazar makes the sad observation that the
land is given to men of violence. *Sanhedrin* 58b.

seem willing to consider that some degree of goodness could be mixed with a proportion of badness.[48]

In light of what we are told in the opening chapters, of Job being a man of impeccable moral credentials, it would seem that in chapter 22, in order to illustrate his theological position that man is not suffering without sin, Eliphaz exaggerates the misdeeds of Job. The very nature of polemics always involves overstating one's position.

At the conclusion of Chapter 22, Eliphaz beseeches Job to change his ways and draw closer to God: "Put yourself in harmony with him and make peace and thus you will attain to well being. Accept instruction from his mouth and place his words in your heart. If you return to the Almighty you will be rebuilt. . . . When you pray to him he will hear you, and you will pay your vows in thanksgiving. Even the guilty will escape punishment, escaping through the purity of your hands." (Job 22:21–23, 27, 30)

The approach employed by Eliphaz here is counselor centered. It is directive. The object has been to uncover the mistaken ideas and harmful attitudes of the patient's behavior and get the patient to modify them. The approach is the very opposite of the approach popularized by Carl Rogers referred to as client-centered therapy, which calls for a phenomenological approach to human experience. Rogers approach is one which deals with the world as the patient sees it, rather than with objective realities. Within this phenomenological world, it is the individual's concept of himself that is most important.[49] Here, Eliphaz presents therapy from the vantage point of the reality as understood by the therapist himself.

It is no accident that the very last words placed in the mouth of Eliphaz by the author of Job are words which, although directed to Job, will apply later to Eliphaz and Zophar and Bildad.

---

48. Kahn, p, 84.
49. Garfield, p. 320.

Eliphaz, in trying to impress upon Job the abundance of God's mercy, says that if Job admits that he has sinned, God will forgive other guilty people of their sins. Job's purity of hands will be an instrument for saving others. And so it was, except the wicked that escape punishment are none other than Eliphaz, Bildad, and Zophar. For, in God speaking to Eliphaz in Job 42:8, the text records: "Now then take seven bulls and seven rams and to my servant Job offer them as a burnt offering for yourselves. My servant Job must intercede for you for only to him will I show favor and not expose you to disgrace for not speaking the truth about me as did my servant Job."

The contrast between the alleged wickedness of Job leveled against him by Eliphaz in chapter 22 and the role of Job being an interceder on behalf of Eliphaz, Bildad, and Zophar is most striking. For the role of an interceder who prayed on behalf of his people was reserved for the prophets.

THE VICTIM INTERCEDING FOR FRIENDS

In brief, Eliphaz made a valiant effort to reach Job, but he was totally unprepared for a vastly changed Job. For all of the teachings of religion had been challenged by a shattering personal experience. Job must choose between tradition and experience, between the body of convictions and beliefs accumulated by the generations on the one hand and the testimony of his own conscience and reactions on the other hand.[50]

George Bernard Shaw once said that the smartest man he ever met was his tailor. For whenever he would visit him, the tailor would always measure him anew, never assuming he was the

---

50. Robert Gordis, *Judaism*, vol. 4, no. 3, Summer 1955, p. 197.

same size, recognizing that there stood before him a new man. Job had grown through his own personal experience. He was no longer willing to accept a theology predicated on the theory that there is a direct correlation between suffering and sin. Eliphaz and the other friends were totally unprepared for the new Job.

However, there are redeeming features to the approach used by Eliphaz. Eliphaz enables Job to reconcile himself to his loss and reestablish a relationship with God. First, as indicated earlier, he was there with Job. Job was not alone. Secondly, by constantly asking him to accept his guilt, Eliphaz and Job's other friends were trying to convey the idea that Job had control over his fate, for if Job would repent and redirect his heart to God according to Job's friends, the pain would surely subside, and God in his infinite mercy would forgive him and return Job to his earlier position of eminence.

Finally, by challenging Job, God let his friend utilize a cure that is at the very heart of psychotherapy. "It is only the bereaved who bury their feelings, their anger, guilt, sorrow, and the rest that are in for serious trouble."[51]

The lesson of the talking cure is that feelings should be expressed. The mourner who wants to find the road back must express his or her feelings openly—there must be weeping and wailing and anger expressed in an appropriate manner. The person who fails to express his or her feelings ends up like a heated kettle which can't blow off steam and finally builds up the inner pressure until it just simply explodes. There has to be a vent and safety valve.[52] Clearly, Job expresses his feelings of loss, anger, and helplessness, and in some measure it's due to the presence of his friend, Eliphaz.

---

51. Freese, p. 182.
52. Ibid., p. 183.

4

LISTENING

When I began my career in the rabbinate, I always felt good when people would compliment me on delivering a fine sermon. With the passge of years, I've come to appreciate that the greatest compliment that can be paid to a rabbi or any clergyman is to refer to him or her as a good listener. When we listen, we strengthen the other person's security in expressing his or her feelings. We pave the way for deeper feelings to be shared with us. A helpful gesture that can lead to active listening may include periodically summarizing what the other person has said. By doing so, we encourage the other person to continue, and we keep him focused on the issue at hand. At times, all that is needed to indicate we are listening is a slight nod of the head, or simply saying "mm" in a way that demonstrates care and concern. The art of listening is so valuable that people are willing to pay hundreds and thousands of dollars to be in a setting where they feel that someone is genuinely listening to them. Listening for the pastoral counselor often requires striking a balance between silence, which may project a disinterest, and being overtalkative, which may communicate keeping the person at arms length and being anxiety ridden over what he or she has said. No advice given by us can ever be effective without first passing the litmus test of being trusted as good listeners.

GREATEST COMFORT, "BE QUIET, LET ME SPEAK"

Job's friends come to comfort him. They console him by sitting together with him for seven days and seven nights without saying a word. They engage in the mourning rites together with him as they rent their robes and threw dust over their heads toward the heavens. Then Job breaks the silence by lamenting his cruel fate. From that point onward, we have a series of speeches by the friends and by Job. The friends' words sought to bring Job comfort, but instead they were like thistles and thorns which stung Job. Their words not only rang hollow on the eardrums of Job, they seemed to have exacerbated the pain. In one instance, Job turns to them and bitterly arraigns them for speaking too much and offering all kinds of rationalizations for the tragedy that overtook him. In 13:5, Job sarcastically mocks his friends by saying: "If you would keep silent this would count as a mark of your wisdom." He continues: "And now hear my arguments, listen to the pleadings of my lips." (13:6)

On another occasion, in a state of frustration and anger, he interrupts Zofar with the following: "Listen carefully to my words and this will count as your consolation." (Job 21:2) In other words, if you seek to comfort me, the greatest comfort you can afford to me is to be quiet and let me speak.

Sigmund Freud's discovery of the value of using free association came from his spontaneous response to an interjection of a woman patient. Up to that time, Freud was given to urging, pressing, and questioning his patients in his attempts to uncover the roots of their symptoms in their early life. Ernest Jones, Freud's foremost biographer, notes that on one historic occasion, however, the patient, Frl. Elizabeth, reproved him for interrupting her flow of thought by his questions. He took the hint and thus made another step towards free association.[1]

In free association, the patient is asked to say anything that enters his mind. We make no attempt to censor his remarks or to make his words seem socially appropriate, logically consistent, or relevant. The technique of free association is based on the theory that the id (instinctual drives) and repressed memories are clamped up and in search of discharge. By eliminating the social requirements of everyday conversation and interaction, the analyst attempts to encourage the patient to lower his defenses and confront repressed memories.[2]

When God appeared to King Solomon in a vision in the night and offered him whatever his heart desired, the wise king did not ask for wealth, nor power, nor fame. He asked for instead, "A listening heart to judge the people and to be able to discern between good and evil."[3]

King Solomon perceptively understood that listening is not done only with the ears but with the heart. A listening heart is one that would eschew being judgmental. A listening heart would try to create a completely nonthreatening situation and let the other person experience openly his feelings. Through his close empathetic listening, such a therapist would sense meaning when the patient is trying to express himself, perhaps in a halting fashion. He would put this meaning into words as clearly as he could, perhaps in the form or with the inflection of a question to indicate that he is trying to follow the patient rather than to lead him. A listening heart would fully identify with the statement from Eth-

---

1. J.H. Kahn, *Job's Illness, Loss, Grief and Integration*, (Oxford: Pergamod Press, 1975), p. 82 The quote of Ernest Jones is from a volume which he wrote entitled Sigmund Freud: Lifework, (London: Hogarth Press, 1953, vol. 1), p. 268.

2. *Psychology Today*, Delmar, CA: CRM Books, 1977; p. 639.

3. 1 Kings 3:9.

ics of the Fathers, "Do not judge a man until you have arrived at his place,"

A listening heart would be aware of the difficulty of finding the right kind of words to the bereaved. The Zohar states *Man D'Ael L'Nachaman L'Avel Baei L'Yasda Milin B'Kadimutah*, "The man who wishes to provide consolation for the bereaved must prepare in advance words to say to him."[4] The listening heart would try to empathize with Job as he says, "I loathe my life. I will give free rein to my complaint; I will speak out in the bitterness of my soul." (Job 10:1) Or when he says, "Therefore I will not restrain my speech, I will speak out in the agony of my spirit; I will complain in the bitterness of my soul." (Job 7:11)

A listening heart is the best medicine for a suffering heart. It is interesting to note how the Talmud recognizes the need for the suffering individual to give free reins to his emotions. In the book of Proverbs, we read: When heaviness is in the heart of man he should subdue it.[5] However, there are some matters that cannot be muzzled. So the Talmud records the following exchange of opinions between Rav Ami and Rav Asi. Rav Ami states 'that the passage means he should dismiss it from his mind. Rav Asi recognized, however, that at times such an approach would be therapeutically damaging. Thus, he revocalizes the word *yashhenah* to read *yesinenah* meaning he should converse, or talk it over with another person.[6] Displaying the same kind of sensitivity to the pain of one who is ill, the Talmud states: He who visits the sick takes away one-sixtieth of his pain.[7] Rashi, recognizing the power of companionship to help the process of one being restored to good health, adds, "And if sixty people were to visit him and each took

4. Zohar, Vilna Edition 1882 vol. 3, p. 176.
5. Proverbs 12:25.
6. *Yoma* 75a. Rashi adds that someone else may provide proper counsel to him.
7. *Nedarim* 39b.

away one-sixtieth of his illness, immediately he would be restored to good health."[8] Or, in another passage quoted in the Talmud, we read, "Blessed be he that considereth (*maskil*) the poor. The Lord will deliver him in time of trouble." (Psalms 41:2)

The Talmud says the poor refer to the sick.[9] The word *maskil* is derived from the same root as the word *sechel* meaning "a certain intuitive feeling that reflects good common sense." Thus, the passage from Psalms could perhaps read, "Blessed is he, who possesses the right kind of *sechel* and is able to understand the needs of the sick."

Any student in medical school has heard repeatedly the sound advice of how important it is to listen to the patient. Before the physician offers a diagnosis, he is expected to listen to what the patient has to say. The good physician who has sensitivity and compassion will not only hear the words of the patient but also pay close attention to every nuance of the patient's emotions as he expresses himself. He will observe carefully the patient's body language as he describes to the physician what ails him. The Talmud reminds us that the patient's medical opinion in some instances is considered more valid than the physician's medical opinion. For example, Rav Yannai said in regard to breaking a fast on Yom Kippur that if the sick person says that he needs food and the physician's diagnosis is that he can continue to fast without harming himself, the patient's diagnosis takes precedence.[10]

The aphorism "the heart knows its own bitterness" (Proverbs 14:10), which in the Talmud is used in regard to the individual knowing best when he must break a fast, has many far-reaching implications. What it underscores is that there are subjective feelings that must be considered very seriously, because at times there is no objective way to determine how ill a patient is. Thus, at

---

8. Rashi, ad locum.
9. *Nedarim* 40a.
10. *Yoma* 83a, *Shulhan Aruch* Orach Hayim 618:1.

times we have no other resources but than to listen to the words of the patient.[11]

Often, the patient's premonition of impending death reflects more than a fear of death, but a healthy and accurate intuition that we dare not dismiss. This kind of feeling is reflected in the Midrash, which relates how Jacob asked God that before he died he be granted a period of illness. Jacob turns to the Almighty and says, "Master of the Universe, (at the present time) a man dies without a period of illness and he doesn't have an opportunity to discuss matters with his children. If a person would be ill for two or three days (before he expires) he will have an opportunity to confer and settle matters with his children." God then responded by saying, "You claim something which will be good. I will introduce starting with you a period of illness before a man expires."[12] Erlich states that this Midrash conveys the following two central ideas: 1) a patient can rightly determine at times when he will die; and 2) we must listen to the words of one who is ill.[13] For in the aforementioned Midrash, God promptly listens and carries out Jacob's request and introduces illness prior to death so that man will be given an opportunity to make final arrangements.

Medical science today can often prolong a life for a longer period of time than any previous generation of mankind. The price that must be paid in many instances is for an individual to be in agony and pain for extended periods of time. Thus, Jacob's request brings with it a mixed blessing. There are those individuals like Jacob who gathered his children around him and gave them a last will and testament, that are able to use their period of

---

11. Dov Erlich-Mashmaut Hargashot ha-Choleh, L'Piskka Hilchatit L'Gabei Shabbat in *Halachah U'Refuah*, edited by Moshe Hershler (Jerusalem & Chicago: Machon Regensberg, 1980), p. 187.

12. Bereshit Rabah 97

13. Dov Erlich, ibid., p. 187.

illness prior to death to straighten out their affairs and put their houses in order. And conversely, all too often, the period of illness becomes a degrading experience for the patient which strips him of his dignity. Often, it not only causes him unbearable pain, but it also exacts its toll on loved ones who carry emotional scars as they must painfully endure witnessing those they care for suffer greatly.

What the Midrash of Jacob reminds us is that even though the period of illness prior to death may have questionable benefits, it was introduced into this world because we must listen to the sick person and honor his request.

JACOB'S AND ELKANAH'S FAILURES

The difficulty of cultivating the art of listening to what the suffering individual genuinely desires is reflected in the following two biblical stories.

The first one tells about Rachel, the wife of Jacob, who like the first two matriarchs of Israel, Sarah and Rebecca, suffers from sterility. After Jacob's other wife, Leah, Rachel's sister, gives birth to four sons, Rachel turns to Jacob and desperately and pathetically cries out, "Give me children or else I die." (Genesis 30:1) Rachel's remark must be understood in the context of a civilization in which a women's worth and self-esteem is greatly enhanced by giving birth to children. Jacob, rather than offering a reassuring or comforting word to a woman whose self-esteem is low owing to her sterility, lashes out in anger at his wife and says, "Am I instead of God that has prevented from you the fruit of the womb?" Rachel needed empathy. Instead, she receives a theological statement that would be appropriate for a debate among two scholars. Jacob appears to be saying that what Rachel is requesting reflects the belief that man can manipulate supernatural forces and that man can bend God's will to serve man's purpose. Nachmanides indicates that the difference between the sacrifice offered in pagan societies and the Torah is that in the Torah, the one bringing the sacrifice does so with the hope that he will draw closer to God. In contrast, in paganism the one bringing the sacrifice wishes to have divine powers draw close to him.[14] Thus Jacob angrily reminds Rachel that her request was inappropriate and represented a rebellion against God.

Where Jacob erred however is that the depressed and agitated spirit who feels hurt does not need theological illumination. While both Nachmanides and another medieval exegete, Rabbi David Kimchi (Radak), seek to defend Jacob's retort, the Midrash condemns Jacob for his lack of sensitivity. The Midrash attributes to God the following words: "Is this the way you answer a woman weighted down with such bitter experiences?"[15] It would seem that Jacob's error bears affinity to the error most ascribed to the friends of Job. Instead of empathizing with Job as they did during the first seven days of mourning, in the ensuing dialogues in the book, they presented to him a number of carefully thought out theological arguments as to why Job was subjected to great suffering.

Job's friends had overlooked the fact that the wounded and crushed in spirit need not theological arguments to penetrate the mystery of human suffering, but more importantly Job needed compassion that raises the self-esteem of the defeated, the confidence of the depressed, and the hope of the forlorn.

In another episode in the book of Samuel, we find Hannah, the distraught and depressed wife of Elkanah, who also is afflicted with sterility. She, like Rachel, was in a predicament where a second wife of Elkanah, Peninah, had given birth to children. The

---

14. Nechama Leibowitz, *Iyun B'Sefer B'Reshit* (Jerusalem: Jewish Agency, 1970), p. 232.

15. Bereshit Rabah 71:10.

book of Samuel relates how Hannah would make her annual pilgrimages to Shilo and there beseech God to help her bear a child. She was weeping, would not eat, and was bitter. (1 Samuel 1:7, 10) Elkanah, upon seeing the way she behaved, turned to his wife and said: "Hannah, why do you weep and why do you not eat, and why is your heart grieved? Am I not better than ten sons?" (1 Samuel 1:8) Elkanah's remark appears to be insensitive, unfeeling, and tasteless. Here again is a woman whose self-esteem is shaken to the core in not being able to bring one child into this world. Why would her husband, who is portrayed as a pious man who made annual pilgrimages at Shilo, respond so callously to her pathetic cry by saying arrogantly that he is more precious to her than ten sons? The Midrash also appears to be disturbed by what appears to be such a brutal statement demonstrating no compassion for a woman broken in spirit. Thus the Midrash points out that when Elkanah says "I am better than ten sons," the word used for "I" is *Anochi* and not *Ani*. The fact that *anochi* is used gives an entirely different meaning to the text.

Anochi is associated in the minds of the readers of the Midrash with the opening of the Ten Commandments: *"Anochi" (I am) the Lord your God who brought you out of the land of Egypt."* When *Elkanah says "Anochi,"* he is using a euphemism for God. In effect, what Elkanah is declaring is that God is better than ten sons.[16] In other words, Elkanah was trying to reach out to his wife and remind her that Hannah had not been abandoned by God. He was empathetically trying to tell her that God cares deeply for "you." Elkanah sought to fortify faith, to inspire confidence, and to provide reassurance that all would be well. The Midrash was embarrassed by the unwarranted and surprising insensitivity of Elkanah and attempted to have Elkanah's remarks mirror the sentiments of a purported pious man, who was a frequent visitor to the temple of Shilo.

---

16. Yalkut Shimoni 1 Samuel 1:8.

One of the most effective ways of demonstrating to the sick that we are empathetic and listening to him is to pray on his behalf. Jewish law established that a visit to one who is ill must also include prayer. Thus, the Rama, in his gloss to the *Shulhan Aruch*, writes, "He who visits the sick and does not pray on his behalf has not fulfilled the *mitzvah*" [of visiting the sick]. (Yoreh Deah 335.4) A visit to the sick is qualitatively different than a social call, for it has the dimension of prayer, which is an intrinsic part of the mitzvah.

EVERYMAN'S QUESTION—IS GOD LISTENING?

The pain experienced by the sick is to him singularly unique. Praying on his behalf is a way of declaring that despite our knowledge, wisdom, and ability to bring healing, we are limited. The person in pain is apt to feel abandoned even when a friend is present, because he can never fully convey to others what he is enduring. Prayer is also our declaration that God has not and will not abandon the suffering individual.

Based upon his groundbreaking work, *Healing Words: The Power of Prayer and the Practice of Medicine*, a physician, Larry Dossey, provides abundant evidence that praying for oneself or others makes a scientifically measurable difference in recovery from illness and trauma. While Dossey emphasizes that praying is not a replacement for medical treatment, it is a very effective addition to it.[17]

It has been suggested that prayer resembles radio, television, and telephone signals, all forms of energy that we transmit across great distances. The question that we have all asked is, "Does God

---

17. Larry Dossey, *The Power of Prayer and the Practice of Medicine*, (San Francisco: Harper, 1993), see preface xv–xx.

listen to our prayers?" But before God listens to our prayers, we ourselves are expected to listen to our prayers.

The art of listening is one that the Halachah recognizes is not only often absent when one person tries desperately to reach out and communicate with another human being. The same inability to listen is often conspicuously absent when man attempts to pour out his heart in prayer to God. Thus, the Halachah states in regard to the laws pertaining to the Shma: "One must hear what one utters with his mouth."[18]

Similarly, in regard to the law pertaining to the proper way to recite the *amidah* (silent devotion), we read in the codes the following: One should not pray the *amidah* in his heart, but rather he should move his lips so that he will quietly be able to hear the words he is reciting.[19]

The ability to listen perhaps is not far from the literal meaning of a famous talmudic passage in which we learn the following: "Much have I learned from my masters even more from my colleagues, but most of all from my pupils."[20] How could one possibly learn the most from those he teaches? If the teacher will on occasion listen to his pupils, his thinking will be crystallized and become clearer as a result of their insight. Their challenges and probing questions will enable the teacher to attain insights which hitherto were unavailable to the teacher.[21]

The ability to listen is tested in visiting the house of mourning, for the law states that even social amenities such as an exchange of

---

18. Hilchot Kriat Shma, *Orach Hayim* 62:3, The Mishna Brerurah adds that if he just reflected in his heart on the words of the Shma, he has not properly discharged his obligation to recite the Shma.

19. Hilchot Tephilah, *Shulhan Aruch* 101:2.

20. *Taanit* 7a and *Makkot* 10a.

21. Story about death of the pupil of Rabbi Johanan, Rish Lakish; see for an understanding of what the teacher can learn from his pupil, *Baba Metziah* 84a.

hello should not take place between mourner and comforter.[22]
The comforter does not say anything until the mourners first
speak.[23] Dr. Robert E. Kavanaugh, ex-priest, teacher, and University of California psychologist, recalls how a young priest at his
first solo wake once approached a mourner with a "How are
you?" only to be met with "How the hell do you think I am" from
a tormented widow left with four children when her husband
suddenly died.

Often, I have found that the bereaved will tell all the details of
the last day, or the last hour, again and again, particularly if the
person died suddenly. The need to talk, to complain, to mope, to
get it off one's chest, and to be listened to, is great.[24]

In a climate of trust, the bereaved may be able to express his
feelings of guilt about having failed or harmed the deceased or not
having loved him enough. He may be frightened by his occasional
feelings of hatred, perhaps a wish for the patient to die quickly, or
to get it over with, so that he could no longer have to watch and
participate in the suffering. There may also be guilt about the fury
against the dead person who has left him with all the pain of loss.
To have these feelings accepted and understood as a normal part
of bereavement is true therapeutic help which a counselor or good
friend can give.

THE LEAD ROLE WITHOUT A WORD

The ability to listen and just to be together with one in anguish is
the greatest form of comfort that can be offered. That idea is

22. Yoreh Deah 385:1; *Shulhan Aruch.*
23. Yoreh Deah 385:1; *Shulhan Aruch.*
24. Lily Pincus, *Death and the Family—The Importance of Mourning* (New York: Pantheon Books, 1974), p. 257.

mirrored in the following interpretation based upon a comment offered by the medieval exegete Rashi on a story that appears in Genesis. In the eighteenth chapter of the book of Genesis, we read of three visitors who came to visit Abraham. Rashi, drawing from Midrashic literature states that each visitor came with a different assignment. One came to inform Sarah that she would give birth the following year. The second visitor came to apprise Abraham of the destruction of Sodom, which was morally bankrupt, and the third came to heal Abraham. According to the Midrash, Abraham was in the process of convalescing and recuperating from surgery. For in the previous chapter of Genesis is recorded how Abraham underwent *brit milah* (the circumcision rite) at the ripe old age of ninety-nine. The setting of the biblical narrative, according to Rabbi Hama, the son of Hanina, was the third day of his circumcision.[25]

When reading the biblical narrative, we learn that Abraham was informed that his wife, who had been barren until then and who was advanced in years, would give birth the following year to a boy. We also learn by inference that Abraham was informed of the impending destruction of Sodom.[26] For the text records how Abraham attempts to avert the disaster that awaits Sodom by interceding before God on behalf of the residents of Sodom. The fact that Abraham pleads at length with God not to destroy Sodom in the event that righteous people are to be found in the city would lend credence to the interpretation which states that one of the messengers reported to Abraham that Sodom would be destroyed.[27]

---

25. *Baba Metziah* 86b

26. See Genesis 18:1–16.

27. The biblical text does not say that one of the visitors related to Abraham that Sodom would be destroyed. It does, however, record the following: "And the men (a reference to the visitors) rose up from thence, and looked out towards Sodom and Abraham went with them

One searches however in vain in the Bible to find a reference for any kind of healing that the Midrash suggest was administered by the angel Raphael.[28]

The answer that is homiletically rich and psychologically sound, although I cannot trace its source, is that the mere presence of the third messenger, who according to the Midrash is the angel Raphael, is in itself therapeutic. Social isolation and the absence of human companionship can impede the individual's opportunities for recovery. Health and human companionship go hand in hand with each other.

THE HANDMAID ACTING AS SARAH'S MOTHER

Another Midrash relates that when Abraham was engaged in binding Isaac upon the altar, Satan went to Sarah and appeared to her in the figure of an old man, very humble and meek, and said to her: "Do you know what Abraham has done to your son today? He took Isaac, and built an altar, slaughtered him and brought him up as a sacrifice. Isaac cried and wept before his father, but Abraham didn't look at him nor did he have compassion upon him." After saying these words to Sarah, Satan left. Sarah thought Satan to be an old man from among the sons of men who had been with her son. Sarah lifted up her voice and cried bitterly, saying:

O my son, Isaac, my son, O that I had died this day instead of you. I grieve for you. After I have reared you and have

---

to bring them on the way." (Genesis 18:16) Rashi notes that the word *va yashkifu*" meaning, "they looked" indicates evil. In other words, it was made clear to Abraham that Sodom would be destroyed. Juxtaposed to the afore-mentioned passage is the beginning of Abraham's plea to God on behalf of the residents of Sodom.

28. Raphael means "God will heal." See Numbers 12:13.

brought you up my joy is turned into mourning over you. In my longing for a child I cried and prayed till I bore you at ninety. Now you have served this day for the knife and the fire. But I console myself, it being the word of God and you performed the command of your God for who can transgress the word of our God in whose hands is the soul of every living creature? You are just O Lord our God for all your works are good and righteous, for I also rejoice with the word which you command and while my eyes weep bitterly my heart rejoices.

And Sarah laid her head upon the bosom of one of her handmaids and she became still as a stone.

Afterwards, she pulled herself together, got up, and went about inquiring about her son till she came to Hebron, but not one was able to tell her what had happened to her son. Her servants went to seek him in the house of Shem and Eber and they could not find him, and they searched throughout the land and he was no there. And behold Satan came to Sarah in the shape of an old man and said to her: "I spoke falsely to you for Abraham did not kill his son nor is he dead," and when she heard the word, her joy was so exceedingly violent that her soul went out through joy.[29]

Why should the good tidings that she hears from Satan result in what would appear to be a massive heart attack while earlier a report that Isaac was killed by Abraham did not result in her death? Perhaps what was present the first time when she heard of the death was an empathetic and caring support system. She grieves in an inconsolable fashion. Her initial reaction was a form of denial of what had taken place: "O that would I have died instead of you." This is Sarah's way of controlling events, of

---

29. Louis Ginzberg, *Legends of the Jews*, vol. 1, (Philadelphia: Jewish Publication Society, 1937), pp. 286–287. For study of midrashic Sources, see *Legends of the Jews*, vol. 5, p. 256, footnote no. 256.

substituting her death for Isaac's. This attempt to rewrite one's life history, to change what has taken place, is a common feature of the mourning process. The denial or disbelief is not a total thing, for just enough of reality is allowed to seep through so that the bereaved can slowly come to grips with the reality that is presented to her.

Sarah's response to the report that her son died is also greeted with a certain degree of acceptance. She expresses resignation to the will of God.

All along during her monologue, the reader of the Midrash assumes that the handmaid is listening attentively. She is sharing with Sarah tears, feelings, and thoughts because these give Sarah a feeling of being understood. She wished to be relieved of her sense of loss, emptiness, and isolation.

The handmaid, by letting Sarah weep, serves the role of her mother. Sarah weeps like a child against the handmaid's bosom. The Midrash says that Sarah became still as a stone. One gets the impression that what is being described here is the feeling of empty numbness which overtakes the mourner shortly after hearing of one's death. Mercifully, nature covers the bereaved with a protective emotional blanket within minutes of the death news and there is a cold, empty numbness, a confused, dazed feeling of unreality that takes over.[30]

One patient described this feeling to her doctor in the following words: "During this short moment before the numbness, there is almost a loss of contact with oneself and one sees oneself almost as if from a distance; and then the numbness, the cold, hard protection of unfeelingness almost descends."[31]

Sarah searching for her son once again shows the power of the denial mechanism of man. Searching for the lost person, an almost

---

30. Arthur Freese, *Help For Your Grief*, (New York: Schocken Books, 1977), p. 57.
31. Ibid., p. 57.

automatic universal defense against accepting the reality of the loss, may go on for a long time.[32] Most people are not aware of their need to search but express it in restless behavior, tension, and loss of interest in all that does not concern the deceased.[33] In the case of Sarah, the Midrashic text gives us no clue as to whether her behavior is prompted by suspicion of the veracity of Satan's initial story.

When Sarah hears that Isaac is alive, the shock of the news causes a convulsive change within her, and she expires. Here, what is conspicuously absent is the earlier support system—the presence of the handmaid. The text creates the impression that she was not present when Sarah heard the news, thus reversing what she had been told earlier. Without someone to share in that difficult moment when emotions were high and violent changes were taking place within her, Sarah is unable to cope, and she passes away.

It is noteworthy that while the story of Job as it appears in the biblical text concludes with the friends of Job being censored for not speaking the truth, or for offering what we would call poor therapy, the Midrash responds more favorably to their attempts at offering Job consolation and comfort. The Midrash tells us that the three friends were recompensed by God for their sympathy toward him in his distress. Their names, the Midrash tells us, were preserved, the punishment of hell was remitted unto them, and best of all, God poured out the holy spirit over them.[34]

---

32. Lily Pincus, *Death & The Family, The Importance of Mourning* (New York: Random House, 1974), p. 115.

33. Ibid., p. 116.

34. Yalkut Shimoni Koheleth 973. The Midrash is from a comment to a passage in the book of Koheleth which reads, "It is better to go to a house of mourning than to a banquet hall." (7:2) A contrast is drawn between the great banquet prepared by Abraham on the day that Isaac was weaned, and the visit to Job by three friends following the tragedies

Perhaps the homilists of the Midrash understood that through the interaction between Job and his friends, Job became reconciled to his fate and had his ruptured relationship with God restored. He was able to experience a revelation, an encounter with God as a result of the interaction with his friends. He demanded an answer from God that is a way of controlling God. Instead, he expresses his humility by saying, "I repent in dust and ashes." (Job 42:6) Elsewhere, we will analyze what forces contributed to a changed Job which appears at the end of the book. What is germane for our purpose is that one can make a good case to show that the friends were important instruments for Job's recovery. The very fact that Job became the agent for his friends' recovery while praying for them shows to some degree an appreciation for the help they provided in the past. God was not harsh with the friends and would not let them suffer even though the author of Job finds the friends' methods wanting.

To return to the original point in this section, regardless of the approach used by the counselor or therapist, there must be present the spirit reflected in what King Solomon requested from God, namely a listening heart. This same idea is mirrored in the book of Exodus, where we have a description of the suffering endured by the Israelite slaves in Egypt. Immediately afterwards, the text records: "And God heard their groaning and God remembered his covenant with Abraham, Isaac and Jacob and God looked upon the children of Israel and God took notice of them." In commenting on the words *Va'Yeda Elohim*, which literally mean

---

which overtook him. Abraham's banquet was attended by men of prominence such as Shem and Eber, but the Torah did not deem it to be important to record their names. Conversely, each of the names of the three friends of Job, Eliphaz the Temanite, Bildad the Shuhite, and Zofar the Naamathite are recorded for posterity in the book. Other rewards were forthcoming to them as well because they cared deeply and were willing to share in the suffering of Job.

"and God knew," and which are translated as "and God took notice,"[35] Rashi comments "he set his heart upon them and did not conceal his eye."[36] God listened to their anguish and pain with his heart. It is a different level of listening.

LISTENING WITH THE THIRD EAR

In 1948, Theodore Reik, one of the leading psychoanalysts of his day, wrote a volume entitled *Listening With the Third Ear.* In it he wrote: "The analyst hears not only what is in the words; he hears also what the words do not say. He listens with the 'third ear,' hearing not only what the patient speaks, but also his own inner voices what emerges from his own unconscious depths."[37]

What is within our unconscious depths is a zone of empathy and understanding which enables our listening to reach others and soothe and calm the troubled and aching soul.

35. *The Torah, A New Translation of Holy Scriptures according to Masoretic Text* (Philadelphia: Jewish Publication Society, 1962), p. 101.

36. Rashi, Exodus 2:25.

37. Theodore Reik, *Listening With the Third Ear* (New York: Farrar Straus & Company, 1948), p. 125.

5

WHEN SILENCE IS GOLDEN

I received word that Robert's wife had died. I rushed over to his house to be with him. He was sitting in his living room absorbed in conversation with his relatives. I, not wishing to disturb, pulled up a chair and sat down nearby. We looked at each other for a moment and I slowly nodded my head in an empathetic manner. No words of mine were necessary to let him know that I was trying to understand his loss and pain. There are many ways and many levels in which we communicate to others. One of the most powerful ways may be through silence.

We seem to need noise. We build our offices with soft music piped through the waiting room because we are frightened by silence.

So often, when others speak to us and then are silent, we feel the need to interject and say something. By speaking, we may potentially cut off the person sharing with us something valuable. Often, we speak because we are uncomfortable with silence. At times, a long moment of silence speaks more powerfully than the most eloquent words.

Just as a wordless prayer may be the most heartfelt prayer, so can a shared moment of silence cement a deeper and closer relationship with others.

THE BIBLE'S MOST FAMOUS SILENCE

The Book of Leviticus records the sudden and enigmatic death of two of the sons of Aaron, Nadav and Avihu, who brought a strange fire to the Lord and who were immediately consumed by the fire.[1]

The Midrash relates that the day the tragedy took place was the very day that the dedication of the sanctuary was being held. The happiest day of the year, the day of the consecration of the temple, when Aaron was dressed in the resplendent attire worn by the high priest, now becomes the darkest day of the year. Aaron becomes a bereaved parent.[2]

Aaron's response is often referred to as the most eloquent silence of the Bible as the text records, "And Aaron was silent." (Leviticus 10:3) Rashi comments, "Aaron was rewarded for maintaining silence, for in the next section of the Torah a law will be issued to him alone."[3]

In other words, for accepting God's judgment, Aaron receives a reward, for the next section of the Torah, which deals with laws pertaining to proper etiquette for members of the priesthood officiating in the temple, is addressed to Aaron alone, and not to Moses, nor to Moses and Aaron. Why should Aaron be rewarded for stifling a most natural response of a grieving parent? There are so many other emotions that take place when one is confronted with death. Why is this one singled out? It would seem that what impressed Rashi is that Aaron bypassed the normal grieving process that may include a denial that it happened, such as, "Oh it can't be! Not my sons." Another response, which one could expect

---

1. Leviticus 10:1, 2.
2. *VaYikrah* Rabbah 11:7.
3. Rashi on Leviticus 10:3.

to be expressed, is anger. "Why me!" "God how could you do this to me?" We find no rage and anger mentioned in the Torah by Aaron upon learning of the death of his sons.

There is no indication that Aaron wishes to take a leave of absence from ministering in the temple. As a matter of fact, the rest of the chapter deals with laws pertaining to the priestly functions of the temple, which Aaron participates in. Nor is there any recording of guilt and shame on Aaron's part, which often rises to the fore as a result of the death of a loved one. Aaron does not say anything similar to, "It's my fault. I never should have encouraged them to officiate as priests in the tabernacle. If I wouldn't have said anything, they would not have participated in the consecration ceremony today, nor would they have died." Instead, the Torah records succinctly, "And Aaron was silent." From Rashi's comment that Aaron was rewarded for his silence, one may infer that Aaron immediately reached a stage where he accepted the death of his sons and made his peace with the will of God.

There is no denial, no anger, no rage, no guilt, but rather acceptance of the harsh and cruel fate of becoming a parent who lost two of his children.

The silence here does not stem from ignorance. On the contrary, it stems from a profound understanding of the finitude and limitations of man in comprehending the mystery of death. It is the silence of one who has the wisdom to fathom that the mystery of life and death is beyond our reach.

It is not similar to the silence of Job found in the first and second chapters of Job. For in Job, we have the silence of a repressed anger that is waiting to be released. In Job, we have the silence of one who has been trained to say the conventional words of piety.[4] Job is correct and lives up to his reputation as being a

---

4. See Job 1:22 and 2:10.

man of impeccable moral credentials. His response to a series of tragedies, which leave him a broken and wounded man, is inspiring, courageous, and pious: "The Lord has given and the Lord has taken. Blessed be the name of the Lord." "Shall we accept good from God and not accept evil?"

Job refuses to blaspheme God despite the advice of his wife to release his pent-up anger. In the interim, he is seething and boiling inside. Rashi understood what must have taken place inside the heart of a tormented soul. For on the passage "And Job committed no sin with his lips," Rashi adds, "but in his thoughts he uttered sinful words." The emotions stirring within him could not be contained. Following his silence for seven days and seven nights, Job erupted in a volcanic and explosive manner. One can seriously question the wisdom of Job's early silence when one reads chapter 3. There, we encounter a man who curses life, a man who is so embittered that he wishes his life had never begun.

In analyzing silence, it is important to recognize that it can mean virtually anything that can be said, verbally at least. Silence is charged with those words that have just been exchanged: Words which have been exchanged in the past, words which haven't or will not be said, but which are fantasized and words which may actually be said in the future.[5]

SILENCE SPEAKING LOUDER THAN WORDS

There are instances in which silence speaks as loud if not louder than words. The following story, found in the Talmud, illustrates this point: Rabbi Judah Ben Illai, Rabbi Jose, and Rabbi Shimeon

---

5. Martin L. Knapp in *Foundations of Non Verbal Communication*, edited by Albert Katz and Virginia Katz, (Carbondale, Illinois: Southern Illinois University Press, 1983), p. 181

Ben Yochai were sitting together, and with them was a man called Judah Ben Gerim. Rabbi Judah opened the discussion and said: "How fine are the works of this people?" (The Romans) "They made roads and market places; they have built bridges and they have erected bath houses."

Rabbi Jose *was silent*. Then, Rabbi Shimeon Ben Yochai replied and said: "All they made they made for themselves. They made roads and market places to put harlots there; they built bridges to levy tolls from them; they erected bath houses to delight their bodies."

Judah Ben Gerim went home and related to his father and mother all that had been said.

And the report of it spread until it reached the government. Decreed the government: "Judah, who exalted us, shall be exalted; Jose, *who was silent, shall go into exile; Shimeon, who reviled our work, shall be put to death.*"[6]

This ancient debate in Palestine around the year 130 reflects a period in Jewish history when the people were under the dominion of the Roman Empire. Not all the Jewish people celebrated the splendor of Roman civilization. The issue in this story is not only Roman rule but also Roman civilization.[7]

One can understand why the Roman authorities wanted to execute Shimeon Bar Yochai. To him, the triumph of Roman civilization was shocking, hateful, and repulsive. He knew that all these splendid edifices and public institutions were not built by the Romans to aid the people but rather to serve their own nefarious designs: "All that they made they made for themselves."

But whey should Rabbi Jose, who offered no opinion and was silent, be sentenced to go into exile? Why did they interpret his

---

6. *Shabbat* 33b.

7. Sabbath, *Abraham Joshua Heschel* (New York: Farrar Straus & Young, 1951), p. 37.

silence as some form of protest against Roman civilization or the Roman Empire?

Rabbi Jose was a man who had a reputation of being a homiletician and orator.[8] In Gittin 67a, we are told that once Rabbi Meir and Haninah Ben Ono disagreed with him, yet Rabbi Judah sided with Rabbi Jose because *nimuko imo*, "he was able to substantiate everything."[9] There is a vast difference between the silence of an orator and the average citizen. The silence of one who earned a reputation of being able to provide a reason for everything under discussion is very revealing. The silence of Rabbi Jose in refusing to criticize the Roman Empire conveyed a powerful message. The Romans were probably well aware of his oratorical skills, his critical faculties, and his ability to offer cogent reasons to validate his position. He also had contact with all sectors of Roman society. His prominence as a haggadist is revealed in a conversation that he had with a Roman matron resulting in her conviction of the superiority of the Jewish religion.[10] The Romans thus understood that his silence was a way of spurning their civilization. They probably viewed it as an act of treason. But they could however not mete out a death penalty since there had been no violation of the law of the land. They were however concerned that Rabbi Jose's presence would remind the Jewish community that one of their leaders and spokesmen abhorred Roman civilization. Thus, the expulsion removed the threat from their midst.

In another story told in the Talmud, there is recorded a legend in which Moses ascends to heaven and he sees God occupied in making little crowns for the letters of the Torah. Upon his inquiring as to what these may be for, he received the answer, "There

---

8. *Sanhedrin* 109a & 113a.

9. Rashi adds that he was able to give a reason for everything he said and he was able to settle disputes.

10. Genesis Rabbah 68:4.

will come a man named Akibah Ben Joseph who will deduce Halakhot from every little curve and crown of the letters of the Law." Moses requests to be allowed to see this man. His wish was granted, but he became much dismayed as he listened to Akibah's teaching, for he could not understand it. When they discussed a difficult matter and inquired from Akibah, "How do you know this?" Akibah responded by saying that this was a law that was already established by Moses at Sinai. Moses' spirits were calmed and he then turned to God and said, "If you have someone whose knowledge of Torah is so profound, why did I become the agent through which Torah was given?" God responded: "Silent! So is my way of thinking." Moses then said, "You have shown me his knowledge of Torah. Show me his reward." Moses was then shown how Akibah's body was destined to be exposed for sale in the butcher shop. Akibah would die a martyr's death, as the Romans would scrape off the skin of his body with iron combs. As Moses sees the humiliating fate of this gigantic talmudic figure who in the aforementioned legend is portrayed as being greater than Moses himself, Moses inquires painfully from God: "This is Torah and this is the reward that is forthcoming?" Again God interrupts Moses abruptly, "Silent! That is my way of thinking."[11]

In this legend, on two occasions God silences Moses. In each case, the silence is a way of reminding Moses of his finitude, of the fact that there are some things that man will never comprehend. Only because Moses understands deeply the paradox of a saintly man like Akibah dying in such a humiliating fashion does God order him to be silent. Often, silence is subsumed under nonverbal communication. When we verbalize, we, to a certain degree, are exercising control over something. Anything which is explained is our way of illustrating that we are not helpless. The mere explanation of something is a way of gaining control over the issue at

---

11. *Menachot* 29b.

hand. Particularly the second time, when Moses is told to be silent
upon seeing Akibah's flesh being sold in the market place and his
body desecrated in such a gruesome way, does an answer to Moses'
question become most urgent. How can a just God mete out such
a cruel judgment against one who undoubtedly is one of the most
saintly and venerated figures in all of Jewish history? The question asked by Moses is the same question that Job asks to God. Job
cannot fathom why he has become the victim. For God to answer
the question directly would be a way of man controlling God. For
the answer itself is in effect a way of forcing God to bend to man's
will. Job does not receive a direct reply. Neither does Moses here.

WHEN KNOWING TOO MUCH INDUCES SILENCE

Elie Wiesel, who has written more eloquently about the Holocaust than any writer, speaks of an oath that he took in 1945. The
oath was that he would wait ten years before he would write
anything about the Holocaust. He felt the real truth could never
be communicated. The real vision could never be shared, so why
speak about it?

Wiesel writes:

Twenty five years after the event I wonder whether we
shouldn't have chosen silence then. For some reason I
believe that had all the survivors gathered in a secret
conclave, somewhere in a forest and decided together — I
know it's a poetic image, infeasible, but I feel this sense of
loss of this opportunity, if we had all decided never to say
a word about it, I think we could have changed man by the
very weight of our silence. But then I also believe that
mankind wouldn't have been able to bear it. It would have

driven man and people to madness. This is why I think we spoke.[12]

The silence that Wiesel speaks about is not due to knowing a little. On the contrary, it is the silence of knowing much and recognizing the limitations of the human being to communicate it to others.

Similarly, in Israel the day before the country celebrates Yom HaAtzmaut, Israel's independence day, it observes "Yom HaZikaron," (Remembrance Day) in honor of over eighteen thousand soldiers who have died during the wars that Israel has waged to maintain its independence. The most moving part of Yom HaZikaron comes at 11:00 a.m. when the siren is sounded and everything comes to a screeching halt as a minute of silence is observed. The silence tells us infinitely more about Yom HaZikaron than the customary rhetoric by the politicians who generally speak of how a nation will forever be grateful for the supreme sacrifice made by the fallen soldiers.

The same can be said of the Holocaust. Any explanation of the Holocaust detracts from its uniqueness. If it is unparalleled and unprecedented in the annals of mankind, then on one level, it becomes impossible to speak about it. There will always be a zone in which we will admit our inability to fathom the mystery of the unjustified suffering which befell the Jewish people during World War II.

Wiesel, although writing about the Holocaust, shuns offering explanations. The following is illustrative of his willingness to live with disbelief, with dismay, and with recognition of the fact that some things don't lend themselves to answers which are comprehensible:

---

12. *The German Church Struggle and The Holocaust*, edited by Franklin H. Little and Hubert G. Locke, (Detroit: Wayne State University Press, 1974), p. 275.

Lack of morality and a perverted taste for bloodshed are unrelated to the individual's social and cultural background. It is possible to be born into the upper and middle class, receive a first rate education, respect parents and neighbors, visit museums and attend library gatherings, play a role in public life, and begin one day to murder men, women and children without hesitation and guilt. It is possible to fire your gun at living targets and nonetheless delight in the cadence of a poem, the composition of a painting. One's spiritual legacy provides no screen, ethical concepts offer no protection. One may torture the son before the father's eye and still consider oneself a man of culture and religion, and dream of a peaceful sunset upon the sea. Had the killing been brutal savages or demented sadists, the shock would have been less, and also the disappointment.[13]

Wiesel is writing from the vantage point of one who has searched deeply and who has arrived at knowing that he does not know. Elihu, the brash bystander in the book of Job, cautioned us against thinking that understanding of the problem of theology is attainable: "Beware lest you say, we have attained wisdom."[14]

There are two kinds of ignorance. The one is dull, unfeeling, barren, the result of indolence; the other is keen, penetrating, and resplendent; the one leads to conceit and complacency, the other leads to humility. From the one we seek to escape, in the other the mind finds repose.[15]

---

13. Elie Wiesel, *One Generation After* (New York: Random House, 1965), p. 5.

14. Job 32:13.

15. Abraham Joshua Heschel, *God in Search of Man* (New York: Harper & Row Publishers, 1955), pp. 56–57.

They who travel in pursuit of wisdom walk only in a circle; and after all their labor at last return to their pristine ignorance.[16]

In the section of the Lord out of the whirlwind in the book of Job, the issue of man's inability to understand the world and thus be able to offer a reason for unjust suffering comes up. For example, we read, "Who is this that darkens my plan by words without knowledge?" (Job 38:2) or "Where were you when I laid the foundations of the earth?, tell me if you have any understanding." (Job 38:4)

"Have you trodden on the bed of the sea or walked in the recesses of the deep?" (38:16) or "Do you know the laws of the heavens? Can you establish my order on the earth?" (38:33) Job's affirmation of his own knowledge is an affront to the true possessor of God's knowledge.

The summit of Job's search for a reason why the seemingly righteous suffer is paradoxically found in a passage where he expresses his humility: "Therefore I abase myself, and find comfort in the realization that I am but dust and ashes." (Job 42:6) God's world is beyond Job's comprehension. Significantly, the world *olam* that in post biblical times came to denote "world" is, according to some scholars, derived from the root *alam*, which means "to hide, to conceal." The world is itself hiddenness; its essence is a mystery.[17]

Job finally is comforted in knowing that he is but dust and ashes. In other words, he makes peace with the fact that there are some things in life beyond his control. What prevented Job from finding an equanimity of spirit and calmness of soul is the misguided expectation that he would be able to pierce the veil of the

---

16. Ibid., *Oliver Goldsmith, Citizen of World*, quoted from Heschel, p. 57.

17. Brown, Driver, and Briggs, *A Hebrew and English Lexicon of Old Testament* (Oxford: Oxford University Press, 1906), p. 761, quoted in Heschel, p. 58.

mystery of suffering. When Job says, "I find comfort in the realization that I am but dust and ashes," there are two biblical images that probably did not escape the author. One is Adam, of whom we read in Genesis: "For dust art thou and to dust shall thou return." (Genesis 3:29) For Job, with his new knowledge that he is dust and ashes like primordial man, is reconciled to his mortality.[18] The other image is that of Abraham, who also spoke of himself as being but "dust and ashes," (Genesis 18:27) while he was confronting God over a similar issue that Job faced. Then, Abraham challenged God, who was prepared to destroy Sodom. From Abraham's vantage point, God carrying out the destruction of Sodom would have been tantamount to destroying the innocent together with the wicked. Abraham was able to confront God with the recognition that ultimately he was but dust and ashes. Thus God's ways did not have to comport to Abraham's limited understanding of cosmic justice. And so it was, because in the narrative in Genesis, Abraham finally accepts God's verdict. The biblical text records that after God assured him that Sodom would not be destroyed if there were ten righteous men in the city, "And the Lord went his way, as soon as he finished speaking to Abraham, and Abraham returned unto his place." (Genesis 18:33) Rashi comments, "Since the defender Abraham became silent, the Judge went his way."[19] Here Abraham is portrayed as greeting God's decision with silence. This response contrasts largely with the spirit of confrontation and challenge toward God found in Abraham's dialogue with God. What accounts for Abraham's meek resignation to the will of God is the recognition that he is but dust and ashes. Being but dust and ashes means that he will accept God's verdict even when intellectually he is not able to make his

---

18. *Dimensions of Job*, edited by Nahum N. Glatzer (New York: Schocken Books, 1969). See article entitled "In Dust and Ashes," Hayim Greenberg, pp. 217–224.

19. Rashi ad locum, Gen. 18:33

peace with it. Similarly, Job finally reconciles himself to his fate when he comes to the realization that there are some things he will never understand.

It is interesting to note that usually every new section of the Torah is separated from the previous one by the space of nine letters. However, the last *sidrah* (Torah portion) of Genesis entitled *Vayehi* is "closed." There is only one letter which separates the conclusion of the *sidrah* of *Vayigash* and the concluding *sidrah* *Vayehi*. The Midrash relates that Jacob wished to reveal the eschatology of the Jewish people, namely what would take place at the end of times. But it was hidden from him.[20]

While the sons gathered around the bed of their dying father, the *shechinah* (God's presence) visited him for a moment and then departed quickly. When the *shechinah* left, so did all traces of knowledge of mystery of life also depart from Jacob. Jacob wished to reveal what would be at the end to his sons and spoke unto them, saying: "Gather yourselves that I may tell you that which shall befall you in the end of days." (Genesis 49:2) God said to him, "It is the glory of God to conceal a thing." (Proverbs 25:2) "Such a course of action is not for you. He that goes about a tabernacle reveals secrets; but he who is of a faithful spirit conceals a matter." (Proverbs 11:13)[21]

Thus, silence can be a source of comfort when it permits the sensitive, understanding, and knowledgeable to recognize their limitations, in comprehending why man is forced to suffer. '

Perhaps in the light of the aforementioned, the following translation of a famous passage is not far from the literal meaning of the passage. Shimon, the son of Gamliel, said, "All my life I associated with scholars and I never found better therapy than silence."[22] Or, a similar statement attributed to Akibah, "A hedge

---

20. Genesis Rabbah 96.
21. Ibid.
22. Pirke Avot 1:17.

around wisdom is silence" (Pirke *Avot* 3:17) may also be understood as extolling the therapeutic value of silence.

HIGHEST PRAISE TO GOD

Undoubtedly, prayer has always had the power to satiate man's thirst for companionship with God and to provide comfort in ridding ourselves of the intense loneliness from which we suffer. It is no accident that the Hebrew word for prayer, *Tefilah*, is also the word used to describe the prayer which we recite in a hushed undertone or silently. In Hebrew, it is known as *tefilah b'lahash*, which means "a whispering prayer."

The medieval poet Ibn Gabirol, wrote, "The highest form of worship is that of silence and hope."[23]

The Psalmist wrote, "To thee silence is praise." (Psalms 65:2) The prophet, in trying to express the holiness of the temple, wrote as follows, "The Lord in his holy temple; Let all the earth keep silent before him." (Habakkuk 2:20)

The Talmud relates that a certain reader once prayed in the presence of Rabbi Hannina and said: "O God, the great, the mighty, the revered, the majestic, the powerful, the strong, the fearless, the all wise, the certain, the honorable," and so forth. Rabbi Hannina waited until he finished and then said to him: "Have you exhausted the praises of your master? Why do you say so much? Even the three attributes which we recite (in the whispering of silent prayer: great, mighty, revered), we do so only because our master Moses put them in his law and because the men of the great assembly fixed them in the liturgy. It is as if an

---

23. Abraham Joshua Heschel, *Man's Quest for God* (New York: Charles Scribner's Sons, 1954), p. 41.

earthly king had a million denarri of gold and we praise him for possessing much silver, is not such praise an insult?"[24]

From this tale, we can deduce that the highest form of praise before God is silence. Here is how Heschel articulates the power of silence in prayer: "In a sense our liturgy is a higher form of silence. It is pervaded by an awed sense of the grandeur of God which resists description and surpasses all expression. The individual is silent. He does not bring forth his own words. His saying the consecrated words is in essence an act of listening to what they convey. The spirit of Israel speaks, the self is silent."[25]

A TEACHER'S SILENCE

Silence also contains within it at times the power of defiance which can be a measure of solace to a people stripped of all rights. In the poem "Eleh Ezkarah," which is chanted during the *musaf* service on the day of atonement, the poet gathers episodes of martyrdom among the sages and weaves them into a coherent epic of faith. The background of these events was the resolution of the Roman Empire to blot out all resistance in the province of Judea by forbidding the practices of Judaism.

Following the fall of the last stronghold of the insurgents in 135 C.E., there was a complete prohibition of all Jewish practices on the pain of death. There was to be no observance of the Sabbath, no performance of the rite of circumcision, no study of the Torah, and, to break the continuity of authoritative religious leadership, no rabbinic ordinations.

Ten sages, including Rabbi Akibah and Rabbi Yishmael, continued to teach the Torah. They were finally caught and

---

24. Berachot 33b.
25. Heschel, p. 44.

executed and left to their people an example of heroic faith, to which the masses have often turned for inspiration and guidance. In the "Eleh Ezkarah," the poet describes how, as Rabbi Yishmael is being led to death, a heavenly voice was heard saying, "Ishmael, Ishmael, let no more sound be uttered, lest I turn the world to water and my throne's footstool to sudden chaos. This is my decree; accept it, all of you who loved the law which I created ere the world was made."[26]

The question to be asked is why did Rabbi Yishmael maintain silence? Why did he not cry out in pain and agony, why does the *bat kol* (heavenly voice) make such an extraordinary demand upon him? Contrary to his classical rabbinic opponent, Rabbi Akibah, Rabbi Yishmael was a rationalist. Even when he is dying, he wants to teach us a lesson. God could destroy the world and the world deserves to be destroyed.[27]

Even in such a moment, Rabbi Yishmael's actions are more like a bereaved mourner rather than a victim. Yishmael keeps the tears within himself. In effect he loses contact with himself and he sees himself from a distance. He is still the teacher of Torah. Yishmael will carry on a dialogue with God in his own silent prayers. There is no acrimonious accusation against him, but rather there is one obsession that he has, and that is to ensure the survival of the Jewish people. That will take place through stifling his voice and remaining silent.

The silence here is the silence of a pedagogue who wants to make the "loudest noise possible."

If we assess our own behavior patterns, we will note that often we lower our voices when we have something of utmost importance we want to share with someone else.

26. HaMachzor, *Ben Zion Bokser* (New York: Hebrew Publishing Company, 1959), p. 432.

27. Wiesel, from *The German Church Struggle and the Holocaust*, p. 276.

Among a series of proverbs cited by Koheleth reflecting the conventional adulation of wisdom the wise sage of Jerusalem reminds his readers, "The words of the wise spoken quietly are heard better than the ranting of the king of fools." (Ecclesiastics 9:17)[28]

Our voices are barely audible when we have something extremely important to tell others. Whispering is a signal to the other person to listen attentively. The most soothing and comforting voice is a soft quiet voice. It indicates that our words are measured, that we are deeply concerned lest we say the wrong thing. We may speak haltingly, pausing often, as if we are not sure that our words will be comforting. Speaking in such a manner often communicates far more effectively than a polished speech delivered flawlessly.

In the daily liturgy following the Amidah, we recite the prayer called Tachanun. We turn to God with our heads on our knees as in a penitential mood and we say: "Bend your ear O God and listen." This image of asking God to strain himself to listen to us emanates from one who has something very important to convey. In the Talmud, there appears the expression *Aseh Aznecha K'Afarkasat U'Kneh Lecha Lev Mevin*, "Make your ears like a funnel and acquire an understanding heart."[29] Straining yourself to hear reflects concentration and empathy. When one hears with the "third ear," one acquires a heart that listens and understands.

It is noteworthy that on Tisha B'av, the national day of mourning commemorating the destruction of the two temples, we conduct ourselves as mourners and do not greet others. Should

---

28. See Koheleth, *The Man and His World*, Robert Gordis (New York: Block Publishing Company, 1955), p. 302, footnote on 9:17. The word Nachat, which is often translated in the aforementioned passage to mean with pleasure, is not as good as quietly since "Nachat" in the sense of quietly contrasts with "Zaakat" meaning ranting or shouting.

29. Hagigah 3a, Hulin 89a and Kiddushin, Jerusalem 1:9.

someone not aware of this stricture greet us, we are to respond in a quiet voice with a Koved Rosh, literally, "a heavy head."[30]

Similarly, when we greet someone who has lost his spouse, the codes rule we say, "May you be comforted," with a soft voice and a heavy head."[31]

And what is even more comforting and shows an extraordinary degree of empathy and love is at times silence. When we greet a friend with a heavy heart and convey to him the feeling that our words cannot express the inexpressible, we provide for him a greater measure of comfort. The fact that we do not say hello nor inquire as to his welfare is a supreme expression of the closeness and intimacy we feel towards the mourner. It's a secret way of communicating. It's our way of saying, "I am trying to understand what you are going through. I am here. Whatever I can do, I will try to do."

THE LOUDEST NOISE IN THE WORLD

One of the more familiar chapters in the Bible which speaks of how silence is able to bring us together with one another in a spirit of love is the nineteenth chapter of 1 Kings, which relates God's revelation to Elijah on the mountain. God reveals himself amidst the sound of deepest silence.

Here is the way Rabbi Samson Raphael Hirsh interprets the chapter:

> Where is the man who can read what was revealed to Elijah here without being deeply moved? He was shown a raging hurricane rending the mountains, splitting the

---

30. *Shulhan Aruch* 554:20, Orach Chayim.
31. *Shulhan Aruch* 385:2, Yoreh Deah.

rocks asunder, a terrible earthquake and an all consuming blazing fire and he recognized that all these were only precursors of God—not in the hurricane, not in the earthquake and not in the fire was God. Then suddenly the rage of the storm quieted; the rolling thunder of the earthquake was stilled, the roaring fired down and the world was filled with a complete silence.[32]

Not a bird twittered, not a leaf rustled, all nature held its breath." Then he hid his face in his mantle, in the silent hush of the whole universe, reverently, attentively listening to its creator and master, he recognized he felt the nearness of God. This deep hushed silence is itself a silence that can be "heard," the loudest announcement of the proximity of God, louder than storms and earthquakes and universal conflagration.[33]

---

32. See 1 Kings 19:12.

33. S.R. Hirsch, *The Pentateuch*, translated by Isaac Levy (New York: Haftoroth Judaic Press, 1971), p. 354.

6

GIVE ME YOUR HAND: REFLECTIONS ON NONVERBAL COMMUNICATION

Raph Waldo Emerson once said, "He has seen half of the universe who never has been shown the house of pain." I go to the hospital and often I see in front of me a frightened and despondent patient. He is in discomfort and pain after spending a sleepless night. There have been repetitive blood takings, doctor's visits, discontent with attendants, and the taking of narcotics which don't work. I hear his groaning and see the anguish and fear that is on his contorted face. I am tempted to say something like, "Don't worry. It's going to be alright." Wisely, I choose not to say anything. Instead, I gently take his hand and hold it. I try to have my hand radiate with a healing touch. I feel the energy flow from my hand to his hand. At that moment, I feel I have given him something without having uttered one word.

THE HEALING TOUCH

Our speech-oriented culture is only recently beginning to take note of the profound and overlooked contribution of nonverbal behavior to the processes of communication.

In the realm of feelings, our facial expressions, posture, movements, and gestures are so important that when our words contradict the silent messages contained within, others mistrust what we say. They rely completely on what we do.[1]

We are engaging in nonverbal communication all the time. For example, as we prepare to terminate a conversation, we may not indicate so in words. We simply change positions by moving forward to a more upright and less-relaxed position in the chair. These silent messages signal to others a wish to leave, and when these messages are understood and accepted, the discussion draws to a close by mutual consent and without rancor.

The Talmud reminds the one who comes to offer comfort to the mourner to always be sensitive to the nonverbal communication of the mourner. Thus, for example, when a mourner nods with his head, gesturing that he would prefer if visitors would leave, visitors must comply immediately with the indirect message and leave. This law was codified in the *Shulhan Aruch*.[2] In other words, the comforters were to do what any good therapist would do, and that is observe all those things that are associated with nonverbal communication. We look for clues in the gestures, facial expressions, and movements of the mourners to know how to respond.

Often, the swiftest and most obvious type of body language is touch. The touch of a hand or an arm around someone's shoulder can spell a more vivid and direct message than dozens of words. But such a touch must come at the right moment and in the right context.[3]

Every rabbi or any other clergyman knows from his visitations to hospitals that often the best way we can help one who is suffering, in pain, or confined to a bed is to take the person's hand,

---

1. Albert Mehrabian, *Silent Messages* (Belmont, Cal: Wadsworth Publishing Company, 1971), p. 197.

2. Moed Katan 27:, Shulchan Aruch Yoreh Deah 376:1.

3. Julius Fast, *Body Language* (New York: Evans & Company, 1970), p. 14.

hold it for a while, and clasp it. At times, no words, regardless how soothing or calming they may be, can be as effective in lifting and raising the spirits of the sick, weak, and lonely as holding their hand.

RABBI JOHANAN'S THERAPY

The following three stories found in the Talmud juxtaposed one to the other bears out this point. Rabbi Hiyya Bar Abba fell ill and Rabbi Johanan went to visit him. Rabbi Johanan said to him: "Are your sufferings welcome to you?" Rabbi Hiyya Bar Abba replied: "Neither they nor their reward." Rabbi Johanan said to him: "Give me your hand." He gave Rabbi Johanan his hand and Rabbi Johanan raised him.

Rabbi Johanan fell ill, and Rabbi Hannina went to visit him. Rabbi Hannina said to him: "Are your sufferings welcome to you?" Rabbi Johanan replied: "Neither they, nor their reward." Rabbi Hannina said to him: "Give me your hand," Rabbi Johanan gave him his hand and Rabbi Hannina raised him. Why could not Rabbi Johanan raise himself? They replied: "The prisoner cannot free himself from jail."

Rabbi Eleazar fell ill and Rabbi Johanan went in to visit him. Rabbi Johanan noticed that Rabbi Eleazar was lying in a dark room and he bared his arm and light radiated from it. Thereupon, he noticed that Rabbi Eleazar was weeping and he said to him: "Why do you weep? Is it because you did not study enough Torah? Surely we learnt: The one who sacrifices much and the one who sacrifices little have the same merit, provided that the heart is directed to heaven. Is it because of lack of sustenance? Not everyone has the privilege of enjoying two tables. Is it perhaps because of the lack of children? This is the bone of my tenth son!"

Rabbi Eleazar replied to him: "I am weeping on account of this beauty that is going to rot in the earth." Rabbi Johanan said to him: "On that account you surely have a reason to weep." And they both wept. In the meantime, Rabbi Johanan said to him, "Are your sufferings welcome to you?" Rabbi Eleazar replied: "Neither they nor their reward." Rabbi Johanan said to him. "Give me your hand." Rabbi Eleazar gave him his hand and he raised him.[4]

Let's examine each story. In the first one, Rabbi Hiyya Bar Abba is ill and Rabbi Johanan visits him. During the course of the conversation, he poses a question which ordinarily would appear to be inappropriate given the difficult situation. He asks him: "Are your sufferings welcome to you?" One cannot appreciate this kind of question without understanding the context. We have here a conversation between two scholars, between two students of Torah. Both are familiar with a passage which appears frequently in rabbinic literature: *Havivin Yesurin*, "Pain or suffering is beloved."[5] One must understand that from the vantage point of classical Judaism, suffering is not something without redeeming features. Suffering is not the making of a whimsical and capricious diety that takes delight in causing pain to tormented souls. Nor can suffering be understood as being beyond God's control.

The Bible often speaks of suffering as being a means of disciplining man rather than a means of punishing man. For example, in the book of Deuteronomy we read: "As a man disciplines his son, so does the Lord discipline you." (Deuteronomy 8:5) Or, "Do not reject the discipline of the Lord, my son; do not abhor his rebuke. For whom the Lord loves he rebukes. He gives pain in the son in whom he delights." (Proverbs 3:11–12)

There is the Psalmist's exclamation: Happy is the man whom you discipline O Lord." (Psalms 94:12) There is the warning of

4. *Berachot* 5b.
5. *Taanit* 21a.

Eliphaz: "Happy is the man whom God corrects, do not reject the discipline of the Almighty. For he injures and binds up, he wounds and his hands heal." (Job 5:17–18) Less known but even more striking in the same book are the words of Elihu: "He delivers the afflicted through his affliction; He opens his ear through suffering." (Job 36:15)

The Talmud is also replete with statements which underscore the benefits to be accrued from suffering; "There are three gifts which the Holy one, blessed be he, gave to Israel and each was given through suffering; the Torah, the Land of Israel, and the World to Come."[6] "A man should be appreciative to the Holy One, blessed be he, during a time that he must endure suffering, for suffering draws man to the Holy One, blessed be he."[7]

Or, according to Rabbi Azariah, King David said before the Holy one, blessed be he: "Show me the way of life." The holy one, blessed be He responds: "If you wish life look forward to suffering."[8] Rabbi Johanan said: "Why was Israel compared to an olive?" To teach us that just as the olive does not bring forth oil unless it is beaten; similarly, Israel does not repent, only through suffering.[9] "He who delights with the pain that comes upon him, brings salvation to the world."[10] "The holy one, blessed be he, inflicts suffering upon the righteous in this world in order that they may have an inheritance in the world to come.[11]

From the close of the Tanaitic period we find stories about sages who invited suffering to come upon themselves for fear lest they were guilty of any transgression.[12]

---

6. *Berachot* 5a.
7. Tanchume Teze 2. Midrash Tehilim 16:12.
8. Pesikte D-Rav Kahana 179:2.
9. *Menachot* 53b.
10. *Taanit* 8a.
11. *Kidushin* 40b.
12. See Ephraim E. Urbach *Sages: Their Concepts and Beliefs*

Thus when Rabbi Johanan asked him: "Are your sufferings welcome to you," Rabbi Hiyya Bar Abba knows very well the many citations from both the Bible and Talmud as to how ennobling suffering is. He responds by saying, "Neither they nor their reward." The reference to "their reward" implies that one who is willing to surrender and accept suffering without revolting against God will be rewarded in the world to come. Rabbi Hiyya at that moment was overcome with a tremendous amount of pain and could not relate to all those statements extolling the virtues of suffering. It was at that point that Rabbi Johanan realized that the time was inappropriate to engage his colleague in any discourse on theology and human suffering. Instead, he asks his friend for his hand. And the Talmud records that "he gave him his hand and he raised him." He cured him by the touch of his hand. I do not read the aforementioned text as some faith healing device in which the healer causes a person who is immobilized to stand up, or a blind man to see or a deaf man to hear. "He raised him up" I choose to read as meaning he buoyed up his spirits. He lifted Rabbi Hiyya Bar Abba out of his state of depression. Touching his hand and letting Rabbi Hiyya Bar Abba know that he wasn't being abandoned and that someone cared for him effectuated a positive change in Rabbi Hiyya.

In the second episode, the tables are turned. This time it is Rabbi Johanan who took ill and another friend, Rabbi Hannina came to visit him. Again, we find a scholar posing the question which was a subject of controversy in the circle they were in. Again, we find the one suffering, this time Rabbi Johanan, unable to find a measure of solace in recognition of the fact that suffering has a redemptive quality. This time, Rabbi Hannina did what Rabbi Johanan did in an earlier story, and that is hold onto the

(Jerusalem: Magness Press, 1979), for a discussion on the reasons for suffering according to rabbinic literature, pp. 447–448.

hand of the one who was suffering. And again, the same positive results ensue with the one in pain being lifted out of his depression. When others heard about this story, they posed the question, "Why could Rabbi Johanan not cure himself? Why couldn't he raise his spirits by himself?" In other words, if Rabbi Johanan, who is an astute student of human behavior, is able to cure Rabbi Hiyya in the earlier story, why could he not use a form of autosuggestion to snap out of his own condition? And the conclusion they drew when discussing this case was that the prisoner cannot free himself from jail. Or, put in another way, the patient cannot cure himself. The touch of another human being is qualitatively different than thinking about another human being touching you.

The third case is far more complex and more complete in its reportage. This time, it relates how Rabbi Eleazar took ill and Rabbi Johanan went to visit him. The text records: "He noticed that he was lying in a dark room, and he bared his arm and light radiated from it." The dark room in the context of these three stories probably is symbolic of his inner state of being. He was depressed.

The first step in the genesis of depression is the loss of love of some important individual. The individual who is going to become pathologically depressed finds himself in a position of dependence upon someone else, a wife, a parent, one of his children, or a friend. In this dependence, he wishes to be loved immoderately.[13]

In the first two stories as well as this one, having someone reach out and touch the depressed person becomes an expression of being loved.

In the third story, Rabbi Eleanzar is sitting in a dark room and Rabbi Johanan, who was a handsome man, bares his arm and light radiates from it. What is striking here is the contrast between the

---

13. Mortimer Ostow, *The Psychology of Melancholy* (New York: Harper & Row Publishers, 1970), pp. 13–14.

dark room and the light which radiates from the hand. This becomes symbolic of an attempt to raise him from depression. We are told elsewhere of the good looks of Rabbi Johanan. He used to go to the gates of the *mikveh* (ritualarium). When women left the *mikveh* he would say to himself, "Let them look upon me that they may bear sons as beautiful and as learned as I am."[14]

Or, in another story recorded in that section of the Talmud, Rish Lakish said to Rabbi Johanan, "Your beauty is fitting for women."[15] Thus, in our story of Rabbi Johanan, he tries to direct Rabbi Eleazar's attention away from his depression by focusing on something new. Rather than Rabbi Eleazar continuing to remain dejected and downhearted, Rabbi Johanan tries to get him to think about something else. Crying spells are very common during depression, and Rabbi Eleazar begins to weep. Rabbi Johanan, expressing himself in a very supportive manner, asks him if the weeping is because he has not studied enough Torah. He then reminds him that even though one has not devoted an extraordinary amount of time to Torah studies, he will be rewarded if, when studying, he has studied in a spirit of devotion and willingness to direct his heart to heaven.

Rabbi Johanan continues to inquire as to the reason for his depression, asking him if it is because he has not been blessed with material wealth. Again, Rabbi Johanan attempts to comfort him by telling him that not everyone is privileged to enjoy two tables, a reference probably to both wealth and learning. In other words, Rabbi Eleazar should consider himself privileged to have earned a reputation as a scholar. Rabbi Johanan continues and inquires, "Is it because you don't have any children?" He then showed him the bone of his tenth son. Rabbi Johanan had ten sons and all of them died. His tenth and youngest son died in a tragic accident, having

---

14. *Baba Metziah* 84a.
15. Ibid.

fallen into a boiling pot.[16] It would seem that Rabbi Johanan never got over the loss and in a sense was clinging on to the last vestige of his son. He also used the bone as a means of offering solace to others. He is speaking from the depths of anguish and pain. His words of comfort now have greater credibility.

However, all these attempts did not fully succeed. Rabbi Eleazar then made some puzzling comment accounting for his present state of depression and weeping, "because of this beauty that is going to rot in the earth." This is probably a reference to Rabbi Johanan's beautiful body that one day will go the way of all flesh. Rabbi Johanan then says to him, "On that account you have good reason to weep," and they both proceed to weep. What Rabbi Johanan was successful in doing was deflecting the focus of attention from Rabbi Eleazar's own state of depression onto someone else, in this case Rabbi Johanan's body. Now, when they both weep, it is because of their contemplating man's predicament here on this earth. Man is dust and to dust shall he return. Rabbi Johanan succeeded in changing the whole focus of attention. It is only when he feels that Rabbi Eleazar is no longer depressed that he poses the theological question which intrigued scholars, namely, does suffering have a redemptive quality? And once again the individual who is suffering rejects suffering as having immediate value or any value for what it purports to bring in the future. Then, Rabbi Johanan once again resorts to a remedy which seems to work every time. He asks for Rabbi Eleazar's hand, then takes it and immediately Rabbi Eleazar rises. In other words, this act of love of concern, of steadfast and abiding companionship, restores his spirits and uplifts his lacerated heart.

The reaching out with the hand is one very striking way of communicating in a way that transcends verbal communication.

Each human language is accompanied by a well-developed

---

16. Nissim Gaon's Commentary on *Berachot* 5b. He says that Sherira Gaon and Hai Gaon are the sources of this information.

language of posture, gestures, facial expressions, and intonations which operate in consonance with verbal language to effect communication.[17]

A case in point is when the friends of Job come together from a long distance to comfort Job. The text records: "Now when they caught sight of him from afar they could not recognize him. So they raised their voices and wept and rent their robes and threw dust over their heads toward the heavens."[18] Here, the friends communicate to Job that they are sharing in his grief by participating in all the rites associated with mourning. They weep with him. The rending of the garment, in addition to being an expression of mourning, also involves a financial loss to them. They are willing to express that the loss of Job is their loss by now performing a rite which will mean some tangible loss to them, since one of their garments as a result of the tear will no longer have the same value. They not only throw dust over themselves, which is a sign of mourning, but rather they throw it toward heaven, which is a way of exaggerating and accentuating their grief. And then the most eloquent form of nonverbal communication, of sharing in the pain, is sitting with Job for seven full days and nights without uttering a word.

EYES AND NOSE—THE SILENT MESSENGERS

Ralph Waldo Emerson once said, "The eyes of man converse as much as their tongue and the ocular dialect needs no dictionary, but is understood the world over." Our eyes convey silent mes-

---

17. *Kinesics and Context: Essays in Body Motion Communication*, University of Pennsylvania Publications in Conduct and Communication, (Philadelphia: University of Pennsylvania Press, 1970), pp. 102–103.

18. Job 2:12.

sages, express our personalities, and keep our conversations running smoothly by adding a silent track that displays our intentions and reactions.[19]

In the Book of Samuel we read, "And Saul eyed David from that day forth."[20] In order to understand the meaning of *oyen* "eyed," it is necessary to understand the context. David has defeated Goliath in battle and has emerged as a folk hero. He has become the object of adoration, particularly by the women. A new song springs up among the people. "Saul has slain thousands, David ten thousands." This makes Saul more paranoiac and jealous of David than ever before. Saul eyeing David refers to casting of an envious eye towards one who has risen in popularity and has won the hearts of the masses. It is a glance of the eye that carries with it jealousy, hatred, malice and hostility. If looks can kill, this is the passage that conveys precisely that. The malicious intent of the eye is to be understood by what we read in the verse juxtaposed to David being eyed: "And it came to pass on the morrow that the evil spirit came upon Saul and he raged in the midst of the house; And David played the harp with his hand, as at other times; and there was a javelin in Saul's hand. And Saul cast the javelin; for he said, 'I will smite David even to the wall with it.'" (1 Samuel 18:10, 11) The envious eye here results in attempted murder.

In the first century, rabbinic scholars debated as to what constitutes the worst feature in a man. Rabbi Eleazer said it was the evil eye, an opinion seconded in another generation by a rabbinic scholar, Rav, who blamed the evil eye for ninety-nine deaths out of every one hundred.[21] "Eat not the bread of him that hath an evil eye," the author of Proverbs reminds us.[22]

---

19. Evan Marshall, *Eye Language: Understanding The Eloquent Eye* (Toronto: New Trend Publishers, 1983), pp. 9–15.
20. 1 Samuel 18:9.
21. *Yerushalmi Shabbat* 14:14, *Baba Metziah* 107b.
22. Proverbs 23:6.

The Talmud tells us that Simeon Bar Yohai and Rabbi Johanan could, with a look, transform people into a heap of bones.[23] When Rabbi Eleazer Ben Hyrcanus was shut out of the place of teaching, every spot upon which he turned his eye was burned up; even a grain of wheat upon which his glance fell was half burned, while the other half remained untouched and the pillars of the gathering place of the scholars trembled.[24]

There is a popular folk interpretation on the passage which tells about the last will and testament offered by Jacob to his sons, Shimon and Levi. Jacob chastises his sons by saying, "Let my soul not come into their secret, unto their assembly let my honor not be united, for in their anger (*b'apam*) they slew a man and when pleased they maim oxen."[25]

One interpretation calls attention to the fact that the word anger is derived from the word *aph*, meaning "the nose." *Aph* and *apam* meaning "their anger" are related, for when one is angry the nostrils flare up. The folk interpretation offered is that simply with a twist of the nose as a gesture of disapproval, we are capable of killing a person's reputation.

A failure to understand the pivotal role that body language can play in communicating feelings and thoughts is reflected in an interpretation which is suggested by some bible scholars on a passage in the book of Job. We are told that when Job learned of the death of his sons and daughters, he rose and tore his robe and shaved his head. And he fell on the ground and *va'yishtahu* which is translated in Marvin Pope's commentary as "he worshipped."[26] Pope, in commenting on the word *va'yishtahu* writes: "The verb here used is the common term for obeisance before royalty or

23. *Baba Metziah* 84a; *Baba Kama* 11a; *Shabbat* 33b.
24. *Baba Metziah* 58b.
25. Genesis 49:6.
26. *The Anchor Bible*, Job, translated and introduced and notes by Marvin in H. Pope (Garden City, New York: Doubleday, 1965), p. 3.

divinity and occasionally even before one's peers." (Genesis 23:7; Exodus 18:7; 1 Kings 2:19) The act consisted of falling down and touching the face to the ground.[27] However, as pointed out by Gruber, Job's adoration would be incongruous in the context of Job 1:20–22. Certainly nothing else in Job's response to the news of the death of his seven sons and three daughters suggests that he engaged in adoration. The nearest Job came to engaging in adoration is his reciting the formula "The Lord has given and the Lord has taken. Blessed be the name of the Lord." Just as the use of this formula in modern Jewish funeral services in no way transforms the ceremony from one of grief to one of adoration, so does it not transform Job's response to tragedy, from mourning to worship. Surely, had the author of Job 1:22 understood either Job 1:20 or Job 1:21 as an expression of adoration, there would hardly have been a need for him to add "Yet in all this did Job not sin or charge anything unseemly to God." (Job 1:22)

Understood neither as adoration nor as submission to God's decree but as nonverbal expressions of grief, these gestures constitute Job's refusal to accept the death of his sons and daughters as a matter of course.[28] In other words, bending over and falling to the ground are expressions of grief.

Another instance of significant body language being expressed in Job is to be found in the second chapter, where it is recorded that the three friends of Job arranged to meet to go *lanud lo vl'nahamo*, "console and comfort him." (Job 2:11) *Lanud lo* literally means "to nod their heads or to tilt their heads." It is a way of commiserating with him. It is an opportunity for one to use his body to show empathy and share pain with another. Words cannot dispel the pain, so we must use something else to convey our heartfelt condolence.

---

27. Ibid., p. 15.
28. Mayer Gruber, *Aspects of Non-Verbal Communication in the Ancient Near East* (Rome Biblical Institute, 1980), p. 471.

The friends bending over and nodding their heads as an expression of commiserating with Job contrasts sharply with what Job remembers about his former happy days before all the tragedies struck him. Thus, in another chapter, we find Job romanticizing about the good old days. He recalls the time when old men rose and stood before him. The Targum, the Aramaic translation of the Bible, on the words *vishishim ḳamu amadu*, adds "elders rose and stood, they stood upright, and now as he mourns his friends lower their heads."[29]

The Targum, in an early section of the Bible, translates the phrase *l'nefesh hayah* "a living soul," *l'ruach m'malela*, "a spirit that speaks."[30] But it is not only the spirit that speaks; the body does too.

In a volume entitled, *Sparks of Light*, which deals with counseling in the hasidic tradition, we read: "In shtetl times as in our own, the language of human body was often more eloquent than that of the mind. Consequently, the rebbe would concentrate keenly on the hasid's non-verbal physical cues—especially his posture and stance.

"As part of the *yehidut* (a hasid's private encounter with his rebbe) protocol, the hasid was expected to stand in a posture of awe and submission to his rebbe. Yet, the rebbe was highly sensitive to whether this posture appeared customary or forced by the occasion. He knew that the proud man stands more self-consciously when assuming the posture of a supplicant; the same stance fits the beggar like an old shoe. Our habitual bearing is observable when we assume another stance; certainly the ordinary shtetl Jew was no trained actor, able to camouflage his characteristic body language. Thus, the rebbe scrutinized this nonverbal realm like an open book."[31]

---

29. Targum on Job 29:8.
30. Targum on Genesis 2:7.
31. Edward Hoffman and Zalman M. Schachter, *Sparks of Light:*

One's character is revealed through the way he carries his body. The prophet Isaiah, when he speaks of the moral depravity of the Jewish community, cites the indiscretions of young women who conduct themselves as harlots. He says "Since the daughters of Zion are haughty and walked with stretched forth necks". . . . (Isaiah. 3:15) A neck which is stretched out reflects the condition of one who also wishes to reveal other parts of her body. It becomes a means of seducing and arousing sexual feelings. It is interesting to note how the *kipah* (skullcap) which the male Jew wears is connected with the significance of the body to convey the proper kind of a message. For example, in the code of Jewish law, we read, "It is prohibited for a man to walk *b'komah zekufah* "with a haughty stand"; nor can he walk four cubits without a headcovering.[32] The juxtaposition of a haughty or arrogant kind of stand alongside of the requirement to wear a covering over the head very strikingly conveys to the reader the importance of carrying oneself with humility.

Since our primary focus in this book is on comfort, let us return to a discussion of what perhaps is one of the key rites in the process of bringing comfort to the bereaved and see the role that body language plays in it. Undoubtedly, the eulogy serves a very important function in giving mourners an opportunity to experience on a certain level the presence of the deceased for a further period of time before bidding him a final farewell. It also enables the mourners and the community to express grief.

Gruber points out that in Babylonian Jewish Aramaic, to eulogize is literally causing others to beat the breast.[33] It's a means of expressing grief which brings in its wake a cathartic release.

Counseling in the Hasidic Tradition (Boulder, Col.: Shambhala, 1983), pp. 99–100.

32. *Shulhan Aruch* Orach Haim 2:6.

33. Gruber, *Non-Verbal Communication in the Ancient Near East*, ibid., p. 435.

Thus we read in the Talmud, *Rafram aspadat l'chalateh b'be knishta*, "Rafram eulogized his daughters-in-law in the synagogue." That the primary sense of Hebrew, *sfod*, is to beat the breast is mirrored in the following statement found in the Talmud: *Amar Ula hesped al lev dictiv al shadayim sofdim, tipuach b'yad kilus b'regel*, "'Ula' said Hesped (Eulogy) 'is striking the hand upon the breast as it is written in Isaiah, beating upon the breast.'" (Isaiah 32:12) Tippuah is striking the hand upon the other hand, Kilus is tapping with the foot.[34] Already in the biblical period, the act of beating the breast becomes the mark of mourning and the word *sfod* takes on two meanings, both "beating the breast" and "mourning."

Ki holech haadam el bet olamo v'savevu ba'shuk hasofdim, "So man goes to his eternal home while the hired mourners walk about in the streets." (Ecclesiastes 12:5) *Sfod* in the sense of beating the breast, is to be found in Isaiah 22:12; Joel 2:12; Esther 4:3; II Samuel 3:31; Isaiah 32:11–12.[35]

Thus, the beating of the breast as a result of the *hesped* (eulogy) becomes an important vehicle for expressing grief and offering the necessary release of pent up feelings and emotions.

The Talmud also states that weeping for the dead is mandatory. When one neglects to weep for a man who was virtuous, the warning is unmistakable. That person will as a punishment find himself in mourning for his own children.[36] On the other hand, a man's sins are forgiven if he sheds tears for the dead.[37] In contrast, laws in a number of Greek cities decreed that the funeral procession should be conducted in silence. Plato, who required that all the people walking in a procession would be outside the city limits before daybreak, would have liked loud mourning restricted to

34. *Moed Katan* 27b.
35. Gruber, ibid., p. 447.
36. *Shabbat* 105b; *Moed Katan* 25a.
37. Loc. cit.

the house.[38] To this observer, it would seem that American society has patterned itself after Greek customs. The result is that often there is not the healthy release of bottled up emotions. Most people feel uncomfortable when a mourner weeps loudly during a funeral service. We are the products of a society that extols stoic silence in the face of death.

CLOTHING AND NONVERBAL COMMUNICATION

The most striking Jewish expression of grief is the rending of garments by the mourner before the funeral service. It is appropriate to place the clothing we wear under the rubic of nonverbal communication because the clothes we wear communicate an important message to others. For example, a new outfit generally promotes feelings of gaiety and happiness. Thus, according to Jewish law, one is not permitted to wear new clothes during the first thirty days following the death of a near relative.[39] Nor is one permitted to wear new clothes during a three-week period from the seventeenth of Tamuz through Tisha B'Av, the ninth day of Av. These days recall the period leading up to the destruction of the Temple that stood in Jerusalem and was destroyed on Tisha B'Av.[40] The Bible records many instances of rending the clothes after the news of death. Among those who rent his clothes is Job, who in addition also shaved his head. Maurice Lamm, in his volume entitled *The Jewish Way in Mourning & Death*, writes: "The rending is an opportunity for psychological relief. It allows

---

38. Dov Zlotnick, *The Tractate Mourning*, translated From the Hebrew with introduction and notes, (New Haven, Conn.: Yale University Press, 1966), p. 24.
39. *Shulhan Aruch* Yoreh Deah 241:10.
40. Kitzur *Shulhan Aruch* 122:2.

the mourner to give vent to his pent up anguish by means of a controlled, religiously sanctioned act of destruction." Maimonides, according to the interpretation of B.H. Epstein (Torah Temimah on Leviticus 10:6), notes with sharp insight that this tear satisfies the emotional need of the moment, or else it would not be permitted as it is a clear violation of the biblical command not to cause waste. For this reason, we may assume the tear for the parents must be made with bare hands.[41]

In *Mourning & Melancholia*, Freud points to the sadistic impulses present in all ambivalent relationships. In melancholia, which he regarded as a pathological form of grief, the sadistic impulses were commonly turned against the self.[42] Those seven relations whom we must mourn for all have in common the fact that we have an ambivalent relationship with them. Thus, since man will turn against himself and will want to tear his flesh and the hair, which symbolizes the loss of one's own flesh and blood in sympathy for the deceased, a substitute was created in the form of rending the garment. There is a school of thought that "Keriah" (rending one's clothes) as a sign of mourning represents a substitute for attempts to disfigure one's own body.

Lamm also indicates that the halachic requirement to expose the heart (that the tear for the deceased parents must be over the heart) indicates that the tear in the apparel represents a torn heart. The prophet Joel (2:13) chastises the Jews to rend the heart itself, not only the garment over the heart, indicating that the external tear is a symbol of the broken heart within.[43]

In addition to rending of the garment another form of nonverbal communication was to pour dust over the head of the body.

---

41. Maurice Lamm, *The Jewish Way in Death & Mourning* (New York: Jonathan David Publishers, 1969), p. 38.

42. Colin Murray Parke, *Bereavement, Studies in Grief in Adult Life* (New York: International Universities Press), p. 83.

43. Lamm, 39.

Many biblical references indicate that the practice was very prevalent.[44]

The practice is to be found also during the talmudic era, as reflected in the following Mishnah: "What was the order of procedure on the fast days? They use to bring out the Ark into the open space in the town and strew wood ashes upon the ark and upon the head of the chief of the court, and every one there put some on his head."[45]

These mourning rites were powerful ways of internalizing the experience of grief and loss as well as nonverbal ways of communicating to others the period of mourning that one had to endure. They would enable friends and acquaintances to greet the mourner with the necessary sensitivity and compassion.

CAIN'S BODY LANGUAGE

When we pay closer attention to the body language alluded to in the biblical text, we can gain new insights into understanding of the Bible. Another case in point is the recognition that expressions commonly interpreted as referring to ordinary anger are best understood as denoting anger turned upon the self, a prime element in Karl Abraham's and Sigmund Freud's definition of depression.[46]

Gruber cites the passage which relates how Cain, after having his sacrifice rejected by God, responds: "And Cain was very angry and his face fell." (Genesis 4:5) Then God turns to Cain and says, "Why are you angry and why has your face fallen?"

---

44. II Samuel 1:2; 15:32; Neh. 9:1; Job 2:12; Lam. 2:10; Jer. 6:26; Ezek. 27:30; Micah 1:10.

45. *Taanit* 2:1.

46. Mayer Gruber, *The Tragedy of Cain and Abel: A Case of Depression.* (Philadelphia: J.Q.R. N.S. 67, 1978), pp. 89–91.

The bending of the head, or the falling of the face, denotes sadness, according with the scientific observations of depression. Thus, a more correct reading would be, "Cain became very depressed and his face fell and the Lord asked Cain 'Why are you depressed? Why has your face fallen?'" (4:5,6) The Hebrew word *harah* means "anger," but in this case the anger is turned against himself and thus, reading "depressed" makes more sense and lends greater depth and understanding to the feelings of Cain.

Gruber quotes other passages where the Hebrew word for sadness, *etzev*, is juxtaposed to the word *harah* "anger" which in its context means "depression." For example, in Genesis 34:7, the biblical text records *va'yitatzvu haanashim* and the people were sad or "depressed" when the sons of Jacob learned that their sister Dinah had been raped, or in Jonah 4:1, *vayera el yonah raah gedolah vayihar lo*, and Jonah was very depressed when he learned that the people of Ninveh had changed their ways. Certainly, in the context of one who turns to God as did Jonah and says "Take my life from me; for it is better for me to die than to live" (Jonah 4:3), the word *depressed* is most fitting. Another illustration is to be found in 1 Samuel 18:8, where we read *va'yihar l'shaul meod va'yera b'enav hadavar hazeh*, "and Saul was very depressed and the saying displeased him. Saul becomes depressed over the fact that David was the center of attention and the object of adulation by all the people after David defeated Goliath in battle. The people spoke of Saul slaying thousands while David slew ten thousands."[47]

Obviously, readers of all ancient texts are limited in their understanding because of the loss of intonational features in the process of something being written.

When Richard Nixon sent transcripts rather than tapes of presidential conversations to the House Judiciary Committee investigating the question of his possible impeachment, members of

---

47. See Mayer Gruber, *Non-Verbal Communication*, pp. 349–375.

the committee quite rightly complained that transcripts could not convey the full or correct meaning of an utterance—having no voice inflection, stress, or other such nuances—and demanded the tapes. This exchange is a landmark in recognizing the legitimacy of paralinguistic communication, those characteristics of speech that affect its interpretation but are not part of the usually recognized language.[48]

We opened our discussion on nonverbal communication by speaking of the efficacy of human touch to often lift the spirits of the depressed and to offer solace to the bereaved. The language of touch permeates our speech, probably as much as that of sight. Montagu remarks that the entry for touch in the *Oxford English Dictionary* is fourteen columns, by far the longest. We use the metaphor to speak with understanding, with words such as perceive, conceive, grasp, accept, which all come from roots meaning to take hold of. In speaking of emotion, we have many words from sources that refer to physical contacts, attraction, attachment, sentiment, and feeling.[49]

We see also from biblical literature how touch is often associated with a form of communication which transcends verbal communication. Thus, when the prophet is about to witness a theophony, the Bible says, "And he laid it on my mouth and said, lo, this has touched your lips. . . . And I heard the voice of the Lord saying, whom shall I send and who will go for us? Then said I, Here I am, send me." (Isaiah 6:7–8) Or, "Then the Lord put forth his hand and touched my mouth and the Lord said unto me, Behold I have put my words in your mouth." (Jeremiah 1:9)

---

48. Nancy M. Henley, *Body Politics* (Englewood Cliffs, N.J.: Prentice Hall Inc., 1977), p. 7.

49. Ibid., p. 98.

SEMICHAH—ORDAINING THROUGH TOUCH

The magical power of touch is reflected in the ceremony *Semicha*, which symbolized the transference of authority from rabbi to his disciple. "And the Lord said unto Moses, 'Take thee Joshua, the son of Nun, a man in whom is spirit and touch him with your hand.'" (Numbers 25:18)[50]

The priestly blessing, which was one of the most impressive features of the service in the temple at Jerusalem and still holds a prominent place in synagogue worship, is recited by having priests raise their hands.[51] Conversely, when the Torah speaks of those who withhold care and concern from other human beings, it is the failure to use the hand that becomes symbolic of distancing ourselves from others: "Do not close your hand from your needy brother." (Deuteronomy 15:7) When the prophet admonishes the people and reflects upon the crimes of the city of Sodom, which became associated with wickedness and callousness, he says, "And the hand of the poor and needy you did not strengthen." (Ezekiel 16:49)

The Talmud, in describing the ambivalent feeling of the Rabbis towards non-Jews who are candidates for conversion, states, "we should push them away with our left hand and draw them near with our right hand."[52]

Schachter and Hoffman, in their analysis of counseling in

---

50. The Hebrew word literally means to press or lean. From this Hebrew word is derived the noun *semicha* (the act or ordination). Today the certificate of admission to the rabbinate is still called *semicha*. Thus at its inception *semicha* involved one human being touching another human being.

51. See Leviticus 9:22.

52. *Sotah* 49a and *Sanhedrin* 107b.

the Hasidic tradition, write, "Yet another intriguing Hasidic approach to healing was through touch and laying-on-of-hands" Some rebbes relied heavily on this method to treat physical illness. We are told that Rabbi Shalom of Belz once attributed the healing power of his fingers to their involvement in Torah study. Rabbi Nachman of Bratzlav taught healing based on subtle diagnosis of bodily pulse. He reported that he experienced energy depletion each time he engaged in laying-on-of-hands.[53]

When the people question the power of God to provide for their needs in the desert, God reassures Moses by using the imagery of the hand. "And the Lord said unto Moses 'will the hand of the Lord be cut off? You will see whether my word will come to pass or not.'" (Numbers 11:23) It would be unthinkable that the people would no longer be touched by the presence of God. The removal of the hand becomes symbolic of the removal of God's concerns from the arena where men struggle to find happiness and meaning to life. Our hands stretched out ready to touch the suffering human being is a veritable act of assuring the sufferer that neither man nor God has abandoned him.

---

53. Hoffman, p. 147.

7

RESPONDING TO TRAGEDY

*Upon receiving news that someone has passed away, the tra-
ditional Jewish response is "Baruch Dayan HaEmet, Blessed
are you O Righteous Judge." This prayer expresses faith in the
ways of God in the face of death, which appears to mock all
human strivings. A colleague of mine said that when he heard
of the death of a young man who had been run over in an
automobile accident, he refused to say the words "Baruch
Dayan HaEmet." He believes that there is a natural order in
this universe that acts independently of God's will. From his
vantagepoint, the natural order of the universe is morally
neutral. From what occurs in nature, we cannot infer the
morality and immorality of those affected.*

*If anything, tragedy should induce within the pastoral
counselor and all those who counsel the bereaved a deep sense
of humility. Honest doubt in God's righteousness can at times
be a prelude to genuine religious faith.*

*The enduring lesson of the Book of Job is that Job's
friends, who espoused the traditional theological perspective of
their day, were wrong, while Job, who espoused so-called
religious heresies, was deemed by God as being righteous.*

*Intellectual honesty should lead us to conclude that no one
has ever been able to satisfactorily reconcile God's love of man
with the presence of evil, which fails to discriminate between
the righteous and wicked. As shown in this chapter, there have
been voices in the Jewish tradition that have given different
responses to human suffering. The responses have enabled
some light to penetrate through the darkness that surrounds*

the mystery of human suffering. No single voice has been able to speak to all generations. The voices cited in this chapter that responded to the destruction of the Second Temple may not speak to those who seek to offer theological responses to the Shoah.

What all these voices appear to have in common is the following thought: Though all of us reluctantly, against our will, must walk at some point in our lives through the valley of the shadow of death, God has given us the strength and the willpower to lift ourselves up out of that valley and see the sunlight of the day. The shadow and darkness may remain, but the sunlight does penetrate and does illumine our way.

EVERY MAN HAS HIS BREAKING POINT

When tragedy struck Job, he lamented his cruel fate. Eliphaz, upon hearing him, reminds his friend Job that Job was always a source of inspiration and comfort to others. He says: "Your words have upheld the stumbling and you have strengthened the weak-kneed." (Job 4:4) Later, Job, after hearing his friend's words, replies by saying, "What is my strength that I should wait and what my end that I should be patient? Is my strength the strength of stones or is my flesh made of bronze?" (Job 6:11–12) In other words, Job questions his ability to avoid a total breakdown. Every man has his breaking point. There is only so much that any one person can take. Despite giving vent to such feelings, there is no indication in the text that Job's anguish brings about a disorder that results in his inability to function. On the contrary, the whole book is devoted to his questioning in a clear and forthright manner the accepted religious viewpoints of his day. Job is forever challenging the arguments advanced by his friends, remaining firm in his contention that he has not committed such grievous wrongs to warrant the misfortunes that have occurred to him. Job is not only convinced that his friends are wrong in accusing him of having sinned, but that they also misrepresent the teachings of God which they purport to uphold. "Is it for the sake of God that you speak falsehood, on his behalf that you utter lies? Will you show partiality toward him? Is it for God that you are arguing? Will He declare you in the right if you show partiality to one side? Will not his majesty affright you and his awe fall upon you?" (Job 13:7, 8, 10, 11)

In other words, Job is telling his friends that even though they are projecting themselves to be guardians of the faith and the defenders of God, they are doing God no service in lying to defend him.

He goes on to say that he doesn't care so much what happens to him personally. What is more crucial is that his integrity be maintained before God. What is more important than his physical well-being is that in his lawsuit against God he be exonerated: "He may slay me, I'll not quaver. I will defend my conduct to his face. . . . Now listen closely to my speech, my declaration be in your ears. See now I set forth my case. I know I will be acquitted. Who will contend with me? I would be silent and expire."[1] (Job 13:15, 17, 18, 19)

---

1. The other interpretation to Verse 15 is "Though he slay me, yet I will trust in him." This interpretation derives from an ingenious emendation by the Masoretes who suggest that the reading should be "lo" spelled with the vocalic consonant way rather than alef, which stands in the text. According to Rashi the sense is though he slay me I will not be separated from him, but will constantly hope for him. Both the consonantal text and the context support the opposite sense. At the risk of death . . . Job will defend, argue, and plead his innocence before God. His concern is not with his life to be delivered from his suffering or be restored to prosperity, but to maintain his integrity and be vindicated before God.

Job maintains his self-esteem. He is not willing to surrender his position to placate his friends, who from Job's vantage point falsify God's teachings. As Nathaniel Branden writes, "Self-esteem requires and entails cognitive self-assertiveness which is expressed through a policy of thinking, of judging and of governing action accordingly. To subvert the authority of one's rational understanding—to sacrifice one's mind in favor of feelings which cannot justify or defend—is to subvert one's self-esteem."[2]

Job will not accept unearned guilt. At the same time, though he has seriously challenged the conventional theology of his day, he will not abandon the ethical system of that faith. Instead, he clings on to his self-esteem. Robert Gordis puts it this way:

Out of his anguish Job makes another basic contribution to higher religion. He insists that, though his unjustified suffering must arouse universal pity, righteous men will not be deflected from the good life by the spectacle of their undeserved misery. Thus Job, boldly cuts the nexus in utilitarian morality between virtue and prosperity making righteousness its own justification.

Upright men will be horrified at this, and the innocent will rise up against the godless. But the just will hold fast

The Anchor Bible, translated with an introduction and notes by Marvin H. Pope (Garden City, NY: Doubleday Company Inc., 1965), pp. 95–96.

For a discussion of the Keri and Ketib to the word *lo* in 13:15 see also Amos Hacham, *Sefer Iyov*, (Jerusalem: Mosad Harav Kook, 1970), p. 89. Hacham indicates as is found in talmudic discussion in last chapter of Sotah that there were both Tannaim and Amoraim who were of the opinion that Ketib with the vocalic consonant way should be upheld.

2. Nathaniel Branden, *The Psychology of Self Esteem* (Los Angeles Cal.: Nash Publishing Corp., 1969), p. 111.

to his way, and he who has clean hands will increase his strength. (Job 17:8, 9)[3]

Another illustration of Job maintaining his self-esteem is reflected in his desire to understand his plight and willingness to hear out his friends despite the fact that their words hurt and pain him. Pleadingly, Job utters, "Teach me and I shall be silent, and where I have erred make me understand." (Job 6:24) Branden says, "If man is to achieve or maintain self-esteem, the first and fundamental requirement is that he preserves an indomitable will to understand. The desire for clarity, for intelligibility and comprehension falls within the range of his awareness is the guardian of man's mental health and the basis for his intellectual growth."[4]

Job's refusal to admit guilt may be a way to work through the tragedy that overtakes him. His response is different than the other responses to tragedy found in both biblical and rabbinic theology. The rabbis asserted that when an individual is afflicted with suffering, he should examine his own ways, for perhaps he is responsible for what occurred. "When a person sees that affliction has come upon him," said Rabba, "he should first examine closely his own conduct. Should he fail to find a moral defect which might account for his suffering he might attribute it to his neglect and the study of Torah. Should this not prove to be the cause, he might then regard his suffering as a chastisement of love aiming to test and refine his character."[5]

Max Arzt notes that the Yom Kippur liturgy is suffused with the belief that sin alienates man from God, Who is the righteous one of the world (*Yoma* 37a), and that the sinner is in desperate need of reconciliation and atonement. This idea is tersely ex-

---

3. Robert Gordis, *The Book of God and Man* (Chicago: University of Chicago Press, 1965), p. 86.

4. Branden, p. 108.

5. Berachot 5a.

pressed in the Book of Isaiah: "Your iniquities have separated between you and your God." (Isaiah 59:2)[6]

The aforementioned idea is mirrored in the holiday Musaf Amidah service, where we read: "Because of our sins were we exiled from the land." Job's friends are persistent in trying to teach Job that even suffering of the righteous has its justification and that man suffers because he has sinned. In light of the evaluation above, where we cited Branden's observations concerning the need to maintain self-esteem in face of unjustified accusation, how are we to understand an admission of guilt as a successful therapeutic way of trying to face a tragedy?

Whenever evil strikes, we may justifiably conclude that we are innocent. Although we may be blameless in the present situation, previous irrationalities and failures to think may lead us to a general sense of distrust so that we are never fully certain of our moral status.

The solution to this problem lies in recognizing this form of uncertainty for what it is, identifying it as a system and striving to be objective and factual in one's self-appraisal. The struggle to achieve a rationale for feeling guilty, will in itself contribute to the regaining of self-esteem.

Following the chain of catastrophic events which led to the destruction of the temple in Jerusalem, the subjugation of the Jewish community under the Roman Empire, the unsuccessful revolt by Bar Kochba against the Romans in the second century in Palestine, and large segments of the Jewish population being led off to Rome, the self-esteem of the Jewish community was severely challenged. How does one feel inwardly strong when confronted by the whole might of Rome, made doubly impregnable by its long tradition of invincibility? How does a Jewish community

6. Max Arzt, *Justice and Mercy: Commentary on the Liturgy of the New Year and the Day of Atonement* (New York: Burning Bush Press, 1963), p. 193.

which views itself as the chosen people come to grips with the enormity of tragedies which were to overcome the Jewish community of Palestine during the first and second centuries? We have a statement by Josephus that 1,197,000 of Jerusalem inhabitants were killed or captured by Titus in the year 70 C.E. The number is not greatly reduced by the fairly cautious historian Tacitus, who, writing a few decades later, gives an estimate of 600,000 Jewish fatalities alone. The Bar Kochba War (132 C.E.) cost Palestinian Jewry according to Dio Cassius 580,000 killed in action, in addition to countless others who died of hunger, disease, or fire. All of these figures are doubtless highly exaggerated, but they give us an idea of the tremendous impressions made on contemporaries by the staggering Jewish losses. "All of Judea," adds Dio, "became almost a desert." The ravages of the war against Trajan cannot be statistically computed, but the great Egyptian Jewish center never recovered from the shock, while the community of Cyprus was completely wiped out. The sum total of the casualties and victims of malnutrition and disease in the seven decades from 66 to 135 must have been enormous. We may also take it for granted that at least some Jewish captives sold into slavery were likewise lost to the Jewish people. Certainly many of the children who were carried off were brought up as Gentiles in a non-Jewish environment."[7]

ASSERTING POWER IN A POWERLESS SETTING

How does one retain self respect and self confidence to face the future in the wake of such enormous losses and the virtual collapse of the Jewish community on a social, political, and religious level?

---

7. Salo W. Baron, *A Social & Religious History of the Jews*, vol. 2 (New York: Columbia University Press), p. 102.

The consciousness of powerlessness undoubtedly accompanied the Jewish people during its many defeats at this time. Powerlessness is the inability to help determine what should be the destiny of the good in contrast to the wicked. Job, who maintained his innocence, cries out bitterly and sarcastically: "It is all one—I say—the blameless and the wicked he destroys alike. When disaster brings sudden death he mocks the plea of the innocent. The land is given over to the hand of the evildoer who is able to bribe the judges. If not he, who then is guilty?" (Job 9:22–24)

Associated with powerlessness is a further dimension of alienation, namely, meaninglessness. This occurs when the individual is unclear as to what he ought to believe when the individual's minimal standards for ability in decision-making are not met.[8]

Rather than blaming the foreign enemy, Jewish leadership followed the old prophetic line of self-accusation and ascribed the downfall to the people's own transgression. In doing so, they were affirming their spiritual strength, for they believed that if they would now repent, redemption would come to the Jewish people and the world. Typical of this mentality is the statement found in the Talmud, "If Israel was to observe two Sabbaths in accordance with the Halacha immediately, they would be redeemed." (*Shabbat* 118b) Or, "Great is Teshuvah in that it bring Redemption, as it is written 'unto Zion shall a redeemer come and unto them that turn from transgression in Jacob.'" (*Yoma* 86b)

A nation that was physically impotent could assert itself and retain its self-esteem by feeling that its future and destiny were still in its own hands. In effect, what was being said in the aforementioned hyperbolic statements regarding Teshuvah was that we can determine our own future. We are not pawns of the Roman Empire. We are not to be made objects of their whims and caprices. We ourselves can change the world by our piety and by

---

8. Dorothe E. Soelle, *Suffering* (Philadelphia: Fortress Press, 1975), p. 11.

our willingness to have our lives governed by the teachings of our faith.

The psychologist Alfred Adler developed a theory of compensation, which can be related to the response of the Jewish people to situations where they were physically impotent and robbed of sovereignty for close to two millennia. Adler said, "If in the organ environment interaction, the balance threatens to turn against the organism, it responds through attempts at compensation."[9]

Recognizing the glaring deficiencies that all people are endowed with, Adler wrote: "The greater the inferiority feeling the more urgent and strange will be the need for a safe guarding guideline and the more distinctly will it emerge. As in organic compensation the effectiveness of psychological compensation is linked with increased activity and brings about striking often superior and novel psychological phenomena."[10]

The Jewish community had been visited with many physical ravages. After the unsuccessful revolt by Bar Kochba had been thwarted in 135 C.E., physical ravages to be sure were most appalling. Not only had Jerusalem become a non-Jewish city, but most of Judea, formerly the core of Jewish settlement, was completely dejudaized. After the fall of Bethar, vestiges of Jewish life disappeared from most of Judea.[11] With the potential for being totally demoralized by the ravages of war and the might of Rome, the rabbis compensated their loss by asserting the superiority of the people by virtue of their acceptance of the Torah. Midrashic homilists, who served the same function that rabbis do today in delivering sermons, always reminded the people how unique, special, and blessed were they by virtue of having their lives

---

9. *The Individual Psychology of Alfred Adler*, edited and annotated by Heinz L. Ausbacher and Rowena R. Ausbacher (New York: Bask Books Inc., 1956), p. 23.

10. Ibid., p. 98.

11. Baron, p. 123.

guided by the Torah. For example, the Midrash states, "At the very moment Israel received the Torah, sixty myriad of ministering angels descended from heaven and set crowns upon the heads of the chosen people."[12] Another midrash states, "As each Israelite pledged loyalty to God, vowed to obey the Torah and promised to fulfill the *mitzvot*, he was kissed by one of the divine emissaries."[13] Still another Midrash reassures the unique relationship between God and the Jewish people by saying, "From the time Israel accepted the Torah with such forthrightness and desire she was called by God, my people."[14]

Possession of this prized gift, the Torah, very well compensated for their abject condition of being physically impotent. Their superiority was established by virtue of the determination of the people to cling to the Torah and not abandon its teaching despite their undesirable happenstance and circumstance.

GOD FAVORING THE PURSUED

There were obviously a number of people who were demoralized and frightened by being placed in an inferior position of being persecuted and pursued by the enemy. The following Midrash sought to lift the spirits of the people and have them gain a new perspective. The Midrash states: "And God seeks the one who is being pursued," (Ecclesiastes 3:15) Rabbi Judah, the son of Simon, said in the name of Rabbi Jose, the son of N'Horah, "The holy one,

---

12. Midrash Tehillim 103:8, Pesikta de Rav Kahana 16:3, vol. 1, p. 266. *Shabbat* 88a, The source here says that each of the children of Israel were adorned with two crowns. Later, when Israel sinned, the crowns were removed by the angels. In the future, they will be restored.

13. Song of Songs, Rabbah 2:2.

14. Ruth Rabba Proems, no. 1.

blessed be he, always holds accountable the blood of the pursued by those who pursue."

You should know that such is the case, for we see that Abel was pursued by Cain and God chose Abel as it says, "The Lord paid heed to Abel and his offering, but to Cain and his offering he paid no heed." (Genesis 4:4) Noah was pursued by his generation and God chose only Noah, as it says "For you alone have I found righteous before me in your generation." (Genesis 7:1) Abraham was pursued by Nimrod and God chose Abraham, as it says, "You are the Lord the God who chose Abram." (Neh. 9:7) Isaac was pursued by the Philistines and God chose Isaac, as it says, "And they said, We now see plainly that the Lord has been with you." (Genesis 26:28) Jacob was pursued by Esau and the Holy One blessed be he, chose Jacob, as it says, "For God chose Jacob as his unique treasure." (Psalms 135:4) Joseph was pursued by his brothers and the Holy One, blessed be he, chose Joseph, as it says, "This he ordained in Joseph for a testimony." (Psalms 81:6) Moses was pursued by Pharaoh and the Holy One, blessed be he, chose Moses, as it says, "Therefore he said he would destroy them had not Moses, his chosen stood before him in the breach." (Psalms 106:23) Saul was pursued by the Philistines and the Holy One, blessed be he, chose Saul, as it says, "And Samuel said to all the people, Do you see him whom the Lord has chosen, that there is none like him among all the people?" (1 Sam. 10:24) David was pursued by Saul and the Holy One, blessed be he, chose David, as it says, "And he chose David his servant." (Psalms 78:70)

Israel is pursued by other nations and the Holy one, blessed be he, chose Israel, as it says, "And the Lord has chosen you from among all other peoples on earth to be his treasured people." (Deuteronomy 14:2)[15]

God's championing the cause of the underdog was a tremen-

---

15. Leviticus Rabbah 27:5.

dous boost to a weak nation that had been humiliated by military defeat. The aforementioned Midrash not only took the sting out of the crushing defeats but more importantly was able to convert the liability—physical weakness—into an asset. To be weak was even considered to be a badge of honor. The esteem of the people was not lowered as a result of persecution and defeat, for God was with the persecuted.

THE WEAKNESS OF PHYSICAL POWER

Another genre of rabbinic literature takes the physical strength of foreign nations and shows it to be for naught compared with the moral superiority of the Jewish people. The Talmud records: "Whenever you find the words of Rabbi Jose the Galilee in a haggadic statement make your ears as a funnel." (In other words, be very receptive to what will be said.) It is not because you are the most numerous of peoples that the Lord set his heart on you and chose you, for indeed you are the smallest of peoples. God spoke to Israel saying, "I desire you, for even when I confer greatness upon you, you humble yourself before me. I made Abraham great and in return he said, 'I am but dust and ashes.' (Genesis 18:27) I made Moses and Aaron great and they said, 'For who are we that you should grumble against us?' (Exodus 16:7) I conferred greatness upon David and he said, 'I am a worm and not a man.' (Psalms 22:7) But the nations of the world are not that way. I made Nimrod great and he said, 'Come let us build us a city and a tower with its top in the sky to make a name for ourselves.' (Genesis 11:4) I made Pharaoh great and he said, 'Who is the Lord that I should listen to him and let Israel go?' (Exodus 5:2) I made Sancherib great and he said, 'Who are they among all the gods of the countries that have delivered their country out of my hand that the Lord should deliver Jerusalem out of my hands?' (II Kings 18:35) I made Nebuchadnezzar great and he said, 'I will ascend above the heights of the clouds. I will be like the Most High.' (Isaiah 14:14) I made Hiram great and in turn he said, 'I am a God and I sit in the seat of God.'" (Ezekiel 28:2)[16]

The flaunting of physical prowess by the non-Jewish world did not impress the expositor of the aforementioned Haggadah. To him, it was sheer haughty arrogance, which was the worst feature that an individual could have. The humble would one day gain supremacy just as God's still quiet voice would make a louder noise than the bombastic loud sounds of the wind, earthquake, and fire.[17]

However, it was not primarily the arrogance of the surrounding nations that conferred a favorite nation status upon the Israelites. They curried favor with God because there was intrinsic holiness which God had bestowed upon them. The following midrash reassured the people of its special status. Elijah said, "Once I was going from place to place and a man approached me and asked me questions concerning words of the Torah. He said to me, 'My master. There are two things in my heart and I love them dearly—Torah and Israel, and I don't know which of them comes first.' I answered him. 'It is the practice of the people to say that Torah supersedes everything else, but I contend Israel that is holy takes precedence.'"[18] Midrashic expositors went so far as to claim that the creation of the Jewish people was more precious than anything which God created. Rav Berachia said: "Heaven and Earth were created only for Israel as it says, 'In the beginning God created the heaven and earth.'" (Genesis 1:1) And *reshit* (first), which comes from the word *b'reshit* is only Israel as it is

---

16. Hulin 89a.
17. See 1 Kings 19:11–12.
18. Tana Dvei Eliyahu 15.

written, "Israel is holiness unto the Lord the first fruits of his produce." (Jeremiah 2:3)[19]

The favorite nation status of Israel is granted to her because she has embraced the Torah. The Torah from the vantage point of Israel is a potent weapon which will protect her. Rabbi Abba Bar Kahana stated in the name of Rabbi Johanan that one hundred and twenty myriads of angels descended from heaven when Israel accepted the Torah. One angel set a crown upon the head of each Israelite while another angel girded him with a weapon.[20]

There was always the uncertainty regarding Israel's future owing to its weak position and political powerlessness.

In the following midrash the rabbis are telling the people that their continued allegiance to the Torah will cause God to carry out everything that is written in the Torah. At times it will appear as if God had deserted the people, but he will return to them. When he returns, God will be amazed that the people have maintained their fidelity. The midrash written in response to the destruction of the temple attempts to comfort them through the reassurance that the covenant is eternal.

"This I recall to mind, therefore I have hope." Rabbi Abba B. Kahana said: "This may be likened to a king who married a lady and wrote her a large *ketubah*, 'marriage document.' So many state apartments I am preparing for you, so many jewels I am preparing for you, and so many silver and gold I give you." The king left her and went to a distant land for many years. Her neighbors use to vex her saying, "Your husband has deserted you. Come and be married to another man." She wept and sighed but

---

19. Leviticus Rabbah 36, Yalkut Shimoni Isaiah 43.

20. Midrash Tehilim 103:8. For an in-depth analysis of the psychological support that adherence to the Torah offered to the Jewish people from the vantage point of the Midrash see, *A Study of Midrashic Responses to Group Trauma*, Melvin Jay Glatt, (New York: Jewish Theological Seminary, 1979), pp. 78–112.

whenever she went into her room and read her *ketubah* she would be consoled. After many years the king returned and said to her, "I am astonished that you waited for me all these years." She replied, "My lord king, if it had not been for the generous *ketubah* you wrote me then surely, my neighbor would have won me over."

So the nations of the world taunt Israel and say, "Your God has no need of you; He has deserted you and removed his presence from you. Come to us and we shall appoint commanders and leaders of every sort for you." Israel enters the synagogues and houses of study and reads in the Torah, "I will look with favor upon you . . . and I will not spurn you" (Leviticus 26:9–11), and they are consoled.

In the future, the Holy One, blessed be he, will say to Israel, I am astonished that you waited for me all these years. And they will reply, "If it had not been for the Torah which you gave us . . . the nations of the world would have led us astray." Therefore, it is stated, "This do I recall and therefore I have hope." (Lamentations 3:21)[21]

The aforementioned Midrash extols the fidelity of the children of Israel to the Torah. Despite the loss of status and prestige which resulted from the destruction of the Temple and the humiliating and crushing defeat during the Bar Kochba revolution, the Torah would serve as an inner support system that would sustain the group. Adherence to the Torah would pave the way for the Messiah and the Messianic era. The people were comforted in the belief that the Messiah and Messianic era would usher in an era of peace for Israel and all nations of the world. The nations of the world would extol Israel not because of its superior political powers, but because they would recognize Israel's spiritual superiority.[22]

The following from the writings of the noted twentieth cen-

---

21. Lamentations Rabbah 3:7.
22. For a discussion of Messiah and Messianic era, and comprehen-

tury psychologist Alfred Adler explains the significance of the concept of the Messiah and the Messianic era for the Jewish people: "In each mind there is a conception of a goal or ideal to get beyond the present state to overcome the present deficiencies and difficulties by postulating a concrete goal for the future. By means of this concrete goal, the individual can think and feel himself superior to the difficulties of the present because he has in mind his successes of the future."[23]

The people were convinced that the setbacks of the present would be short-lived. They would be followed by the dawn of a better day. Illustrations abound in both biblical and rabbinic literature on the transience of the abject condition of humiliation and of the suffering and destruction which the Jewish community would have to endure.

One story relates how Rabbi Gamliel, Rabbi Eleazar Ben Azariah, Rabbi Joshua and Rabbi Akibah were walking and they heard noise at a distance of 120 miles from the home of a Roman named Petaliah. They began to weep and Rabbi Akibah laughed. They said to Akibah, "Why are you laughing?" He asked them what was the reason for their crying. They responded by saying: "These idolaters bow down to images and bring frankincenses to idols. They are resting securely and are at peace. The contrary is with us that even our holy temple is being burned by fire." Akibah responded, "It is precisely for that reason that I laugh. For if this is the reward of those who go contrary to God's will, namely that they sit securely, so much the more will be the reward and the future of those who act in accordance with his will."[24] The Talmud then records another episode of the same rabbis who were going up to Jerusalem. When they reached Mt. Scopus, they rend

sive bibliography on subject see *Principles of the Jewish Faith, Louis Jacobs (New York: Basic Books), pp. 368–397.*

23. Ausbacher, p. 99.
24. *Makkot*, 24a.

their clothes. When they reached the Temple Mount, they saw a jackal emerging from the holy of holies. They began to weep and Akibah began to laugh. Akibah's colleagues wept upon seeing the most sacred spot of the temple trampled upon by a jackal. The contrast between the holy of holies, which no one could enter into during the entire year, with the exception of the high priest, who was permitted to go into it but once a year on the day of Yom Kippur, and the reality of the sacred spot which was now so desolate and barren, caused them to cry. Akibah laughed, offering them the reassurance that one day Jerusalem would be heavily populated. Akibah quoted passages from the prophets to prove his point. When he concluded, his colleagues said to him, "Akibah you have comforted us. Akibah you have comforted us."[25] Akibah's laughter brings consolation to them. Akibah's laughter is one of determination, a tenacity, a healthy kind of stubbornness and defiance of the dreadful consequences. The grave national picture in which Jerusalem is razed to the ground does not demoralize him. The unsuccessful revolt by Bar Kochba which Akibah supported and whom Akibah thought was the Messiah did not vanquish the indomitable spirit of Akibah.

FEELING SUPERIOR THROUGH LAUGHTER

What does laughter represent psychologically? The oldest and probably still most widespread theory of laughter is that laughter is an expression of a person's feeling of superiority over other people.[26]

---

25. *Makkot*, 24b.

26. John Morreal, *Taking Laughter Seriously* (Albany, N.Y.: State University of New York Press, 1983), p. 4.

In the second chapter of the book of Psalms, the Psalmist speaks of the enemies of Israel who plan to overthrow the newly crowned king of Israel. The attack upon Israel would be a revolt against God, Who willed someone to be king over Israel. "The Kings of the earth stand up and the rulers take counsel together against the Lord and against his anointed: Let us break their bands asunder and cast away their cords from us." (Psalms 2:2–3)

The surrounding nations reason that it would be better to make an onslaught when the king has ascended the throne and not wait until he has grown more formidable by reorganizing and strengthening his forces.

But then the Psalmist continues by pointing out how futile and absurd are the machinations of these nations. The Psalmist writes: "He mocks at them. . . . Truly it is I that have installed my king on Zion, my holy mountain." (2:4, 6) Hence, through laughter, God expresses His superiority over that which man plans and contrives.

It is folly to think that the calculated planning of man will determine the outcome of a human situation. The theme of the psalm is an exemplification of the Yiddish proverb: *A Mensch Tracht Un Got Lacht* — "A man thinks and God laughs."

Laughter is an expression of a person's feeling of superior adaptation to some specific situation or to his environment in general. Laughter takes the physical form it does, the baring of the teeth, because originally laughter was a physical challenge or threat to an enemy. This showing of the teeth in laughter as in the aggressive behavior of dogs is a way of asserting one's physical prowess.[27]

The person with a sense of humor can never be fully dominated even by a government which imprisons him. Laughter will put the individual above the situation to some extent and will

---

27. Ibid., p. 6.

preserve a measure of freedom, if not of movement at least of thought.[28]

Akibah's laughter is not only the venting of nervous energy, but, more important, it is a serious act of defiance against Imperial Rome. Furthermore, it is not the hollow laughter of the insensitive person who avoids reality in his attempt to find life amusing. Akibah's laughter has credibility, for he himself bears eloquent testimony to the seriousness of life by dying a martyr's death at the hands of the Romans.

In *Berachot* 61b, there is recorded the martyr's death of Akibah. The Talmud also cities another episode in which Akibah's laughter provides consolation even at a time of great suffering. The Talmud relates how Rabbi Akibah once came to visit Rabbi Eliezer, who was ill. Other students were also present. Everyone wept with the exception of Akibah. They said, "Why do you laugh?" He said, "Why do you weep?" They said, "How shall we not weep when the book of the law (i.e., the learned master) is in pain?" Akibah said, "That is why I laugh. So long as I see that the master's wine did not become sour, or his oil rancid, or his honey corrupt, or his flax ruined, I thought, perhaps (though God forbid) the Master has already received this world (i.e., his reward) but now that I have seen the master in pain I rejoice."[29]

Akibah's laughter here stems from the conviction that there is something that God has in store for us beyond the challenge that we always face in the present. He comforts his colleagues here by reassuring them of the existence of the hereafter.

---

28. Ibid., p. 101.

29. C.G. Montefiore, Ancient Jewish & Greek Encouragement and Consolation, (Bridgeport, Conn.: Hartmore House, 1971), p. 21.

THE PRESENT DOESN'T DETERMINE THE FUTURE

When we turn to the Bible, we encounter many instances when Israel is called upon to look beyond an impending tragedy into a future that would bring them consolation. Two illustrations are most striking. One is recorded in the thirty-second chapter of Jeremiah. The incident takes place in the tenth year of Zedekiah's reign, about 588 B.C.E., while Jeremiah was confined in the court of the guard. We are told that Jeremiah had a foreboding feeling which he felt to be the word of the Lord that his cousin Hanamel would come to him and ask him to buy a piece of property in Anathoth to which he, Jeremiah, held the right of redemption.

The legal situation is that described in the law recorded in Leviticus 25:25. This law stipulates that in the event of a man's being forced because of poverty or debt to sell all or part of his inheritance, the next of kin had both the privilege and the duty of redeeming the property in question and thus keeping it in the family.[30]

By all accounts, this was a poor business investment since Jerusalem would be destroyed the very next year by Nebuchadnezzar. Anathoth, where the purchase took place, was only four miles northeast of Jerusalem near the present day village of Anata, which preserves the ancient name.

The transaction was carried out according to proper legal procedures. The transaction was intended to be symbolic of God's promise, a promise which, as we see in other verses in the same chapter, Jeremiah himself dared to believe. He felt that beyond the impending tragedy, normal life would once again be resumed in the land.

---

30. *Jeremiah Anchor Bible*, translated with an introduction by John Bright, (Garden City, N.Y.: Doubleday, 1965), p. 239.

In Jeremiah 32:15, we read: "For this is what the Lord of Hosts, the God of Israel has said: 'Houses and fields and vineyards shall once again be bought in this land.'" And then Jeremiah 32:16 and 32:24–25 show Jeremiah's pessimism regarding the prudence of such an investment: "Then after I had given the deeds of purchase to Baruch Ben Neriah, I prayed to the Lord as follows: Ah my Lord! Look! The siege ramps are already thrown up to take the city. And through sword, starvation and disease the city is delivered to the Chaldeans who attack it. What you threatened has come to pass—as you see. Yet you, Lord God, said to me: 'Buy the field, pay for it and have the transaction witnessed, when the city is delivered up to the Chaldeans.'" Jeremiah here displays stubborn courage in redeeming the field of Anathoth even though he knew very well that the temple would be destroyed and the people would be taken into exile. He felt frustrated. He was filled with anguish and black despair. But he suppressed these feelings and took a leap of faith by purchasing the land.

Jeremiah does not abandon hope as the final collapse nears. The purchase was made to signify that Israel has a future in her own land. On one level, Jeremiah felt that he was doing a foolish thing. But the compulsion of God's word again overpowered him. Knowing his God as a God who never abandoned his people, he, who could see no hope, acted in hope nevertheless.[31]

Another illustration of refusing to let the present determine the future deals with a question posed by the people to the prophet Zechariah. The historical background is the condition which confronted the Jews who returned from the first exile. The people turn to the prophet and they ask about the need to fast on the fast of the fifth, month which is probably the fast of Tisha B'Av. The prophet does not answer the question directly but later he assures the people that the current days associated with fasting and sad-

---

31. Ibid., introduction to Book CXVll

ness will eventually be days of joy and happiness. "Thus saith the Lord of Hosts; the fast of the fourth month, and the fast of the fifth, and the fast of the seventh and the fast of the tenth shall be to the house of Judah joy and gladness and cheerful feasts." (Zechariah 8:19)

The following statement in the Pesikta takes the darkest day in the calendar and it converts it also into the most joyous: "Abaye said, the Messiah will come on Tisha B'Av for they establish this day as a day of mourning during these times. But the Holy One, Blessed be He, will convert it into a holiday as it is written, And I will convert their mourning into joy." (Jeremiah 31:12)[32]

PARALLEL BETWEEN JOB AND ZION

I have devoted some attention to this study analyzing the book of Job, which deals with the suffering of the individual. At the same time we have offered some insights as to how the rabbis came to grips with the national traumatic experience of the destruction of the temple. There is a strong connection between the two, as reflected in the words of the Midrash, which states, 'All that which took place to Job also took place to Zion.'[33] Often, the modern Western reader may find this shift from individual pain to collective pain of the people disconcerting. But as Robert Gordis points out, the key lies in the Hebrew concept of "fluid personality." "The Servant Songs (in the second part of the book of Isaiah) have long proved difficult, since they contain certain features that

---

32. Pesikta quoted in "Sefer Haagadah" Revnitzki and Bialik (Tel Aviv: Dvir Publishing Company, 5720), p. 306. A similar quote may be found in Meir Ish Shalom's Edition of Pesikta Rabati, Tel Aviv 5723, end of ch. 28, p. 136a.

33. Pesikta Rabati 26.

obviously refer to the people collectively and others that mirror individual traits. The servant is both the community and the individual who represents it."[34]

The concept of fluid personality is generally assumed to be based on the idea of primitive psychology propounded by Levy-Bruhl and E. Durkheim.[35]

It may be suggested that the age-old problem of "I" in the psalms finds its solution in the same psychological phenomenon. In countless psalms, the poet seems to be describing his own personal lot in unmistakable terms and then imperceptibly the ground shifts to his group or to his people as a whole.[36]

An illustration of the fluid personality may be found in Psalms 51, which opens with an account of how King David is burdened with guilt feelings for taking Bat Sheva away from Uri, the Hittite, her husband who was sent out by David on a suicide mission. This psalm goes very deep into human suffering after sin:

Be gracious unto me O God according to thy mercy. According to the multitude of thy compassion blot out my transgressions. Wash me thoroughly from mine iniquity. And cleanse me from my sin. For I know my transgressions; and my sin is ever before me. . . . Behold, I was brought forth in iniquity, and in sin did my mother conceive me. Behold, you desire truth about that which is hidden, make me, therefore, to know wisdom about secret

---

34. Robert Gordis, *Poets, Prophets and Sages, Essays in Biblical Interpretation* (Bloomingdale, Indiana: Indiana University Press, 1971), p. 234.

35. Ibid., p. 234. Theory may be found in Durkheim's volume *Elementary Forms of Religious Life*.

36. Ibid. For statement of problem Gordis calls attention to the introduction to the Standard Commentaries of W. R. Harper, R. Kittel, and Hans Schmidt.

things. Purge me with hyssop, and I shall be clean. Wash
me and I shall be whiter than snow. Make me to hear joy
and gladness. Let the bones which you have crushed exult.
(Psalms 51:3–10)

There is almost total despair expressed here by David. His
situation is so desperate that only God can help him get rid of the
overwhelming guilt feelings that weigh heavily upon him. The
most admirable part of this chapter is the frank expression of guilt
to which David admits. Maurice Samuel points out that today
when we speak of a guilt complex it is generally taken to be a
condition of which a person must rid himself not by recognizing
that he is guilty (because that's the guilt complex); instead he is
supposed to get rid of any impression as to having been a wrong-
doer. Here, David knows what he did and he was guilt. It wasn't
a guilty complex, it was a genuine guilt.[37]

Near the end of the psalm, David says: "You do not want me to
bring sacrifices; You do not desire burnt offerings. True sacrifices
to God is a contrite spirit; God, you will not despise a contrite and
crushed heart." (Psalms 51:18,19)

Maurice Samuel points out the contrast here to most tenden-
cies of modern psychologists, whose aim it is "to build up a man";
to make one feel, "No, I wasn't guilty. I had a complex; there were
circumstances which led me to it." But David says specifically,
"True sacrifice to God is a contrite spirit," to know you have been
wicked and to be shattered by it.[38]

Just at this point does the voice of David become the voice of
the people. David and the Jewish people become fused in one.

---

37. Mark Van Doren and Maurice Samuel, *The Book of Praise,
Dialogues on the Psalms*, edited and annotated by Edith Samuel, (New
York: John Day Company, 1975), p. 50.
38. Ibid., p. 51.

After expressing the desire of God that he be given a broken and a contrite spirit, we have the emergence of what Gordis refers to as the fluid personality: "May it please you to make Zion prosper; rebuild the walls of Jerusalem. You will delight in sacrifices offered in righteousness, in burnt offering and whole offering; Then will they offer bullocks on your altar." (Psalms 51:20–21)

THE MOST PERFECT THING—A BROKEN HEART

The problems of the individual become the problems of the nation. The Psalmist here expresses a notion somewhat akin to what centuries later would be said by the Kotsker Rebbe: "The most perfect thing in this world is a broken heart." In other words, there is no sham or pretense to a broken heart. It is authentic and honest. It represents the quintessence of truth.

The Psalmist here is the spokesman for the people. The impetus to the Psalmists' bearing his heart lies in David's personal individual experience. But his individuality blends with that of the group and the society with which the poet is associated, or with the entire people of which he is a part.[39]

The fluid personality is similar to what modern psychoanalysis has suggested in the phenomenon of what is referred to as identification. This is defined as the "self definition of the Ego in terms of some other person initially the father or the mother. . . . Identification is the mechanism underlying grouping. . . . Each

---

39. Another illustration of the fluid personality is to be found in the book of Hosea where the prophet's bitter experience with his wife, Gomer Bat Divlayim, who committed adultery, becomes symbolic of the people of Israel's career of infidelity and degradation by worshipping a pagan diety, Baal. See Gordis, ibid, pp. 234–239.

member of the group identifies himself with the leader who thus replaces the parent of the family group."[40]

Identification may also be defined as the method by which a person takes over the features of another person and makes them a corporate part of his own personality. It is not necessary for a person to identify with someone else in every respect. He usually selects and incorporates just those features which he believes will help him achieve a desired goal. There is a good deal of trial and error in the identification process because one is usually not quite sure what it is about another person that accounts for his success. The ultimate test is whether the identification helps to reduce tension; if it does, the quality is taken over, if it does not, it is discarded.[41]

When the Midrash states that "all that happened to Job happened to Zion," it was a way of attempting to reduce tension among the Jewish people. For whatever calamities and tragedies it would have to face, there was the assurance that ultimately it would find comfort in the realization that everything worked out for the people just as it did for Job, even though initially everything looked so hopeless for him. God did not abandon him. Job was vindicated and was compensated for his losses. He lived to a ripe old age. Similarly, whatever losses and pain endured by the Jewish community, they would be transient and everything would work out.

Amos Hacham, in his commentary on Job, shows many linguistic parallels between Job and Lamentations. The latter book records an eyewitness account to the destruction of the first temple. He does not conclude that the author of Job borrowed from the author of Lamentations or that the author of Lamentations used material found in Job. There may have been literary

---

40. *Encyclopedia of Social Studies*, (New York, 1946), vol. 2, p. 584b.

41. *Theories of Personality*, second ed. Calvin S. Hall and Gardner Lindzey (New York: John Wiley & Sons Inc., 1970), pp. 45–46.

styles which poets drew from and it is conceivable that both authors drew from the same source.[42] He does not draw any distinction between the complaints of the individual and that of the group. In keeping with the idea of the fluid personality, both are interchangeable. Likewise, whatever linguistic parallels there exists between Job and Psalms should not lead one to conclude there is borrowing, one from the other. Rather, the individual and the group both responded in a similar way to the pain of separation, death, and loneliness.[43]

Earlier, we indicated that one of the most famous lines in the Hebrew Bible which the Masoretes emended to read "though he slay me I trust him" probably makes more sense if we read it in accordance with the translation based upon the original reading, "Though he slay me I will not quaver." But in coming to grips with the theme of this chapter, "Responding to Tragedy," it is an undeniable fact that the Masoretic reading made a profound impression on countless generations of readers who interpreted this most widely quoted passage as an example of supreme submission to the will of God.

Elie Wiesel points out that in reading books of the medieval period such as *Shevet Yehuda* or *Emek HaBacha*, we learn of entire communities wiped out by invaders, crusaders, and avenging armies. Centers of learning, great and small, were obliterated overnight. Another enemy come and gone, another Jewish community apparently dead and yet twenty-four hours later, the community comes back to life.

Wiesel writes: "You read these stories and sooner or later you cannot but wonder: Why did so many victims of so many tragedies go on proclaiming their faith? Why didn't they quit? Why didn't they choose to end their suffering and the suffering of

---

42. *Job*, Amos Hacham, (Jerusalem: Mosad HaRav Kook, 1970), pp. 27–29.

43. Ibid., p. 24–25

their children by converting assimilating—dissolving into society? They could have. Certainly as individuals. But they didn't. Why?

"A story is narrated in Shevet Yehuda about Jews who fled their village and their country. They boarded a ship that eventually they had to abandon. They landed on a desert. Hunger, thirst, disease befell them; many died. Among them was a pious man whose wife had died of hunger. He continued his march, hoping to reach a Jewish settlement. His two children were too weak, so he carried them. When he finally realized that he was the last survivor, the pain was so sharp he fainted. When he came to, he looked around first, and then he looked up to the sky and addressed God: 'Master of the Universe, I know what you want; you want me to stop believing in you, but you won't succeed; you hear me, you won't succeed.'"[44] After the book of Job was written, its hero was best remembered primarily for what we learn about him from reading the prose tale. There he is depicted as a righteous man who retains his faith despite the gravest of provocation. The other Job of the dialogue who rebels against the injustice of undeserved suffering, who challenges God, was not that familiar to readers of the Bible.

The Talmud casts Job into the same mold of Abraham, who is a paragon of one who meets supreme tests of faith. Just as God tested Abraham when He asks him to bind Isaac, likewise did He test Job. The Talmud elaborates on the biblical saga by saying that Satan had sojourned through earth and he reports back to God saying that he has found none so righteous as Abraham. It is then that God tells Satan that there is another man, Job, whose faith is exemplary and there is no one on earth like him, a man blameless and upright.[45]

44. Jewish Digest, Sept. 1972, article by Elie Wiesel.
45. *Baba Bathra* 16a.

On the other hand, the book of Job differs dramatically from the story of Abraham in the following respect: Whereas in the story of Abraham and the binding of Isaac the child is not killed; in the book of Job, the children are killed. Both books have a test. For Abraham, it is the test whether or not he will kill his child, but for the test of Job, among other things, it is his response to the killing of his children.

Actually Job never achieved the status of Abraham as an exemplar of unflinching faithfulness. There are several reasons why Job is foreshadowed by Abraham, the "knight of faith," and never has had such a powerful spell over the minds of Jews as did Abraham. Firstly, Job is in the third strand of Biblical literature and Abraham is in the first strand. The five books of Moses supersede in sanctity the other two strands of biblical literature. Secondly, the historicity of Job is itself challenged in rabbinic literature, as one school of thought contends, that Job was only a parable.[46] Thirdly, Job was not viewed as a member of the Jewish people, and thus his popularity would never match Abraham, whose stories were read in the synagogue whenever the Torah reading was from those portions of the Torah where the events of his life are recorded.

There are traditions that connect Job with Jethro and Balaam, who were consulted by Pharaoh on the question of the genocide of the Israelites; Job's woes are regarded as punishment for failure to protest this crime.[47] Rabbi Yizchak Zeev Soloveichik, known as the Brisker Rav, interprets Job's suffering as divine retribution for being silent when consulted by Pharaoh in regard to the extermination of the Jewish people. Soloveichik says it is human nature that when one feels pain, one screams. Job, however, was silent when he heard of Pharaoh's plan to destroy the Jews. His silence

---

46. *Baba Bathra* 15a.
47. *Sanhedrin* 106a, *Sotah* 11a.

proves that he failed to share in their pain and suffering. Therefore, he was afflicted with unbearable pain.

The binding of Isaac was recorded in the morning liturgy, and a passage from Nehemiah, which speaks of God choosing Abraham, was also part of the daily liturgy. The "Amidah," which is recited thrice daily during the Shaharit, Minhah, and Maariv services, speaks of the God of Abraham, Isaac, and Jacob. Job, being in the third strand of literature, the Ketubim, was never read in any of the religious worship services. Other parts of the Ketubim, like the Books of Song of Songs, Ruth, Lamentations, Ecclesiastics, and Esther, were read on different festivals. Many of the psalms were incorporated into the daily liturgy, but Job was never read publicly.

JOB, THE MAN WITH NO HISTORY

The legends surrounding Job did not reach as wide of an audience among the Jewish people as did the stories of Abraham. Abraham, whom the Bible states was the first Jew, thus became associated in the minds of the people with a willingness to submit and surrender to God's will. The history of martyrdom, which represents the ultimate in self-sacrifice, was traced back to him. Also, Job was associated with the issue of theodicy, which was viewed as being insoluble. He became in a certain sense an individual without a history. Traditionally, when the Jewish psyche would think of an individual's willingness to surrender to the will of God, personalities like Abraham, Akibah, Hanah, or Hannaniah Ben Teradion would come to mind.

Job, to the masses, was linked more with an insoluble theological issue rather than with a historical figure or a historical period in which the destiny of the Jewish people was at stake.

Another important mode of responding to tragedy finds its origin in a midrashic comment attributed to Miriam, the sister of Moses. The Talmud tells us that following the Pharaoh's edict that all male children were to be cast into the river, Amram (the father of Moses, Aaron, and their sister, Miriam) divorced his wife, Yocheved. This example was followed by many of the Israelites. They were devastated by the decree and they reasoned that it would be pointless to bring Jewish children into the world, for the children would be subjected to death. If they could not bring Jewish children into the world, they felt the institution of marriage was itself no longer valid. Miriam, Moses' eldest sister, said to her father: "Father, your decree is worse than Pharaoh's decree. The Egyptians aim to destroy only the male children, but you include the girls as well. Pharaoh deprives his victims of life in this world, but you prevent children from being born and thus you deprive them of the future life, too. He intends to destroy, but who knows whether the intention of the wicked can persist. You are a righteous man and the enactments of the righteous are executed by God, hence your decree will be upheld."

Amram recognized the correctness of her contention and went to the Sanhedrin and put the matter before them. The members of the court spoke and said: "It was you that separated husbands and wives and from you should go forth the permission for remarriage. Amram then made the proposition that each of the members of the Sanhedrin return to his wife and wed her clandestinely, but his colleagues repudiated the plan, saying, "And who will make it known to the whole of Israel?"

Accordingly, Amram stood up publicly under the wedding canopy with his divorced wife, Yocheved, while Aaron and Miriam danced about it, and the angels proclaimed, "Let the mother of the children be joyful!" His remarriage was solemnized with great ceremony, so that the men who had followed his example in divorcing their wives might imitate him now in taking them again unto themselves. And so it happened and from the reunion of Amram and Yocheved, Moses was born.[48]

The response of Miriam to the critical moment in Jewish history according to the aforementioned tale is based upon negative factors. She does not urge her father to remarry her mother because of the bond of affection between the two or because they are well-suited for each other or any other similar reason. Rather, she states her plea based on the fact that Amram will not want to give Pharaoh a victory: "Your decree is worse than Pharaoh's decree." She pleads with her father not to shatter Jewish existence into fragments, which would result if the Jewish family ceased to exist. This is precisely what would have taken place had Miriam not succeeded in convincing her father of the folly of his behavior.

Miriam's response to her father's decision to divorce his wife finds its analogy in a central point articulated by a twentieth century theologian, Emil Fackenheim. He spoke of the need to affirm Jewish life following the Holocaust by carrying out what he called the 614th commandment of the Torah, "Not to give Hitler a posthumous victory." The Torah, according to the rabbinic tradition, contains 613 commandments. Thus, in speaking of a 614th commandment, Fackenheim cleverly dramatizes the need to advance what on the surface appears to be a new teaching.

Fackenheim writes: "The authentic Jew of today is forbidden to hand Hitler yet another posthumous victory."[49]

Fackenheim contends that something radically new has happened, and that is we must face the fact that Hitler did win at least one victory—the murder of six million Jews. Although the very name Hitler should be erased rather than remembered, we cannot disguise the uniqueness of his evil under a comfortable generality,

---

48. *Sotah* 12a, *Baba Batra* 120a, Shmot Rabbah 1:19, Also see Ginzberg, *Legends of Jews*, vol. 2, p. 262.
49. Emil Fackenheim, *The Jewish Return into History* (New York: Schocken Books, 1978), p.22.

such as persecution in general, tyranny in general, or even the demonic-in-general.[50]

According to Fackenheim, the implications of this 614th mitzvah are as follows: First we are commanded to survive as Jews lest the Jewish people perish. We are commanded, second, to remember in our very guts and bones the martyrs of the Holocaust lest their memory perish. We are forbidden, thirdly, to deny or despair of God, however much we may have to contend with Him or with belief in Him, lest we perish. We are forbidden finally to despair of the world as the place which is to become the Kingdom of God, lest we help make it a meaningless place in which God is dead or irrelevant and everything is permitted. To abandon any of these imperatives in response to Hitler's victory at Auschwitz would be to have him yet win other posthumous victories.[51]

A radical response to tragedy is recorded in another section of the Talmud, where we learn that a lot of men were demoralized and depressed over the destruction of the Second Temple. They decided not to marry or to bring any children into the world. But this outlook did not prevail, for carried to its logical conclusion, it would mean an end to the Jewish people.[52]

In other words, the Jewish community decided not to give Rome another victory, which would have been achieved if people no longer married, for without Jewish children coming into the world, Jewish life would cease to exist.

The Talmud, in the same section, also records how other forms of asceticism became popular, owing to the deep depression which set in following the destruction of the Second Temple. There were those that decided to abstain from eating meat and drinking wine, since the institution of animal sacrifices ceased and

---

50. Ibid., p. 23
51. Ibid., pp. 23–24.
52. *Baba Batra* 61a.

libations were no longer offered as part of the temple cult.[53] Their outlook was rejected by the rabbis, who decided to go on and build upon the ruins and re-create Jewish life as a religion which affirmed life. It was destined to become a religion which would develop a positive and healthy attitude to the material world as mirrored in the following statement: "In the future man will have to give an account (Before the heavenly tribunal court) for all that which his eyes saw and which he failed to enjoy." [54]

Jewish endurance in the face of catastrophe became the normative response of the Jewish community following the destruction of the Second Temple. Eli Wiesel writes: "And out of the temple in flames came a tale of hope the most magnificent tales of all, a work of art, the Talmud."[55]

There was now a collective commitment to Jewish group survival for its own sake as mirrored in the tale of Miriam and Amram and the other talmudic tale which speaks of the rise of asceticism following the destruction of the Second Temple.

All could readily understand that the price of forgetting the destruction of the Second Temple was conferring upon the Romans another victory.

The same defiant spirit is to be found in Job, for Job in the throes of trying to lift himself out of a state of deep depression speaks not only of going down to "Sheol," the realm of death, but of his hopes descending with him. He says, "Indeed I have marked out my home in Sheol and spread out my couch in darkness. To the pit I call, you are my father and to the worm my mother and sister. Where then is my hope? My hope, who can see it? To the chambers of Sheol it descends. Together we shall go down to the dust." (Job 17:13–16)

In commenting on Job 17:16, Amos Chacham renders *Badei*

53. Ibid.
54. Jerusalem Talmud *Kidushin* 4:12.
55. Wiesel, ibid.

Sheol "the loneliest places of Sheol." "I will go down to Sheol. My hopes will also go down to Sheol. And tragically my hopes will be there all alone."[56] One could not paint a picture filled with greater despair than that found in the seventeenth chapter of Job. Yet despite that, Job in the same section, makes it clear that the righteous life is to be lived for its own sake and not for the desire of reward. God is viewed as his adversary. Bitterly, Job cries out: "God has set me as a byword among people, I am one in whose face men spit. My eye has grown dim from grief and all my limbs are like a shadow. Upright men will be horrified at this and the innocent will rise up against the godless. But the just will hold fast his way and he who has clean hands will increase his strength." (Job 17:6–8)

At this juncture, his close relationship with God has broken down. But despite the anger he feels in living in a world which mocks and taunts those that live a righteous life since no reward will be forthcoming for them, he will not succumb. He will defiantly live a righteous life not in affirmation of a covenant which was struck between God and him, but rather because the righteous man refuses to have life humiliate him.

Miriam refused to have Amram's despair win out lest Pharaoh emerge victorious. The rabbis did not let asceticism spread rampant, lest Judaism would cease to exist. The righteous man in chapter seventeen of Job does not desist from being righteous even when everything in life seems to vindicate hopelessness and absurdity.

LIFE—A PLEDGE RETURNED TO GOD

A more traditional form of response to tragedy was to view life itself as a pledge which has to be returned to its original owner. A

---

56. Amos Hacham, ibid., p. 135.

popular tale which offered solace particularly to bereaved parents is one which tells of two sons of Rabbi Meir who passed away while their father was in a house of study on a Sabbath afternoon. Rabbi Meir's wife placed them on a bed and spread a sheet over them. When Rabbi Meir returned home on a Saturday evening and inquired as to the whereabouts of their two sons, she did not answer directly. She let him recite *havdalah* (the ceremony marking the conclusion of the Sabbath) and prepared a meal for him. Upon concluding the meal, she engaged in conversation with Rabbi Meir. Rather than confront him directly with the tragic news of the death of their children, she posed a question to him. She told her husband of a deposit that had been entrusted to her and now the man had come to claim his deposit. She inquired if she is responsible to return the deposit. When Rabbi Meir answered in the affirmative, she gently led him into the room where their two dead sons were to be found. When Rabbi Meir saw his two dead sons, he was grief stricken and broke down completely. He spoke of his sons as his teachers, for they "enlightened me with their Torah."

She then reminded Rabbi Meir of his answer to the query she posed to him. At that point Rabbi Meir quoted the immortal words from Job: "The Lord giveth, the Lord taketh, Blessed be the name of the Lord." Rabbi Hanninah tells us the Midrash related that her words provided Rabbi Meir with comfort. And the wife of Rabbi Meir is deserving of the accolade "A woman of valor who may be found?"[57]

CAN EVIL BE GOOD?

Another popular tale which represents a perspective to suffering which was accepted by many was the talmudic story of Nahum

---

57. Midrash Mishle, chapter 31.

GamZu, who was blind and crippled with both legs being crushed and whose body was covered with sores. He conducted himself in a manner free of complaints for the seemingly miserable lot meted out to him. His disciples were pained by the fact that such a saintly man was so terribly afflicted. They asked how can such a righteous man suffer so much. He answered, "I myself am the cause for once on a journey a man asked me for food and I answered, wait until I unload my asses. But before I did so the poor man expired. So I fell on my face and said: My eyes which had no consideration for your eyes, let them become blind. My hands which had no mercy upon your hands, may they become cripple. My feet which had no pity upon your feet, may they be crushed. And I could not find any satisfaction until I had said, May my whole body be covered with sores." His disciples said to him: "Woe is unto us that we must see you in such a condition." And Nahum GamZu replied: "Woe would have been unto me had you not seen me in such a condition." And why was he called the man of GamZu? Because whenever anything would happen to him, he would say *gamzu l'tovah* (this is also for good).[58] The Talmud continues with the story of how a group of Jewish people desired to send a present to a king. The question as to who should go was discussed and Nahum GamZu was selected, for he was accustomed to miracles. He was given a box full of precious stones and pearls, which were stolen at night. The thieves replaced the box with earth. When he awakened in the morning and discovered that the stones and pearls had been replaced with earth, he said, "This is also for good." When he arrived at the King's palace, the box was opened and the king was livid with anger when he saw the box filled with earth. His immediate impulse was to kill all the Jews, since he reasoned that they sought to mock him. In the talmudic tale, Elijah appears as one of the King's advisors and he

58. *Taanit* 21a.

suggested that the earth was special in that it was the same earth, which when used by Abraham against his enemies, was effective in destroying them. In accordance with this advice by Elijah, the earth was used against an enemy that till that point was invincible, and the enemy was conquered. The earth was then deposited in the king's treasury and the box once again filled up with precious stones and pearls. Nahum was sent away with an escort and rewarded with many precious stones and pearls.[59]

In the first story, Rabbi Meir views his sons' death as a homecoming after his wife gently and with great sensitivity led him to the realization that everything given to us eventually must be returned.

Abraham Joshua Heschel writes, "If life is sensed as a surprise, as a gift defying explanation, then death ceases to be a radical negation of what life stands for."[60]

The idea of death being a return and not being a final destination is reflected in the language of the Bible. In the Bible, to die and be buried is to be gathered to one's people. (Genesis 25:8) "They were gathered to their fathers." (Judges 2:10)

As Jews throughout the centuries heard the story of Rabbi Meir and his wife, reconciling themselves to the loss of their sons, they were able to feel comfort in the realization that death was a homecoming, to use the felicitous phrase of Heschel.

Rabbi Meir found a measure of solace in the recognition of the fact that his sons' lives were spent in devotion to Torah. Rabbi Meir and his wife were able to attain a new level of faith, which is grounded in the recognition that in order to believe one must learn to accept.

The tale of Rabbi Meir and his wife was not just a dramatic

59. Ibid.

60. Abraham Joshua Heschel, "Death as Homecoming" in *Jewish Reflection on Death*, edited by Jack Reimer, (New York: Schocken Books, 1974), p. 59.

vignette which strengthened Jewish morale, but its spirit was reflected later in the code of Jewish law, which states that the first words uttered when one hears of death are *Baruch Dayan Emet* (Blessed is the truthful Judge). Job's acceptance of the blows that befell him as the will of God, "The Lord giveth, the Lord taketh, Blessed be the name of the Lord," became indelibly etched in the psyche of the Jew as the kind of response that one was expected to make upon hearing of the death of a close one.

In the second story of Nahum GamZu, one detects a need to see a world whose overriding principle can be traced back to the account of creation in the Bible, *Creatio Ex Nihilo*, "God created a world out of nothing, out of an earth which is formless and chaotic. His making order out of chaos culminates with God ruminating on all creation after the universe was created and seeing 'it was very good.'" Nahum's response *gamzu l'tovah*, "this is also good," was rooted in the belief that the evil could be transmuted into good.

Nahum's response is a repudiation of the philosophical idea that there is randomness in the universe. The idea of things happening without any reason, that we live in a world that not even God can control, was alien to Biblical and rabbinic faith. The idea of a chaotic evil world where tragedies occur because God is impotent to stop them was spurned by Nahum GamZu. If every-thing God created was good, then Nahum was convinced that his setbacks would be transmuted one day into good.

Victor Frankl tells of a patient of his who held to the belief that God's acts were not random ones, and how he as a psychiatrist drew upon them to effect therapy. He relates how a rabbi who lost his first wife and their six children in Auschwitz, where they were gassed, had remarried, and now it turned out that his second wife was sterile. The rabbi evaluated his plight in terms of despair, since there was now no son to say Kaddish for him after death. Frankl then asked the rabbi if he ever hoped to see his children again in heaven. His question was followed by an outburst of tears, at which point the real reason for the rabbi's despair came to the fore. He explained that since his children died as innocent martyrs, they were found worthy of the highest place in heaven, but as for himself, he could not expect as an old sinful man to be assigned the same place. Frankl suggested to the rabbi that this perhaps was the meaning to his suffering that he, the rabbi, could be purified through these years of suffering so that finally he, like his innocent children, would become worthy of joining them in heaven. Frankl then quoted a passage from Psalms where it is written that God preserves our tears: "You keep count of my tossings, put my tears in your flask! Are they not in your book?" (Psalms 56:9) "So perhaps none of your suffering was in vain," concluded Frankl. And then for the first time in many years, the Rabbi was able to find relief from his suffering.[61]

"Gamzu l'tovah" carried with it a message of inner buoyancy. It served as a basis for comfort and encouragement. It afforded a perspective which had a salutary effect on the psyche of many. The story of Nahum had a psychologically stabilizing and uplifting effect.

"Gamzu l'tovah" represented an orientation which was able to see something positive amidst the pain and suffering. Obviously, it had its limitations in providing a satisfactory answer as to the suffering of the seemingly innocent. But there are instances where, through a mental disorder or tremendous anguish and pain, that an individual is able to seek and find the understanding which takes him to a higher development of personality.

CREATIVE ILLNESS

Jack Kahn, in his volume *Job's Illness: Loss, Grief and Integration*, quotes from H.E. Ellenberger, who discusses the emergence of

---

61. Victor Frankl, *Man's Search For Meaning*, ibid., pp. 189–190.

revolutionary psychological theory in the works of Fechner, Jung, and Freud as the result of what he called a creative illness. Each of these innovators underwent periods of mental disturbances at the time of their most intensive productivity.

A creative illness succeeded a period of intense preoccupation with an idea and search for a certain truth. . . . Throughout the illness the subject never loses the thread of his dominating preoccupation. He suffers from feelings of utter isolation, even when he has a mentor who guides him through the ordeal. The termination is often rapid and marked by a phase of exhilaration. The subject emerges from his ordeal with a permanent transformation in his personality and the conviction that he has discovered a great truth or a new spiritual world.[62]

A discussion of Jewish responses to tragedy would be incomplete without mention of the idea of the *z'chut* (merit), which is acquired by the sacrifices of others, especially a predecessor. Every morning in the *Shaharit* service, we implore God to remember the *akedah* (the binding of Isaac). We ask God to treat us with compassion in recognition of the obedience of Abraham. On Yom Kippur, we recite the "Eileh Ezkerah," hoping to acquire merit on the basis of the sufferings of our predecessors. Ostow points out that in the Goldschmidt Mahzor, the "Eileh Ezkerah" is followed by the verse: *Chasidim eylu v'harigatam Av harachamim z'chor otham, z'Chutham uz'chut avotham Yaamdu L'Vanecha b'eyth Tzaratham*, (Lord of mercy remember these righteous and their murder. May their merit and the merit of their fathers protect your children in time of need).[63]

The concept that the death of others acquires *z'chut*, "merit,"

---

62. Jack Kahn, ibid., p. 155.
63. *Judaism & Psychoanalysis*, edited by Mortimer Ostow (New

for us is demonstrated by the simple fact that we demand and expect special consideration by virtue of having been the victims of the Holocaust. On the most literal level, many Jews demand and expect financial restitution payments.

Jews, for example, expect restitution from the banks of Switzerland, who stole deposits from Jews during World War II and helped German Nazis hide the money they looted from the Jewish victims of the Holocaust. Jews expect compensation for the sham perpetrated by some of Switzerland's banks, who after the war turned away survivors and heirs of victims of Holocaust with lies, obfuscation, and impossible-to-satisfy demands for proof of relationship to those who were deceased. However, the special consideration that Jews expect goes beyond financial restitution. For it is impossible to measure in dollars and cents how the victims were rebuffed, denied, and humiliated in their efforts to recover their money and survive in a postwar world that showed them nothing but indifference, prejudice, and hate. On the political and social level, we expect that all non-Jews will understand that we are entitled to special consideration. We do not literally ask for special privilege. But nevertheless, we expect it.[64]

THE HOLOCAUST—ACQUIRING SPECIAL CREDIT

Ostow also points out that enemies of the Jewish people, like revisionist historians who attempt to rewrite the history of World War II, claiming that the Holocaust never took place, agree with

York: KTAV Publishing House Inc., 1982), "The Jewish Response to Crisis,B by Ostow, pp. 253–254.

64. Tom Bower, *Nazi Gold* (New York: Harper Collins, 1997). This book presents the full story of the fifty year Swiss–Nazi conspiracy to steal billions from Europe's Jews and Holocaust survivors.

us on the point that the Holocaust experience does acquire a special credit. By falsifying the past and denying the reality of the Holocaust, they thereby deny the Jew of that special *z'chut*.[65]

In rabbinic literature, the death of the righteous results in a special credit being conferred upon the living, for their death atones for the sins of the generation.[66]

In reading the end of the Book of Job, one walks away with the feeling that God is censoring the friends of Job by telling Eliphaz that none of them spoke the truth as did Job. God in effect is saying that Job's suffering does acquire credit, a kind of *z'chut*. For otherwise how could the friends be condemned for such a valiant defense of traditional dogma as they make in the dialogue? How could Job be commended for his vehement attacks on their doctrine and the God they presumed to defend? It would seem that Job, as a result of the suffering has indeed acquired merit. He is permitted to vent his wrath against God because, as the psalmist says, "God will not despise those who are broken in spirit."

In our daily communications, there is always an aura of respect and humility that is with us as we confront those who have suffered deeply. We are more tolerant, patient, and understanding with them than we are with others. By continuing to face the daily exigencies and struggles of life, they in effect are granted a special status.

This concept of *z'chut*, "merit or credit," goes beyond the rabbinic concept of *ein adam nitfas al tzaaro* in which a person is not held accountable when in pain.[67] The affirmation of the tradition by the one who suffered is given far greater weight than the expressions of piety uttered by those untested.

The pious belief in God's kindness articulated by the author of the third chapter of Lamentations, "The kindness of the Lord has

---

65. Ostow, ibid., p. 255.
66. *Moed Katan* 28a.
67. *Baba Bathra* 16b.

not ended, His mercies are not spent. They are revered every morning—Ample is your grace" (Lamentations 3:22–23), has credibility in light of him projecting himself as a witness and a victim to the suffering of the Jewish people. He opens his dirge with the words "I am the man who has known affliction under the rod of his wrath. Me, he drove on and on in unrelieved darkness." (Lamentations 3:1–2)

Similarly, the Psalmist declaring "I shall not die but live and declare the works of God" (Psalms 118:17) becomes all the more of a powerful statement of faith because juxtaposed to it we find the verse "The Lord hath afflicted me but he hath not given me over to death." (Psalms 118:18)

Suffering can embitter as well as enoble. All too often, it is the former that prevails. The fact that from the biblical period through the rabbinic period it received a positive polarization was, in itself, a source of comfort to all generations of Jews. It was not an attitude plagued by dark psychologies or by masochism, by a love of suffering to explain their vulnerable existence and miserable way of life that prompted the rabbis to say *Havivin yesurin*, "Beloved is suffering." Rather, acceptance of suffering as a virtue was due to the realization that suffering contained some redeeming features.

It is no accident that in projecting the end of days when the Messiah would usher in an era of lasting peace the rabbis speak of that period as being preceded by *Hevlai Mashiach*. The Hebrew word *hevlai*, which literally means pangs or throes of birth, is attached to various other words to denote the suffering and tribulations that are the price of any major initiation. Thus, *hevlai* stands, among other things, for suffering including labor pains, the suffering of hell, human sufferings, and the pre-messianic cataclysms that will befall mankind during *Hevlai Mashiach*.

Thus no birth, growth, death, or rebirth can evolve without a bitter toll of "pangs." Any major initiation, whether in the past or the future, carries with it its pangs. The final initiation into redemption at the end of time is no exception: It also will involve pangs of redemption and messianic cataclysms. Redemption and the Messiah are the sweetest, most blissful, most wonderful glorious joyful, absolutely most desired objects one could ever wish for. It would be unrealistic to expect an initiation into the utmost of everlasting joy without first going through untold pangs. As a matter of fact, for this kind of ultimate wish fulfillment, the pangs to endure may well be the most cataclysmic of all.[68]

Nahum's response of *Gam Zu L'Tovah*, "this is also for good," is but one of many statements which offer consolation to those whose lot was unbearable. Perhaps it is not only the strong conviction of an extraordinary individual that is able to transmute the bad into good but that also of a persecuted nation determined to make sense out of what at times appears to be a senseless world.

---

68. Jay Y. Gonen, *A Psychological History of Zionism* (New York: Mason Charter Publishers Inc., 1975), pp. 4–5.

8

MAKING YOUR PEACE WITH GOD

We stand in good company if periodically our faith is shaken. The psalmist gave vent to a feeling that even the most pious among us has expressed when he bitterly cried out, "My God, My God, why have you forsaken me?"

While the focus of this chapter is reconciling ourselves with God after being hurt, it's important for the pastoral counselor to understand that often a crisis in faith represents a crisis in a relationship with a loved one. Not being able to make one's peace with God may be a camouflage for one not being able to make peace with one's parents. I cannot conceive of walking with another person through an unrelenting pain, despair, anxiety, suffering, and anger at God without exploring with the person his or her relationship with loved ones. Our function is not to theologize with people but rather to help them find those inner resources of strength that will enable them to rise above their pain and anger.

Had the author of the Book of Job chosen to write about a man who gravitated towards atheism after having everything precious stripped from him, we would have wept with Job. However, the thought of atheism was alien to all biblical writers. Instead, the author chose to present to us a Job who through his suffering is able to arrive at a deeper understanding of God. He presents to us a Job who stands above his own ego and wisdom and transcends his own needs as he reaches out to affirm God.

Jewish history bears eloquent testimony to individuals who in the darkest of moments were certain of God's nearness

and presence and who in speaking to him proclaimed, "In your
light we shall see light." (Psalms 36:10)

The voice of the psalmist filled with anger towards God
that lamented, "Why do you hide your face? Why do you
forget our affliction and oppression?" Psalms 44:25 is coun-
terbalanced by another voice within the same book which
declared, "As for me the nearness of God is my good." (Psalms
73:28) The challenge of the pastoral counselor and all those
who seek to help people in distress and pain is to listen empa-
thetically to the voice lashing out angrily at God, while at-
tempting to strengthen the other voice that allows God to enter
into one's life.

WHERE IS MY FATHER?

In the Book of Genesis, it is told that when Jacob took ill, he
called for his son Joseph, the viceroy of Egypt, and requested
that when he dies, Joseph should take his body and bring it back to
Israel to be buried alongside his fathers. Joseph reassures his ailing
father that he will honor the request. Jacob had Joseph take an
oath that he indeed would bring his body to the land of Israel.
After the oath was administered, the Torah states, "And Israel
bowed down upon the head of the bed." (Genesis 47:31) Rashi,
commenting on the words "upon the head of the bed," quotes the
Talmud in saying, He (Jacob) turned himself toward the divine
presence. Hence the rabbis said that the divine presence is above
the head of one who is sick.[1]

Often during a period of serious illness, man often reflects
more deeply on his relationship with God. Man begins to ask the

---

1. *Shabbat* 126b *Nedarim* 40a

ultimate questions. There is an attempt on the part of man to put "his house in order." A man who was seriously ill when I visited him in the hospital said to me, "Rabbi, I made my peace with God."

The Book of Job is about a man who tries to grope with the Mount Everest of all questions, namely why does a person who perceives himself as living in accordance with the teachings of God suffer so much? The most critical pain that Job sustains from the vantage point of the author is not as a result of the losses in his family, the death of his children, or the loss of his wealth, or the excruciating physical pain he must endure. It is his perception of losing God, or more correctly being abandoned by God that looms largest in his mind. There are constant expressions of feeling deserted and persecuted by God. Job bitterly cries out: "For the arrows of the Almighty are in me; my spirit drinks in their poison; God's terrors are arrayed against me." (Job 6:4)

"Therefore I will not restrain my speech. I will speak out in the agony of my spirit, I will complain in the bitterness of my soul. Am I the sea or a monster of the deep that you place a guard about me? When I think, 'my couch will comfort me, my bed will share the burden of my complaint', then you terrify me with dreams and frighten me with visions so that I prefer strangling death rather than existence." (Job 7:11–15) "If I call him, would he answer me? For he crushes me for a trifle and increases my wounds without cause." (Job 9:16–17) "For you take pride in hunting me like a lion, time and again you show your wonders against me. You constantly send new witnesses against me and increase your hostility toward me; wave after wave of foes assails me." (Job 10:16–17)

"He (God) has fenced in my ways so that I cannot pass, he has set darkness upon my paths. My glory he has stripped from me and removed the crown off my head. He has broken me down on every side and I perish; my hope has he uprooted like a tree. He has kindled his wrath against me and treats me like a foe." (Job

19:8–11) "But I go to the east and he is not there; to the west, and do not perceive him; to the north, where he is concealed and I do not behold him. He is hidden in the south, and I cannot see him." (23:8–9)

The very name of Job suggests the idea of one who is persecuted and one who feels deserted. The most probable view is that Iyyob (Job) is a Hebrew folk etymology of a previously existing semitic name being a passive participle noun form of the very "Ayab," to hate, hence the hated or persecuted one.[2] If the name was understood as meaning "enemy" it may have been chosen to symbolize the principal's attitude toward God, his adverse reaction to the suffering inflicted on him. According to Rabbah, Job blasphemed when he used the term *tempest* in 9:17 meaning "Perhaps a tempest passed before thee which caused the confusion between Job (Iyyob) and enemy (Oyeb).[3]

Marvin Pope suggests that the name Iyyob was not simply an invention of the author of the book. He shows how in one of the Amarna Letters dating from about 1350 B.C.E., the prince of Ashtaroth in Bashan bears the name Ayyab, an older form of the biblical name. Still earlier, about 2000 B.C.E., in the Egyptian Execration Test, there is mention of the Palestinian chief named "ybm", which is almost certainly to be vocalized "Ay (y) abum" (with the nominative ending "um" that was later dropped). The name Ayya Bum also appears in the Akkadian documents from Mari and Alalakh dating from the early second millennium B.C.E. W.F. Albright has explained the name Ay (y) abum as contracted from Ayya-abu (m)— "Where is my father?"[4]

If Iyyob is then derived from a word meaning where is my

---

2. Robert Gordis, *The Book of God & Man* (Chicago: University of Chicago Press, 1965), p. 67.

3. *Baba Bathra* 16a, *Niddah* 52a.

4. Marvin Pope, *Job*, Anchor Bible Series (Garden City, New York: Doubleday & Company, Inc., 1965), p.6

father, we have revealed in the name what seems to pain Job deeply, namely that God has deserted him. He is constantly awaiting an answer from God, certain of his vindication. A feeling of being abandoned and a feeling of being persecuted on the part of Job are to be found throughout this book. However, it is erroneous to try to ascribe different forms of mental illness to Job owing to feelings that are perfectly healthy and justified in wake of the tragedies that have overcome him. All too often, as pointed out by Abraham Maslow, psychology has dwelled more upon man's frailties than upon his strengths, it has thoroughly explored his sins while neglecting his virtues. Psychology has voluntarily restricted itself to only half of its rightful jurisdiction and that the darker, meaner half.[5]

Maslow has propounded a theory of human motivation which differentiates between basic needs and metaneeds. The basic needs are those of hunger, affection, security, self-esteem, and the like. Metaneeds are those of justice, goodness, beauty, order, unity, and so forth. The basic needs are deficiency needs, whereas the metaneeds are growth needs. The basic needs are proponents over the metaneeds in most cases and are arranged in a hierarchical order. The metaneeds have no hierarchy—they are equally potent and can be fairly easily substituted for one another. The metaneeds are as instinctive or inherent in man as the basic needs are, and when they are not fulfilled, the person may become sick.[6]

METANEEDS MORE THAN BASIC NEEDS

In the Book of Job, the focus is more on Job's metaneeds than on his basic needs. It, as stated earlier, is not his suffering over the loss

---

5. Calvin S. Hall and Gardner Lindzey, *Theories of Personality*, (New York: John Wiley & Sons, Inc., 1970), p. 326.

6. Ibid., pp. 327–328.

of children, property, or good health that disturbs him most. It is rather over how could a just and good God cause him to suffer so much? In a world where there is order in which goodness brings in its wake reward, and evil yields punishment, he cannot fathom why he is suffering. When God does appear out of the whirlwind which will be discussed later, he tries to show Job that there is order—and meaning, which is imperfectly grasped by man. The Lord out of the Whirlwind chapters attempt to address themselves to the metaneeds of Job.

Maslow speaks of a group of self-actualizing people like Lincoln, Jefferson, Walt Whitman, Thoreau, Beethoven, Eleanor Roosevelt, and others who should be the focus of clinical observation to discover what characteristics distinguish them from the ordinary run of people. Characteristics he found in this creative group that most of them have were: 1) a profound mystical or spiritual experience; 2) their intimate relationships with a few specially loved people tended to be profound and deeply emotional rather than superficial; 3) they resisted conformity to the culture; and 4) they were realistically oriented.[7]

All too often in the psychological literature dealing with Job, there has been a preoccupation with Job's illness rather than with Job's ability to arrive at new levels of understanding in his relationships with God.

The aforementioned characteristics of healthy individual could easily be applied to Job, as we shall demonstrate.

Firstly, it was a mystical or spiritual experience that enabled Job at last to reconcile himself to his condition and to make his peace with a God whom Job perceived as having hurt him unjustly. For it was only after the Lord appeared to Job out of the whirlwind that Job declares that his deepest wish has been granted, namely that God has not ignored him and that He has

---

7. Ibid., p. 328.

responded to him. Although it is beyond the scope of this study to offer a literary analysis of God's long-awaited response to Job, it is necessary to briefly state some of the problems Bible scholars face when examining this section of the book. Job pleads with God to step forward and explain to him why he has suffered. For example, he says "But I wish to speak to the Almighty. I desire to argue my case with God." (Job 10:2) "He may slay me I'll never quaver, I will defend my conduct to his face." (Job 13:15)

When God finally speaks to Job, He challenges Job to understand the nature of the creation of the world. The different parts of God's world, like heaven and earth, stars and sea, morning and night, lights and darkness are described. Job is asked if he knows the mystery of what brings snow, hail, and floods into the world. God asked Job if he knows anything about rain, dew, the frost, or the clouds. Then there are a number of animals that are described such as the mountain goat, the wild ass, the buffalo, the ostrich, the horse, the hawk and the falcon. Afterwards, there are descriptions of the hippopotamus and the crocodile. And Job is challenged to understand the role they play in God's universe. The universe is unknown to man. The implications of this section are that just as the natural world remains a mystery to man, yet it too reveals an orderliness. The world is not just dictated by random forces. However, what is conspicuously omitted in the section of the Lord out of the whirlwind is a direct answer to the mystery of Job's suffering. In these chapters, it is God's might and power that are underscored. But as pointed out by Robert Gordis, Job has frequently conceded God's might himself during the earlier debates with the friends. It is not God's might but His righteousness that Job calls into question.

"However wise and strengthened a man might be, has he ever argued with God and emerged unscathed? If it be a matter of power here he is! But if of justice, who will arraign him? Who would remove God's rod from me, so that my dread of him would not terrify me? Then I would speak and not fear him, for he is far from just to me." (Job 9:4, 19, 34, 35)

"O that I knew where to find him, that I could come to his dwelling! I would lay my case before him, and my mouth would not lack for arguments. Would he contend with me merely through his great power? No, he would surely pay heed to me." (Job 23:3, 4, 6)

If Job suddenly surrendered before the spectacle of power that he had so passionately challenged in his cry for justice, it would be a stultifying conclusion to a brilliant debate.[8]

Gordis cites a number of answers that students of the bible have advanced to explain how God's response in the section of the Lord out of the Whirlwind provides an answer to the agonizing question which plagued Job, namely, what is the purpose of his suffering? He concludes by saying: The poetic ultimate message is clear: Not only ignoramus, "we do not know," but ignorabimus, "we may never know." But the poet goes further. He calls upon us Gaudeamus, "let us rejoice," in the beauty of the world, though its pattern is only partially revealed to us. It is enough to know that the dark mystery encloses and in part discloses a bright and shining miracle.[9]

But one still fails to see how the aforementioned offers any solace and comfort to the bereaved. Why after God has impressed upon Job both the mystery and the harmony of the world should Job answer contritely, "I have heard you by hearsay, but now my own eyes have seen you. Therefore, I bend myself and repent in dust and ashes." (Job 42:6)

As stated earlier, borrowing from insights advanced by Maslow about self-actualizing people who have a mystical or a spiritual experience, it takes a revelatory kind of experience for Job to make his peace with God. The *searah* " whirlwind" or other such me-

---

8. *The Book of God & Man*, ibid., pp. 127–128.
9. Ibid., p. 134.

teorological phenomena usually accompany a theophony. (Cf. Psalms 8:8–16, 86:15; Nahum 1:3; Ezekiel 1:4; Zechariah 9:14; Exodus 13:22, 19-16.)

I KNOW MY REDEEMER LIVES

After the speeches of God, Job answers, "I had heard of you by hearsay, but now my own eyes have seen you." (Job 42:5) Job becomes convinced of what he has doubted till now, namely that there is God's providential care. He had hoped for the assurance that God was on his side and would vindicate him. This, he had insisted, must come somehow—if not during his life, then later. "Oh that my words were now written; of that they were inscribed on a monument, that with an iron pen and led they were hewn in the rock forever! For I know that my Redeemer lives, though he be the last to arise upon earth! Deep in my skin this has been marked, and in my very flesh do I see God. I myself behold him, with my own eyes I see him, not with another's—my heart is consumed with longing within me!" (Job 19:23-27) Now, after God has spoken to him out of the whirlwind, Job's demand has been met and he reconciles himself to his fate.

Peeke points out that when Job says, "I have heard of you by hearsay, but now my own eyes have seen you," it is the vision of God that has released him from his problem. His suffering is as mysterious as ever, but plain or mysterious, why should it vex him any longer? He has seen God and has entered into rest. The only answer we can get to the problem of pain is, the poet would tell us, this answer: If we know God, no other knowledge matters. We can give no answer to the questions, no solution of its baffling riddles. But since we know God, we can trust him to the uttermost, we know incredible though it may seem that the world's

misery does not contradict the love of God. It was therefore with
deliberate intent that the poet put on God's lips no hint of the
reason of Job's suffering.[10]

The psalmist expressed a similar idea when he said, "Whom
have I in heaven but you, and there is none upon earth that I desire
besides you. My flesh and my heart faileth, but God is the strength
of my heart and my portion forever. . . . It is good for me to
draw near to God, I have put my trust in the Lord God that I may
declare all of your works."(Psalms 73:25, 26, 28)

The psalmist, like Job, does not speak about how enriching
suffering is. Rather, it is the fellowship with God that is enriching
and that fellowship is to be found in adversity no less than in
prosperity.

In Psalms 38, the psalmist, like Job, cries in desperation as he is
overwhelmed by a deep sense of agony and helplessness. "For my
loins are filled with a loathsome disease and there is no soundness.
I am feeble and sore broken. I have roared by reason of the
disquietness of my heart." (Psalms 38:8, 9) The condition described bears affinity to that of Job's condition.

The psalmist is willing to accept his suffering. His enemies are
many and powerful. But what he wants more than anything else is
the assurance that God is not far from him. "For mine enemies are
lively, and they are strong: and they that hate me wrongfully are
multiplied. . . . Forsake me not, O Lord: O my God be not far
from me. Make haste to help me, O Lord my salvation." (Psalms
38:20, 22, 23)

The reassurance that he has not been abandoned by God
comes to the fore when Job has a mystical experience in which he
sees God. It enables Job to reconcile himself to his cruel fate.
Actually, Job's struggle with God finds its antecedent in Jacob's
battle with an emissary of God. Jacob's battle with an angel is

10. Arthur J. Peeke, *Job's Victory in Demensions of Job*, edited by N.
Glatzer, (NY: Schocken Books, 1969), pp. 203–204.

fought anew all the time by men struggling to maintain their faith. After Jacob's wrestling with a nocturnal foe by the river of Jabbok, Jacob says, "I have seen God face to face and have remained alive." (Genesis 32:31) Juxtaposed to that statement, we read of an injury sustained by Jacob: He is limping upon his thigh. He is able to sustain the injury because God's nearness has been experienced. In order that we avoid crude anthropomorphisms in which we speak of seeing a God that cannot be seen, it is important to take note of the following point. In his great code, the Mishneh Torah that begins with the words, "The principle of all principles and the pillar upon which all science rests is to know that there is a first being who brought every existing thing into being," Maimonides does not offer a speculative proof of the existence of God. He states that the source of our knowledge of God is the inner eye, "the eye of the heart," a medieval name for intuition.[11]

"To Jewish thinkers of the past," writes Abraham Joshua Heschel, "the evidence for their certainty of the existence of God was neither a syllogism derived from the abstract premises nor any physical experience, but an insight. The eye of the body is not that of the soul, and the soul, it was believed, does at times attain higher insights."[12]

Yehuda HaLevi maintains that just as the Lord gave all of us a bodily eye to perceive things, he endowed some people with an inner eye or inner sense.[13]

In his poems, he speaks of himself having seen God with the heart rather than with the bodily eye. "My heart saw thee and believed thee. I have seen thee with the eye of the heart."[14]

Job's seeing God is the insight attained by something compa-

---

11. Mishnah Torah, Yesode Hatorah 4:7.
12. A.J. Heschel, *God in Search of Man* (New York: Harper & Row Publishers, 1955), p. 148.
13. Kuzari 4:3.
14. Shirim Nivharim, Shirman quoted by Heschel, ibid., p. 148.

rable to the "eye of the heart," and it gives him the equanimity and
serenity of mind that eluded him earlier.

The Book of Psalms is an eloquent testimony to the ability of
man being able to experience the nearness and presence of God
even when it appears that everyone else has abandoned man. Like
Job who at certain moments felt deserted by his friends, the
psalmist declares, "When my father and mother forsook me, then
the Lord will take me in." (Psalms 27:10) Rashi offers an interpretation on the passage which speaks to the heart of the complexity
of parent and child relationship. Rashi comments, "When people
are engaged in a sexual relationship their intent is to satisfy their
desires. Upon conclusion of the act, and after a climax has been
achieved, each one turns his head away from the other. God
watches the drop of semen and forms the embryo."[15] In other
words, at the moment when the father and mother should be
concerned with the possibility of conception and bringing a child
into this world, each one is more preoccupied with satisfying his or
her own needs and attaining a sexual climax. The embryo, which
is ready to emerge into the world, experiences anxiety because his
parents are preoccupied with other things. This anxious feeling
becomes an omen for what will take place later in life as the child
will never feel certain that his parents will be on hand to help him
in time of need.

Lurking in the minds of many children is the thought that
their father and mother are neglecting them, are not paying
adequate attention to them. "Children at times are exposed to
periods of separation from parents. Separation may produce acute
distress, which may give way to despair or depression. In the
course of normal growth a child must acquire appropriate instru-
mental actions for dealing with his world. He must make a
transition from running to mother to establishing direct behaviors

15. Rashi on Psalms 27:10.

which relieve the frustration but do not evoke rejection, or other punitive consequences from his associates."[16]

Here the psalmist experiences acute pain as he finds it difficult to experience relief from a profound feeling that those who should be most responsible for him, namely his parents, have abandoned him. He is reassured by a feeling that God will adopt him. The verb used here, *asaf", is the same verb used in describing Rachel's condition after she gave birth to Joseph following a number of years of sterility. She calls the baby Joseph, for God has asaf,* "taken away," my shame. Rachel was childless. She viewed herself as being alone in this world. Her self-perception was that of a woman who although alive was dead. After her sister, Leah, gave birth to four children, Rachel turned indignantly to Jacob and, projecting her inadequacies onto him, says: "Give me children, if not I am dead." Rashi, quoting Midrash Rabah, states, "Hence we learn that one who has no children is considered dead."[17]

Thus, from Rachel's vantage point, bringing a child into this world is tangible evidence that God has not neglected her. Similarly, the psalmist in Chapter 27 feels the presence of God despite the fact that he has been abandoned by his parents.

We have illustrated how one of Maslow's observations about self-actualizing people having a profound mystical or spiritual experience applied to Job, who makes his peace with his "undeserved suffering" only after a mystical experience in which God is perceived by Job as having been seen by him. Like the revelation to Moses at Sinai, so did the revelation to Job cause a new and a greater love of God to emerge.

Secondly, Maslow states that self-actualized people have intimate relations with others which tend to be deeply emotional rather than superficial. This description also fits Job as we have

---

16. Wiggins, Renner, Clore, and Ross, *The Psychology of Personality* (Philipines: Addison-Wesley Publishing Company Inc., 1971), p. 175.

17. Rashi, Genesis 30:1.

shown in Chapter 3, "Enter the Comforter," where we examined the relationship of Eliphaz and Job. The relationship of other friends, Bildad and Zophar, was no less intense and close.

The emotional intensity of their relationship is revealed not only in the heated dialogues between Job and them but also in the prologue of the book, when they stay with him for seven days and seven nights, sharing and empathizing with his pain. Even though Job has been wounded deeply by them and accuses them of turning against him and acting more like enemies than like friends, God in the epilogue will expect Job to serve as an interceder on their behalf. They were wrong, says God. They are guilty of speaking untruths about God even though they sought to defend God. But it is a testimony to their enduring friendship that God will tell Eliphaz that Job will intercede on behalf of them. Generally, we intercede on behalf of those we love. Job's friendships are able to withstand even some faulty, erroneous and tasteless remarks made by his friends to him.

REVEALING OUR DARKER SIDE

It was Jonah Ben Abraham Gerondi (Rabenu Yonah), a Spanish rabbi and moralist of the thirteenth century, who, in his commentary on the passage in *Avot*, "Acquire for yourself a friend," adds, "to be his confidant . . . and not to reveal his secrets to others."[18] Job bares his soul and discloses his innermost thoughts, his doubts, anxieties, frustrations, and anger to his friends. For an individual like Job, who projected to the public an image of being a pious and God-fearing man, revealing himself in a way to betray that impeccable image was hazardous. We are only open and revealing

---

18. Rabenu Jonah comment on *Avot* 1:8.

when there is trust and confidence that those to whom is revealed the darker side of our personalities will not hurt us.

Thirdly, Maslow speaks of self-actualizing people as resisting conformity to the culture. Job rejects the conventional theology of his day that viewed suffering as a result of commission of sin.

Again and again, Job challenges God to appear and defend his actions. Again and again, he refuses to accept the reasoning of his friends, who are certain that God is both almighty and just and that the only conclusion possible is that since he is suffering he must have sinned. Job never questions either God's existence or His omnipotence but only God's justice, mercy, and goodness.

I reject a psychiatric diagnosis of disordered behavior attributed to Job. Those who engage in undesirable behavior, those who challenge the so-called "eternal verities" of a faith, have always been perceived as being madmen.[19] Job has a right to insist on the perfection of his behavior and the integrity of his mental state. There is no need to place a clinical label on him.

The depression he experiences is a normal part of the grieving process. Job's inability to regain his confidence in God and experience something which as stated earlier is similar to revelation, until the very end of the book, is understandable in light of a psychological principle already understood by the rabbis who declared, "The divine presence does not rest upon men in a state of depression.[20]

Job must work through his depression before God's presence, nearness, and concern can be felt.

---

19. The Prophet Hosea gives expression to the madness associated with the prophet, "The prophet is a fool the men of the spirit is mad." (Hosea 9:7)

20. *Shabbat* 30b.

DEPRESSION AND
DISTANCING OURSELVES FROM GOD

Centuries later, an eighteenth century hasidic master, whose doctors had just told him that his end was near, wrote of how the gulf between God and man widens during a man's depressed state. The following words, attributed to Rabbi Nachman of Bratzlav, found in Arthur Green's volume on this hasidic master, could easily be applied to Job immediately after he was dealt the severe blows of one successive loss after another.

The reason why people remain far from God is that their minds are not settled. They do not help themselves in this regard. The main thing is to get it clear in one's mind that there is no ultimate meaning to our passions and to those things that bind us to this world. When a person realizes that this is true of all such passions, both bodily desires and those external to the body such as personal glory, then he will surely return to God.

But know that depression keeps one from guiding the mind in the directions that one wills and makes it difficult to come to any inner resolution. Only by means of joy can a person lead his mind where he wants and thus settle his mind. Joy represents the world of freedom, as in "For in joy will you go forth." (Isaiah 55:12) It is by means of joy that a person becomes free and goes forth from exile. When the mind is linked to joy, it is taken out of bondage, and that mind becomes free. Then, that liberated mind can be guided by the will.

This is the meaning of the talmudic phrase "his mind was humored." When one brings joy into the mind, the mind is liberated and may thus be settled. And this humoring of the mind also brings about great unification above.[21]

Green continues:

Translated into a comment on Nachman's personal situation, this teaching is an announcement that he is not going to let his illness get the best of him. The threat of depression is a real one, perhaps now more than ever before. He seeks to escape it by reasserting his own ability to maintain willful control over his own mind. He contrasts himself with those who "do nothing to help themselves", who do not work to fight off the depression that engulfs them in times of adversity. The very fact of such adversity he says, may become an occasion for the renewal of one's religious life.[22]

We need not glorify depression, which is a regression. Depression can nevertheless provide a new opportunity to go through stages of one's development that had been missed in the first round.

The idea of depression causing man to be removed from God is found in the Talmud and subsequently in the code of the Jewish law. The Talmud records: "One whose dead relative lies before him is exempt from the recital of the Shma, and from prayer, and from tephilin." The Palestinian Talmud quoted by Tosafot (*Berachot* 17b) derives this law from the verse in Deuteronomy 16:3, "so that you may remember the day of your departure from the land of Egypt as long as you live." The commitment accepted in

---

21. Arthur Green, Translations from Liqqutim of Rabbi Nachman of Bratzlav. Translation appears in *Tormented Master—A Life of Rabbi Nachman of Bratzlav* (New York: Schocken Books, 1979), p. 244.

22. Ibid., pp. 244–245.

Egypt is applicable to man, who is preoccupied by life and not to one who has encountered death.[23] This period between death and burial is known as *anninut*. The aforementioned law exempting the "Onan" (name for mourner during this period of time) from positive ritual commandments is found in *Shulchan Aruch* Yoreh Deah 341:1.

Emanuel Feldman points out that the reason for the law exempting the Onen from various religious obligations is because death removes man from an intimate relationship with God. Man can no longer serve him, he can no longer perform the *mitzvot*, he no longer possesses the *Nishmat hayyim*, (the breath of life), which is the distinguishing characteristic of the human being.[24]

Actually, this process of temporarily cutting off a full relationship with God continues in some respects into the period of "Avelut," which commences with burial and lasts seven days and, with regards to some aspects, thirty days. The law asks the mourner to behave as if he were dead. He is now an incomplete person and his daily life begins to reflect the fact of his incompleteness. His physical appearance and his body are neglected. . . . Therefore he who has been involved with death . . . refrains from participating in those aspects of life which express a relationship with God or fellowman or himself. His essence as a person has been diminished and thus he does not cut his hair, for cutting the hair is a sign of man's concern with his person. . . . The mourner allows his hair to grow unattended and uncared for; there is no concern with his physical is-ness.[25]

As stated earlier, the thought of suicide passes through the mind of every thinking man who has roamed the face of this earth.

---

23. Joseph B. Soloveitchick, "The Halakhah of the First Day," in *Jewish Reflections of Death*, edited by Jack Reimer, (New York: Schocken Books, 1974), p.77.
24. Ibid., p. 87.
25. Ibid., pp. 88, 89.

Job is not immune from this thought. Repeatedly, he utters statements which may be construed as a wish for death.[26] But when a person who is depressed rejects suicide as an alternative, the nearness to death may be sufficient to wipe out the despair and depression.

This idea finds expression in the following section of Job: "Let his flesh become fresh as in youth; Let him return to the days of his vigor. He then prays to God and finds favor and joyfully enters his presence. He recounts to men how he was saved, and sings to men saying, 'I have sinned and perverted the right, but he did not punish me. He has redeemed me from going down to the pit; so that I might see the light of life.'" (Job 33:25–28)

FIGHTING DEATH, ASSERTING LIFE

The words above cited by Elihu, the young brash bystander, try to raise the spirits of Job by suggesting that man's flirtations with death can become the ground from which a reborn individual emerges. There is a new sense of intimacy and closeness to God that potentially can be achieved as a result of suffering. Similarly, Rabbi Nacham of Bratzlav saw his own illness and imminent death not only as forces that persecuted him but also as forces that enabled him to draw close to God. He writes: "Many fight against me on high." (Psalms 56:3) A person has enemies above in heaven. Thus the rabbi says: "Just as there are enemies below so are there enemies above." When a person has enemies who persecute him, he flees ever close to God. The more a person is pursued, the closer is he to God, since God is everywhere. "If I rise up to heaven, there you are; I go down into Sheol, you are there." (Psalms 139:8)

---

26. See Job 3:3–26, 6:8–10, 10:18–19, 7:15, 9:21, 10:1.

Whenever a person flees, he is fleeing to God. This is the meaning of "Pharaoh drew near." (Exodus 14:10) He drew Israel nearer to their Father in heaven. As he pursued them, they came closer to God.[27]

All the feelings of being persecuted by God, which Job has ventilated, have become like stepping stones leading up to the moment that he feels that God has revealed Himself to him. And once that moment of revelation occurs, the haunting question of why he had to suffer disappears. He no longer feels that he is a persecuted man. Instead, his dominant mood is now one of humility. "Therefore I abase myself and repent in dust and ashes." (Job 42:6)

Job now recognizes that man can no longer have any control over God. He is content with the new insight he has attained, being able to experience in a direct way the presence of God. "I have heard you by hearsay, but now my own eyes have seen you." (Job 42:5)

The reader of the book of Job often walks away confused that no direct answer is given to Job's suffering. How does the presence of God provide healing to the broken-hearted, the wounded, and the anguished? What the author seeks to demonstrate perhaps is that the worst affliction of all is to feel that one is abandoned and all alone in this universe. Being with someone else does not necessarily relieve the loneliness. The contrary is often the case, for at times we experience the most acute form of loneliness amidst big crowds. Nor is the presence of another being, alone with you, able at times to assuage the pain of loneliness. For to stand together with someone who does not understand our pain, at times, only intensifies the pain. Job's loneliness is greatly relieved at the end of the book because paradoxically there is no lonelier being in the world than God Himself.

---

27. *Tormented Master*, ibid., p. 245.

Gilbert K. Chesterton correctly points out that one of the central ideas of the Bible may be called the idea of the loneliness of God. This idea is to be found, for example, in Isaiah 40:14: "With whom hath he taken counsel?" "I have trodden the winepress alone, and of the peoples, there was no man with me." (Isaiah 63:3)[28]

God being all alone is graphically conveyed in the comment by Rashi on Genesis 1:5 "And it was evening and day one day." Rashi notes that according to the order of the text, the word "Rishon" should have appeared. The text should have read, "And it was evening it was day 'Yom Rishon' 'the first day,'" because later the text will say, it was evening and day the second day, the third day, the fourth day, and so forth. Why then does the word "Echad," meaning one, appear instead of "Rishon," meaning first? Rashi answers by saying, because God was alone in the universe. A universe with nothing in it at all, nothing from the natural world let alone a human being, and God, all by Himself in the world, projects dramatically an image of a lonely God who is in need of man. Eventually, He brings into this world a people that is to be a blessing to everyone by turning others to the knowledge of God. But that people, the Jewish people, are destined to be isolated and alone in this world.

"Lo it is a people that shall dwell alone not reckoned among the nations." (Numbers 23:9) Rashi illustrates Israel's loneliness by commenting: "When they are happy no other nation is happy with them." (Ad Locum)

All of us have experienced moments of joy. When it occurs, we want to reach out and share it with others. The popular tune reminds us that "when you smile, the whole world smiles with you." However, Rashi interprets the words "not reckoned among the nations" to mean that when Israel will have its joyous mo-

---

28. G.K. Chesterton in the *Dimensions of Job*, ibid., p. 230.

ments, they will be experienced solitarily. In the ancient world of paganism, Israel's mission was to be misunderstood by the other nations. Its loneliness is always depicted as being shared by God particularly when it suffers humiliation and is rejected by neighboring nations. For example, in Deuteronomy we read: "Then the Lord will turn your captivity and have compassion upon you." (Deuteronomy 30:3) Rashi notes that the text should read *v'heshiv* in the Hiph'il conjugation instead of the Kal conjugation. The Hip'il would make it accusative. In other words, God causes the Israelites to return from the exile. Why then does the text have the Kal conjugation v'shav? Rashi writes, "Our Rabbis derive from here that the divine presence, if one can say so of God, 'was with Israel' in the affliction of their exile and when they are redeemed, he ascribes redemption for himself, (i.e.) that he will return together with them."[29] This divine pathos is replete throughout midrashic literature, which depicts God as forever sharing in the pain of His people who have been uprooted from their comfortable moorings and are now afflicted with the curse of exile.

OUR HUMILIATION AND GOD'S TEARS

The following midrash portrays God as weeping and wailing bitterly over the humiliation of the Jewish people. Balza asked Rabbi Akibah, "Where is all this noise (a haunting, wailing sound) from?" Rabbi Akibah answered, "When God sees the quiet peacefulness of the pagan shrines and their worshippers and contrasts it with the utter ruination of the Temple and the way the Jewish people are tyrannized by foreign oppression he is envious and wails. And immediately the heavens and earth also wail thunder-

---

29. Rashi, Deuteronomy 30:3.

ously as the text reads, 'The Lord shall roar (wail thunderously) out of Zion and utter his voice out of Jerusalem and the heavens and earth shall shake.'" (Joel 4:16)[30] Here it is the cosmos, the entire universe that shares the suffering of God's chosen people.

Through the use of other artistic hyperboles, God is portrayed often as behaving in a way which is characteristic of an individual in deep grief. He is traumatized by Israel's suffering. He desires that His own actions reflect various mourning practices, rites, and procedures. "If a human being had a son who died and he mourns for him, what is it necessary for him to do?" God asks a group of ministering angels. They reply, "He hangs sackcloth over his door." "I will do likewise," God retorts. That is why, explains this midrashic exposition, heavy clouds are in the sky at different times. They are a sign of God mourning. They hang over the entrance way to heaven. As the Bible states: "I clothe the heavens with blackness, and I made sackcloth their covering." (Isaiah 50:3)[31]

God's melancholic gloom and sadness is poignantly expressed in another midrash, which depicts Him weeping inconsolably all by Himself.

Says the Midrash,

Come and see, how much greater is God's compassion than that of the people of Israel, for in every generation we can find righteous, pious men of impeccable integrity who are suffering in exile. The holy one, blessed is he, beats his hands against his breasts and he weeps for them in a clandestine fashion. And why does God weep for them privately (rather than publicly)? For it is humiliating for the lion to weep before the fox, for the teacher to break down in tears before his pupils and for the king to weep

---

30. *Shmot Rabbah* 29:1.
31. Lamentations Rabbah 1:1 Pesikta de Rav Kahana 15:3.

before one of his slaves. Therefore the text records, for if you will not hear me, my soul shall weep in secret places. (Jeremiah 13:17)[32]

When the mourner is in the process of working through his grief, he often is filled with many regrets. Job, when he reconciles himself to God, feels embarrassed over his arrogant request of expecting to know the mystery to the problem of evil. His renewed faith in the justice of God is accompanied by the words, "Therefore I abase myself and repent in dust and ashes." (Job 42:6)

God is not only depicted in midrashic literature as a mourner who has pangs of regrets,[33] but the Bible also describes Him as such. In Genesis we read "And the Lord regretted that he had made man on earth, and his heart was saddened [depressed]." (Genesis 6:6) Rashi, in his commentary on that passage, depicts God as mourning over the impending loss of man just as King David would mourn the loss of his son Abshalom. (II Samuel 19:3) Rashi continues:

And the following I wrote in reply to the heretics: [the following selection from the Midrash] One gentile asked Rabbi Joshua, the son of Karha, saying to him: "Do you not admit that the Holy One, blessed be he, foresees the future?" He (Rabbi Joshua) said to him, "Yes." He (the heretic) said to him, "But it is written: It grieved him at his heart" (he was depressed). He (Rabbi Joshua) said to him, "Was there ever a son born to you?" He (the heretic) said to him, "Yes." He (Rabbi Joshua) said to him, "And what did

---

32. Tanna de-Bel Eliyahu 28. Taken from *Sefer Haagadah*, Chaim N. Bialik (Tel Aviv: Dvir Publishing Company, 1960), p. 289.

33. See Pesikta Rabbati 29:1 and Lamentations Rabbah Proems No. 20.

you do?" He (the heretic) said to him, "I was happy and I made everyone joyous." He (Rabbi Joshua) said to him, "And did you not know that his end would be to die?" He, (the heretic) said to him, "At the time of joy let there be joy and at the time of mourning, mourning." He (Rabbi Joshua) said to him, "So are the works of the Holy One, blessed be he. Even though it is revealed before him that their end would be to sin and to be destroyed, he did not refrain from creating them for the sake of the righteous who are destined to arise from them."[34]

In the aforementioned interpretation, Rashi was compelled to deal with a passage that ran counter to the omniscience of God, a cardinal doctrine of Judaism. How could God ever find himself in a position where He regrets and becomes depressed over something that He brought into this world?

The rabbis accounted for biblical anthropomorphisms by quoting the passage, *Dibrah Torah Kilshon bnei adam*, "The Torah speaks in the language of man." Passages that speak of the emotional state of God's being were understood in a transcendental and metaphorical sense. For our purposes, what is of interest, is that only a mourning God is able to understand the plight of a mourning man. A God who Himself has undergone depression is able to empathize and console a man who has undergone a similar experience.

Job is alone, as his friends fail ultimately to offer him the solace that he needs. God is depicted as also being alone. Job's depression is evident in many sections of the book, just as God is sometimes portrayed as also being depressed. Job needs a strong support system to be able to weather the storm of one tragedy visited upon another tragedy. The God that both biblical, talmudic, and mi-

---

34. Rashi, Genesis 6:6.

drashic writers know of was a God who was filled with pathos and compassion, one who suffered along with His children and identified fully with their wretched situation.

Glatt points out that when God is depicted as mourning over the sufferings of His people, what is being expressed is possibly anger against Him. These homilies portraying God as a mourner could very well be interpreted the following way: "God where are you? Since you are omnipotent why was your saving power not revealed to us?" Such midrashic homilies may have been intended to articulate resentment toward God saying in effect: "I wish you were suffering the way you permitted me to suffer."[35]

In another homily found in the Talmud, God is described as feeling very ambivalent about having to exile His children from the land of Israel. The homily offers a contrast between a period in Jewish history when God is the object of adoration and praised thrice daily by His children, the people of Israel, and the abject condition of exile when Israel sits alone without any children.

Rabbi Jose said,

> It has been taught, I was once walking on a road and I entered one of the ruins of Jerusalem to pray. Elijah (may he be remembered for good!) came and waited for me by the entrance till I finished my prayer. When I finished my prayer he said to me: Peace be unto you, my master, and I said to him: Peace be unto you my master and teacher. And he said to me: My son, why did you enter this ruin? I said to him: to pray. And he said to me: You should have prayed on the road. I said to him: I feared that the passersby might interrupt me. And he said to me: You should have prayed a short prayer. At the same time I learned

---

35. Melvin Jay Glatt, *A Study of Midrashic Response to Group Trauma*, ibid., p. 47.

from him three things: I learned that one does not enter a ruin; and I learned that one may pray on the road; and I learned that he who prays on the road should pray a short prayer. And he said to me: My son, what voice did you hear in this ruin? I said to him: I heard a *bat kol* (heavenly voice) cooing like a dove and saying: Woe to the children for whose sins I destroyed my house and burnt my temple and exiled them among the nations of the world! And he said to me: By your life and the life of your head! Not only this time does it say so, but every day three times it says so; furthermore whenever Israel enters synagogues and homes of study and responds "May his great name be blessed," the Holy One, Blessed be he shakes his head and says: "Happy is the king who is thus praised in his house; how great is the pain of the father, having banished his children; woe to the children banished from their father's table."[36]

In the aforementioned section of the Talmud, in a certain sense, parity is achieved between the suffering of God and man. The banishing of Israel means that God is also now alone. The children of Israel are now orphaned, and God is now the bereaved parent who must face the void of not having His children lavish Him with adoration and praise.

JOB'S HEALING WITHOUT GOD'S ANSWER

The citation above illustrates how the tradition sought to comfort the lonely and the afflicted by portraying a God who Himself

---

36. *Berachot* 3a.

underwent comparable experiences. Similarly, the greatest act of empathy that God is able to perform for Job is to be with him in his hour of pain. As many have pointed out, Job never receives an answer from God. God's appearance out of the whirlwind does not answer the charge; it does not even touch upon it. As Martin Buber writes: The true answer that Job receives is God's appearance, only that distance turns into nearness that his eyes see Him (Job 42:5) that he knows Him again. Nothing is explained, nothing adjusted; wrong has not become right nor cruelty kindness. Nothing has happened, but that man again hears God's address.[37]

How man again or specifically Job hears God's voice, how he experiences His nearness is not revealed to the reader. But one thing should be clear to the modern reader: The regaining of a religious outlook, and once again feeling the presence of God, cannot be minimized in the therapeutic setting.

It was Carl Gustav Jung, Sigmund Freud's rival, who, based upon the hundreds of patients he treated, spoke of the relationship between a healthy religious outlook and man being saved from mental disorders. Jung once remarked:

> During the past thirty years people from all civilized countries of the earth have consulted me. I have treated many hundreds of patients, the larger number being Protestants, the smaller number Jews and no more than five or six believing Catholics. Among all my patients in the second half of life—that is to say, over thirty-five—there has not been one whose problem in the last resort was not that of finding a religious outlook on life. It is safe to say that everyone of them fell ill because he had lost that which the living religions of every age have given to their

---

37. Martin Buber, *At the Turning* (New York: Farrar, Strauss & Young, 1952), pp. 61–62.

followers and none of them has been really healed who did not regain his religious outlook.[38]

Job regains his perspective and belief in the goodness of God through a daytime theophony out of a storm. The author of the book seems to be saying that if God reveals Himself to mortal man and instructs him, there is then no need to doubt God's providence and His concern for all creatures of this world.

The answer to the book, which comes from the realm of revelation and not simply wisdom, gives the book its uniquely Jewish flavor. The healing process takes place as soon as Job experiences the presence of God.

One is often disappointed in not finding any progression in the book from Job's lament over his cruel fate in chapter three to his affirmation of God's ways at the conclusion of the book. The reader is apt to think that God's revelation is something that comes upon Job suddenly, that there is a cataclysmic metamorphosis that suddenly overtakes him.

Such a reading removes the book from the way we ordinarily perceive reality. The following observation of C.S. Lewis is noteworthy in trying to come to grips with the enigma of how Job eventually perceives the presence of God. Lewis writes:

In grief nothing stays put. One keeps emerging from a phase but it always recurs. Everything repeats. Am I going in circles or dare I hope I am on a spiral? Grief is like a long valley, a winding valley where any bend may reveal a totally new landscape. As I've already noted not every bend does. Sometimes the surprise is the opposite one; you are presented with the same sort of country you thought you had left behind miles ago. That is when you wonder

---

38. Carl Gustav Jung, *Modern Man in Search of a Soul* (London: Kegan Paul, 1933), p. 264.

whether the valley isn't a circular trench. But it isn't. There
are partial recurrences but the sequence doesn't repeat.[39]

In the grieving process, for the man of faith there will be
repeated feelings of disbelief and recrimination against God before full-fledged therapeutic grief ensues. It is difficult, as indicated earlier, to find a working-through process in Job's grief.
Perhaps some progression of coming to some kind of reconciliation with his predicament may be found with the appearance of
the young Elihu after the rounds of the theological debates that
Job has with his three friends, Eliphaz, Bildad, and Zofar.

Kahn points out that Elihu exhorts all the friends to join in a
group endeavor to search out the truth:

"Let us examine for ourselves what is right. Let us together
establish the true good." (34:4) He makes them into a group again
by using the words "let us." It would be possible that Job could
become more accessible to Elihu's message by reason of the fact
that he will not be singled out to receive it. As a group phenomenon, this is called universalization and helps to reduce the sense
of isolation and shame.[40]

By Elihu including himself and the three friends in the search,
Job is able to become more receptive to God's revelation, for once
again his pain is being shared by his friends.

When one reads the concluding section of chapter two, one is
impressed by the bonds of intimacy, warmth, and empathy established between Job and his friends. They are with him for seven
full days and nights and engage in all the mourning rites. However, when one moves to the section of the book containing all the

---

39. C. S. Lewis, *A Grief Observed* (New York: Seabury Press, 1961),
pp, 46–47.

40. Kahn, ibid., p. 120. The phenomenon called universalization is
taken from S. Thompson & J.H. Kahn, *The Group Process as a Helping
Technique* (Oxford: Pergamon Press, 1970), p. 63.

speeches, one is left cold by the comfort provided to Job. Elihu's words, in which they together are called upon to solve a problem, solidifies the bond between Job and his friends which had become weakened during all the dialogues. It is this quality of empathy that prompted the rabbis to say, "Either friends like the friends of Job or death."[41]

When Elihu introduces the idea of exploring together why Job has suffered, he and the three friends of Job and Job himself coalesced into a small community sharing in the sorrow of one of its members. The grief of the individual has now re-echoed in the life of the group. Job no longer stands alone in his bereavement. Elihu and Job's three friends have encircled him with the warmth of brotherly sympathy. Elihu has now paved the way for God to appear out of the whirlwind. For in the book, Elihu delivers four speeches, which run from Chapter 32 through Chapter 37. Immediately afterwards, God, in Chapter 38, appears out of the whirlwind.

God's presence and deep involvement in the life of one who is suffering is graphically presented in the talmudic statement attributed to Rabbi Meir: "When a man suffers pain, how does the Shechinah respond? He says my head and my arms are heavy."[42] God, according to Rabbi Meir, becomes weary, one of the symptoms of depression, through the suffering of man. God has internalized into His own being the suffering of man. He has fully empathized with man's condition.

In keeping with the rabbinic statement that just as God is compassionate, so must you be compassionate, as He is gracious, so must you be gracious,[43] the friends of Job, and Elihu, break down the wall that separates the sufferer and all those upon whose way in life the dark shadow have not fallen.

---

41. *Baba Bathra* 16b.
42. *Sanhedrin* 46a.
43. *Sotah* 14a, *Shabbat* 133b.

Once again, through Elihu's initiative, do we find the empathetic bond found earlier in chapter two, where we read: "So they raised their voices and wept and rent their robes and threw dust over their heads towards the heavens." (2:13)

When a person empathizes, he abandons himself and relives in himself the emotions and responses of another person. He is capable of experiencing in himself a mood that is analogous to the mood of the other person as to represent the exact feeling of the other person quite closely.[44]

The power of empathy finds its meaningful expression in

---

44. Robert L. Katz, *Empathy, Its Nature and Uses* (Glencoe, Ill.: Free Press of Glencoe, a division of MacMillan Inc., 1963), p. 4. It is interesting to note that Joseph Albo, in his philosophical treatise, *The Book of Principles*, interprets the 15th chapter of Genesis in which a covenant is struck by severing of different animals into different pieces as symbolic of the empathy that both parties of the covenant should feel toward each other. In Genesis, Chapter 15, Abraham is commanded to take a heifer, a she-goat and a ram, a turtle dove and a pigeon and cut them into pieces. The covenant between the pieces as it is called is understood the following way by Albo.

"The cutting of the animals into two to strike a covenant is symbolic of the tie found between the contracting parties of the covenant. The purpose of the cutting is to tie and bind the love between both parties until they become like one body. One should watch his neighbor like he watches himself. Therefore they would cut an animal into two parts, and the contracting parties passed between the pieces, to symbolize that just like these two pieces were from one animal while the animal was alive, and each part of the body was inextricably interwoven with the rest of the body, likewise the pain felt by one of the contracting persons is always felt by the other. The only thing that is able to separate the different parts of animal is death. Similarly the two people who "cut a covenant", to use the biblical phrase, are like one body and only death can separate them. Based upon this observation, says Albo, if one becomes aware of damage or pain inflicted upon his friend, that he should place himself in a dangerous predicament to save him, just as he would

hasidic circles in the phenomenon called *hitlabshut*. *Hitlabshut* figuratively expressed the rebbe's action in cloaking himself in the garment of the hasid's own thoughts, words, and deeds. These the rebbe examined from within, thereby fulfilling the talmudic command "Do not judge a man until you have arrived at his place. . . ."[45]

"I feel his pain even more than he does," Rabbi Nachman of Bratzlav said of a hasid. "He can at least become distracted from his pain. I cannot." Therein lay the rebbes problem. He had consciously and deliberately entered the dark realm of the hasid's suffering.[46]

However, the rebbe, like any one seeking to help another person in distress, must be in control of his own emotions. If one becomes too emotionally involved with the person in pain, it tends to reduce his effectiveness in helping him.

LIBERATED FROM PRISON OF SELF-CENTEREDNESS

While one cannot underestimate the importance of empathetic understanding of the internal frame of reference of the individual

---

endanger himself to save his own life. Thus the covenant initiated by God in which Abraham cuts the pieces of the animals, followed by God causing smoke and flames to appear which are frequent symbols of the divine presence in biblical theophonies, is, according to Albo, God's way of internalizing into his own being the suffering of man. God has fully empathized with Abraham's condition and Abraham is called upon to reciprocate that abiding and steadfast concern. (Joseph Albo)—This quote is taken from Binah Bamikrah, Isaccar Jacobson (Tel Aviv: Sinai, 1960), p. 23.

45. *Sparks of Light*, ibid,. p. 122.
46. Ibid., p. 123.

that is suffering, the book of Job goes far beyond this point. At the conclusion of the book, Job is liberated from the prison of self-centeredness. As indicated elsewhere in this book, the last chapter records Job experiencing the very presence of God, something he had yearned for from the moment that tragedy overtook him. But experiencing God is often a short-lived encounter. The Book of Numbers, for example, relates the episode of seventy men who undergo a feeling of spiritual ecstasy. (Numbers 11:25) But the text records, when the spirit rested upon them they prophesied but they did so no more. The Sifri adds the comment: "They prophesied that day but never after."[47] There are those whose lives may be illumined by only one mystical experience which is transient.

What could be done for Job to aid him in the building up of a foundation of religious thought which would sustain that unique experience of feeling the presence of God? What would God do, if anything, to avoid having Job relapse into his previous condition which saw him livid with anger and depressed?

In the chapter entitled "Give Me Your Hand" we cited the story from *Berachot* 5b where we learn how Rabbi Johanan was able to provide effective therapy to Rabbi Eliezer by having Rabbi Eliezer remove himself from his egocentric thoughts about his own pain. Rabbi Johanan succeeded in having Rabbi Eliezer focus on something totally unrelated to his own depressive condition.

Similarly, God tries to expand Job's world by having Job pray on behalf of his friends, who have been guilty of untruths in their defense of God. The emphasis is no longer on getting Job to recite his troubles, his feelings, or his fears, but rather to bring the larger world into his life as the preferred path of healing.

Gerald W. Paul, in an article entitled "Expanding the Patient's World," writes: "Since shifting my focus from the patient's diminutive hospitalized world to the living, expansive outside

---

47. Sifri Numbers 11:25.

world, I feel I'm throwing my weight on the side of healing and hope rather than pity and despair. While physicians, nurses, cooks, technicians, and other hospital workers focus on the patients and reinforce their sense of helplessness, I focus on the outside world of connections with people, places and ideas."[48]

Having Job pray on behalf of his friends could not take place earlier in the book while he experienced anger, rage, and depression and when he was more interested in reciting his ailments and grievances. Only after a catalogue of complaints had been uttered by Job and only after working through his emotional and spiritual crisis is he receptive to accepting God's new assignment. Then, in order to facilitate Job's recovery, God provides a new form of therapy, asking Job to cease getting mired down in self-indulgence and self-pity.

The idea of expanding the patient's world bears affinity to a rabbinic concept which states, "He who prays for his friend and he is in need of the same thing his prayers are answered first."[49] The proof text used by one authority to validate this idea is the passage found near the conclusion of the book of Job, "Then the Lord restored the fortunes of Job when he had interceded for his friends." (Job 42:10) Opened to a larger view of reality that now embraces his friends, Job is able to respond to God's goodness and healing power. Only a Job who is on the way to recovery—one who is well integrated—has the capacity to respond to God's invitation to have him pray on behalf of his friends.

---

48. Gerald W. Paul, *Expanding the Patient's World*, in *Ministry*, a magazine for clergy, Nov. 1984, vol. 57, no. 11, p. 16.

49. *Baba Kamma* 92a.

CONCLUDING THOUGHTS

Earlier, we referred to the pastoral function assumed by Moses, David, and God Himself, who is the supreme pastor of Israel. We indicated that the modern day rabbi and clergymen of other faiths have been thrust into a position whereby healing the broken heart and raising those crushed in spirit are important components of their ministry.

In Judaism, *nichum avelim* (comforting the mourners) and *bikur cholim* (visiting the sick) constitute the fulfillment of divine commandments.[1] While they are commandments which are obligatory upon all Jews, the present day trend of rabbis expected to be

---

1. See the "The Meaning of Bikur Cholim" by Norman Lamm presented on November 12, 1995 at the annual conference of the Coordinating Council on Bikkur Cholim. While *bikur cholim* is ordinarily translated as visiting the sick, Lamm states that there is no intimation in the biblical Hebrew that the word *bikur* means "visit." He has not found *bikur* to mean "to visit" in rabbinic literature as well. Lamm suggests that the word *bikur* is related to the word *boker*, which means "morning" or "dawn." When we visit the sick we must open a window for his depressed spirit, bring in light to his darkened soul, let the dawn and what it symbolizes enter the life of the patient.

A different way of understanding *bikur cholim* is that *bikur* comes from the rabbinic word meaning "to examine." The word is used in regard to examining an animal for a blemish to determine if it was fit for sacrificial purposes (Hagigah 9a). Examining the sick would mean to make an assessment of his needs when visiting with him. The world of

experts in offering some kind of counseling to the bereaved or the sick appears to be irreversible. It is reported that the renowned Rabbi Akiva Eger, whose diligence in Torah study and extreme reluctance to spend precious moments in other activities are well-documented, made it a constant practice to visit the sick. Frequently, he would spend the entire night at the bedside of the critically ill patient.[2]

In an article entitled "The Last Day of Maimonides Life," Abraham Joshua Heschel advances the theory that the reason why Maimonides was never able to write a book citing all the sources of his magnum opus, the Mishnah Torah, was due to the fact that he was too preoccupied with his work as a physician aiding those who were suffering. Heschel cites a letter written by the provencal scholar Samuel Ibn Tibbon, who was engaged in preparing a Hebrew translation of Maimonides' philosophical treatise, *Guide for the Perplexed*. Tibbon wanted to visit and consult with Maimonides on some difficulties of the translation. Maimonides responds that he was so weighed down by his responsibilities as a physician that every spare moment that he had was used in studying and teaching Torah, thus he would not be able to meet with Tibbon.[3]

Maimonides' life-long search for personal perfection now finds perfection in the imitation of God. The Talmud extends the concept of imitating the ways of God to visiting the sick: "The

---

the sick is vastly different from the world of those blessed with good health. Therefore, *bikur*, an examination which tries to understand his needs, is in order when comforting one who is ill.

2. Rabbi Shlomo Sofer, Chut Ha Meshulash He-Chadash Tel Aviv, 5723, p. 207. Also quoted in *Judaism & Healing*, J. David Bleich, (New York: KTAV Publishing House Inc., 1981), p. 44.

3. Abraham Joshua Heschel, *The Insecurity of Freedom*, Chapter 20, The Last Days of Maimonides," (New York: Farrar, Straus & Giroux, 1966), pp. 285–297.

Holy One, blessed be he, visits the sick, as it is written, And God appeared to him at Elonei Mamre, so you visit the sick." (*Sotah* 14a)

Maimonides' personal achievement is abandoned for the sake of enhancing God's presence in human deeds to be like God in his actions.[4]

To heal is to do God's holy work. To soothe pain, to prevent grief, to wipe away a tear becomes the supreme privilege of anyone who must come in contact with the helpless, poor, and sick in body and spirit. The alleviation of physical pain is often beyond our control, but alleviation of psychological anguish is something that all of us are capable of providing.

The Talmud relates that the Messiah is sitting at the entrance of the city and he will be recognized by virtue of the fact that he is sitting with those who are suffering all kinds of diseases and binding their wounds.[5] In the same section of the Talmud as cited earlier, the name of the Messiah is Menachem, which means "the one who brings comfort."

The Jewish tradition obligates every one to hasten the days of the Messiah. We do so by offering solace and encouragement to those who suffer, by attempting to motivate them to marshal all their resources and renew their fight for life.

In our study, we have shown that the friends of Job provided companionship at a critical juncture of his life. In their professional capacity, modern day rabbis, as well as clergy of other faiths, must face the ugliness of death and suffering constantly. The problem raised in the book of Job, namely, why seemingly good people suffer, is the Achilles heal of religious faith. What the book

---

4. Heschel, ibid., p. 290.

5. *Sanhedrin* 98a, Rashi adds that the Messiah himself is suffering from leprosy and despite His physical condition He is tending to the needs of each individual leper. He is acting as a nurse carefully binding each sore of the individual who suffers. (Rashi Ad. Locum)

of Job teaches us is that the greatest solace and comfort which God provided for Job was simply being with him. That which was spoken by God doesn't seem to come to grips with answering the riddle of the suffering of good people. It is interesting to note that when I ask mourners to recall what was said to them by friends who visited with them during the period of *shiva*, the overwhelming majority have little if any recollections of the words of condolence spoken. What however stands out vividly in their minds is who came to visit and be with them in their hour of travail. Conversely, they always recall those friends who failed to be with them.

The psalmist speaks of God being with him as he walks through the valley of the shadow of death. It is not the spoken word of God that reassures the psalmist but God's presence. In chapter 73, he goes even further and speaks of feeling the presence of God at all times. In keeping with what we said in the section on nonverbal communication, on how often the touch of another person's hand communicates far more eloquently than words, the psalmist declares, "But I will be with you at all times; you hold me by my right hand." (Psalms 73:23) He concludes by saying, "But it is good for me to draw near to God: I have put my trust in the Lord God that I may declare all thy works." (73:28) What makes the psalmist feel the presence of God is, again, not the spoken word, but rather some experience comparable to the secure feeling of the child whose father takes his right hand. A father takes his little boy by the hand to lead him. The warm touch of father is reassuring to the child. Clasping firmly the son's hand is far greater evidence of father's love than any words spoken by father.

Similarly, the rabbi who is often praised for his ability to speak and who often feels compelled to say something profound to unravel the mystery of the suffering of God's children makes his greatest contribution to the bereaved by being with him or her.

There need not be any explanation of suffering. The rabbi's presence and concern and his entering the dark realm of the bereaved suffering is the greatest act of comfort that he can provide.

When the First Temple in Jerusalem was destroyed, the author of the book of Lamentations, in describing the desolation and suffering of a vanquished nation, cried out: "For these things I weep; mine eye, mine eye runneth down with water because the comforter that should relieve my soul is far from me. . . ." (Lamentations 1:16)

Nothing can be more brutal and devastating than to be alone in a moment of anguish and pain. Conversely, when the rabbis foresaw the advent of the Messiah and looked forward to the Golden Age instead of projecting it in the past, they spoke of Him as having the name of Menachem (the Comforter). The psalmist, with sensitivity and compassion, spoke of the broken spirit as being the sacrifices of God and of God never despising the broken and contrite heart. It remains for us to imitate the ways of God by being comforters to those who desperately need some cogent evidence that they do not stand alone in their moment of pain and agony.

BIBLIOGRAPHY

Arvidson, Rolf. "Aspects of Confrontation" in *Confrontation In Psychotherapy*. Edited by Gerald Adler and Paul G. Meyerson. New York: Science Hall, year, pp. 165–179.

Ausbacher, Heinz L. and Rowena R. Ausbacher. *The Individual Psychology of Alfred Adler*. New York: Basic Books Inc., 1956.

Baker, Wesley C. *More Than a Man Can Take: A Study in Job*. City: Westminster Press, 1946.

Baron, Salo W. *A Social and Religious History of the Jews*. Vol. 2, third printing. New York: Columbia University Press, 1958.

Bereshit Rabbah. Standard Edition, Rom.

Bettelheim, Bruno. *Surviving and Other Essays*. New York: Alfred A. Knopf, 1979.

———. *The Uses of Enchantment*. New York: Alfred A. Knopf, 1976.

Bialik, Chaim N. and Y.H. Revnitzki. *Sefer HaAgadah*. Tel Aviv: Dvir Publishing Company, 5720.

Bible. Masoretic Text.

Birdwhistell, Ray L. *Kinesics and Context: Essays in Body Motion Communication*. Philadelphia: University of Pennsylvania Press, 1970.

Bleich, J. David. "Visiting the Sick" in *Judaism and Healing*. New York: KTAV, 1981, pp. 43–45.

Bokser, Ben Zion. *HaMachzor*. New York: Hebrew Publishing Co., 1959.

Branden, Nathaniel. *The Psychology of Self Esteem*. Los Angeles: Nash Publishing Corp., 1969.

Bright, John, ed. and trans. *Jeremiah*, Anchor Bible Series. Garden City, NY: Doubleday, 1965.

Brown, Driver, and Briggs. *A Hebrew and English Lexicon of the Old Testament* Oxford: Oxford University Press, 1906.

Buber, Solomon, ed. *Eicha (Lamentations) Rabbah*. Vilna: 1899. Reprint: Tel Aviv.

———. *Midrash Mishle*. Vilna: 1893.

———. *Midrash Tanchume*. 2 vols. Lemberg:1883, Reprint Israel: Book Export Enterprises.

———. *Midrash Tehillim*. Vilna: 1897. Reprint Jerusalem: Ch. Vegshal, 1976.

Carr, Arthur C. "Bereavement as a Relative Experience" in *Bereavement is Psychosocial Aspects*. Edited by Schoenberg et al. New York and London: Columbia University Press, 1975, pp. 3–7.

Chesterton, G. K. "Man is Most Comforted by Paradoxes" in *The Dimensions Of Job*. Edited by Nahum N. Glatzer. New York: Schocken Books, 1969, pp. 228–237.

Coordinating Council on Bikur Cholim. *The Meaning of Bikur Cholim*. 1995.

Cossuto, Umberto. *A Commentary of the Book of Genesis*. Jerusalem: Magness Press, 1969.

Dossey, Larry. *The Power of Prayer and the Practice of Medicine*. San Francisco: Harper, 1993.

Dov Erlich-Mashmaut Hargashot ha-Choleh, L'Piskka Hilchatit L'Gabei Shabbat in *Halachah U'Refuah*. Edited by Moshe Hershler. Jerusalem and Chicago: Machon Regensberg, 1980, pp. 185–188.

Encyclopedia of Social Studies. Vol. 2. Article on Identification, p. 584B.

Fackenheim, Emil. *The Jewish Return Into History*. New York: Schocken Books, 1978.

Finkelstein, Louis, ed. *Sifre Dvarim*. New York: The Jewish Theological Seminary, 1969.

Fast, Julius. *Body Language*. New York: Evans and Company, 1970.

Frankl,Victor. *Man's Search for Meaning: An Introduction to Logotherapy*. New York: Washington Square Press Inc., 1963.

Freese, Arthur. *Help for Your Grief*. New York: Schocken Books, 1977.

Friedman, Meir, ed. *Pesikta Rabbati*. Vienna: 1880. Reprint, Tel Aviv: 1962.

Gerber, Israel J. *Job on Trial*. Gastonia, NC: E. P. Press Inc., 1982.

Ginzberg, Louis. *Legends of the Jews*. 7 vols. Philadelphia: Jewish Publication Society, 1954.

Glatt, Melvin J. *A Study in Midrashic Responses To Group Trauma*. New York: Jewish Theological Seminary of America, 1979.

Gonen, Jay Y. *A Psychological History of Zionism*. New York: Mason Charter Publishers Inc., 1975.

Gordis, Robert. "The Temptation of Job, Tradition Versus Experience in Religion." *Judaism* 4, no. 3. (summer 1955): 195–208.

———— *The Root and the Branch*. Chicago: University of Chicago Press, 1962.

————. *Poets, Prophets, and Sages: Essays in Biblical Interpretation*. Bloomingdale, IN: Indiana University Press, year).

————. *Koheleth: The Man and His Word*. New York: Block Publishing Co., 1955.

————. *The Book of God and Man, A Study of Job*. Chicago and London: University of Chicago Press, 1965.

Graetz, Heinrich. *History Of Jews*, vol. 2. Philadelphia: Jewish Publication Society, 1893.

Green, Arthur. *Tormented Master: A Life of Rabbi Nachman of Bratslav*. New York: Schocken Books, 1979.

Greenberg, Hayim. "Dust and Ashes" in *The Dimensions of Job*. Edited by Nahum N. Glatzer. New York: Schocken Books, 1969.

Greenstone, Julius, ed. *Jewish Encyclopedia*. Vol. 5. New York and London: Funk and Wagnalls, 1904.

Gruber, Mayer. *Aspects of Non-Verbal Communication in the Ancient Near East*. Rome: Biblical Institute, 1980.

―――. "The Tragedy of Cain and Abel: A Case of Depression," *Jewish Quarterly Review*, no. 67 (1978).

―――. *Who Is Man?* Stanford: Stanford University Press, 1965.

Hachman, Amos. *Sefer Iyyob*. Jerusalem: Mosad Harav Kook, 1970.

Halevi, A. A., comm. *Midrash Rabbah Shmot*. Vocalized by Y. Toforovski. Tel Aviv: Machabarot L'Safrut, 1959.

―――. *Midrash Rabbah Shmot*. Vocalized by Isaac Z'er Yedler. Vols. 5–7. Bnei Brak, Tifereth Zion: Publication Society, Inc., 1959.

Ha-Levi, Yehuda. *Kuzari*. Edited by A. Zifronti. Tel Aviv: Machbarot L'Safrut, year.

Hall, Calvin S. and Gardner Lindzey. *Theories of Personality*, second edition. New York: John Wiley and Sons Inc., 1970.

Henley, Nancy M. *Body Politics*. Englewood Cliffs, NJ: Prentice Hall Inc., 1977.

Heschel, Abraham Joshua. Death as a Homecoming, in *Jewish Reflections on Death*. Edited by Jack Reimer. New York: Schocken Books, 1974, pp. 58–73.

―――. *God in Search of Man*. New York: Harper Row Publishers, 1955.

―――. *Man's Quest for God*. New York: Charles Scribner's Sons, 1954.

―――. *The Insecurity of Freedom*. New York: Farrar Strauss & Giroux, 1966, pp. 285–297.

―――. *The Sabbath*. New York: Farrar, Strauss & Young, 1951.

―――. *Torah Min Ha-Shamayim B'Aspiklaria Shel Hadarot*. Vols. 1–2. London and New York: Soncino Press, 1962.

Hirsch, Samson Raphael. *The Pentateuch*. Translated by Isaac Levy. Vol. 1. New York: Judaic Press, 1971.

———. *The Pentateuch Haftoroth*. Translated by Isaac Levy, vol. 7. New York: Judaic Press, 1971.

Horovitz, Hayyim S. *Sifre Numbers and Sifre Zutta*. Leipzig: 1917. Reprint, Jerusalem: Wahrmann Books, 1966.

Horovitz, Hayyim S. and Israel A. Rabin, eds. *Mechilta D'Rabbi Ishmael*. Breslav: 1930. Reprint, Jerusalem: Wahrmann Books, 1970.

Jacobs, Louis. *Principles of the Jewish Faith*. New York: Basic Books, 1964, pp. 368–379.

Jacobson, Isaacar. *Binah Bamikra*, Commentary on the Portion of Lech Lecha, Tel Aviv: Siani, 1960, pp. 22–25.

Jackson, Edgar. *Parish Counseling*. New York: Jason Aronson Inc., 1975.

Jung, Carl Gustav. *Modern Man in Search of a Soul*. London: Kegan Paul, 1933.

Kahn, J. H. *Job's Illness: Loss Grief and Integration: A Psychological Interpretation*. Oxford: Pergamon Press, 1975.

Katz, Robert L. *Empathy: Its Nature and Uses*. Glencoe, IL.: Free Press of Glencoe, 1963.

Knapp, Martin L. *Foundations of Non-Verbal Communication*. Edited by Albert Katz and Virginia Katz. Carbondale, Ill.: Southern Illinois University Press, 1983, p. 181.

Kushner, Harold J. *When Bad Things Happen to Good People*. New York: Schocken Books, 1981.

Lamm, Maurice. *Jewish Way in Death and Mourning*. New York: Jonathan David Publishers, 1969.

Landau, Bazalel, ed. *Yalkut Shimoni* Jerusalem: 1960.

Lazerson, Arlyne, ed. *Psychology Today*, second edition. Delmar, CA: CRM Books, 1977.

Leibowitz, Nechama. *Iyun B'Sefer Bereshit*. Jerusalem: Jewish Agency, 1970.

Lerner, Harriet. "Internal Prohibitions Against Female Anger" in *American Journal of Psychoanalysis* 40, no. 2 (1980): 137–147.

Linn, Louis and Leo Schwartz. *Psychiatry and Religious Experience*. New York: Random House, 1958.

Lynch, James J. *The Broken Heart: The Medical Consequences of Loneliness*. New York: Basic Books Inc., 1977.

Mablim. (on Kings 19:9) *Mikraot Gdolot*. New York: M.P. Press, 1974.

Mandelbaum, Bernard, ed. *Pesikta de Rav Kahana*. 2 vols. New York: The Jewish Theological Seminary, 1962.

Mann, James. "Confronttion as a Mode of Teaching" in *Confrontation in Psychotherapy*. Edited by Gerald Adler and Paul G. Meyerson. New York: Science Hall, year, pp. 41–48.

Margulies, Mordecai, ed. *Midrash Vayyikra Rabbah*. 3 vols., second printing. Jerusalem: Wahrmann Books, 1972.

Marshall, Evan *Eye Language: Understanding the Eloquent Eye*. Toronto: New Trend Publishers, 1983.

Mehrabian, Albert. *Silent Messages*. Belmont, CA: Wadsworth Publishing Company, 1971.

Mikraot Gedoloth Neviim and Ketubim, Standard Edition.

Mikraot Gedoloth Torah, Standard Edition.

Mirkin, Moshe Aryeh, comm. *Midrash Rabbah*. 11 vols, second printing. Tel Aviv: Yavnelt Publishing House, 1968.

Mishneh Berurah, Standard Edition. Jerusalem: Torah L'Am, 1960.

Montefiore, Claude G. *Ancienter Jewish and Greek Encouragement and Consolation*, new edition. Bridgeport, CT: Hartmore House, 1971.

Morreal, John. *Taking Laughter Seriously*. Albany, NY: State University of New York Press, 1983.

Moustakes, Clark E. *Loneliness*. New York: Prentice Hall Inc., 1961.

Nathan, Peter E. and Sandra L. Harris. *Psychopatholofy and Society*. New York: McGraw Hill Inc., 1975.

Nissam Gaon, Standard Edition.

Ostow, Mortimer. *Psychology of Melancholy*. New York: Harper and Row Publishers, 1970.

———. "The Jewish Response to Crisis" in *Judaism and Psychoanalysis*. New York: KTAV, year, pp. 235–265.

Parkes, Colin Murray. *Bereavement: Studies in Grief in Adult Life*. Madison, CT: International Universities Press, 1972.

Paul, Gerald W. "Expanding the Patient's World" in *Ministry: A Magazine for Clergy* 57, no. 11 (Nov. 1984): 4–6, 16.

Peake, Arthur S. "Job's Victory" in *The Dimensions of Job*. Edited by Nahum N. Glatzek. New York: Schocken Books, 1969, pp. 197–205.

Pincus, Lily. *Death and the Family: The Importance of Mourning*. New York: Pantheon Books, 1974.

Pirke, de-Rabbi Eliezer. Jerusalem: Eshkol J. Weinfield and Co., 1976.

Pope, Marvin H. *Job*, Anchor Bible Series. Garden City, NY: Doubleday, 1965.

Rabenu Yonah, Standard Edition.

Rank, Otto. *The Trauma of Birth*. New York: Harcourt Brace and Company, 1929.

Rashi, Standard Edition.

Reik, Theodore. *Listening with the Third Ear*. New York: Farrar, Strauss, and Company, 1948.

Ruth Rabbah, Standard Edition.

Saver, Moshe. *Machlool Hamaamarim V'Hapitgamin*, 3 vols. Jerusalem: Mosad Harav Kook, 1961.

Schachter, Zalman M. and Edward Hoffman. *Sparks of Light: Counselling in the Hasidic Tradition*. Boulder and London: Shambhala, 1983.

Schwartz, Matthew B. "The Meaning of Suffering: A Talmudic Response to Theodicy" in *Judaism*, Fall 1983, pp. 444–451.

Shepard, Martin. *Someone You Love Is Dying*. New York: Harmony Books, 1975.

Shir Hashirim Rabbah, Standard Edition.

Shmvlavich, Hayim Lev. *Sichot Musar*. Israel: n. p., 1980.

Shulchan Aruch, Standard Edition.

Soelle, Dorothe E. *Suffering*. Philadelphia: Fortress Press, 1975.

Sofer, Shlomo. *Chut Ha-Meshulash He-Chadesh*. Tel Aviv, 5723.

Soloveitchik, Joseph B. "The Halakha of the First Day" in *Jewish Reflections on Death*. Edited by Jack Reimer. New York: Schocken Books, 1974, pp. 76–83.

Spero, Shubert. "Is Judaism an Optimistic Religion?" in *Treasury of Tradition*. Edited by Norman Lamm and Walter S. Wurzburger. New York: Hebrew Publishing Company, 1967, pp. 203–215.

Sundberg, Norman D. and Leona E. Tyler. *Clinical Psychology*. New York: Appleton Century Crofts, 1962.

Talmud Babylonia, (Bavli) Standard Edition.

Talmud Palestinian, (Yerushalmi) 7 vols. New York: M. P. Press, 1976).

Tanna de-Bei Eliyah. Jerusalem: Lewin Epstein Bros., 1976.

Targum, Standard Edition.

The Torah: A New Translation of Holy Scriptures According to the Masoretic Text. Philadelphia: Jewish Publication Society, 1962.

Urbach, Ephrayim E. *Chazal*. Jerusalem: Magness Press, 1975.

———. *Sages: Their Concepts and Beliefs*. Jerusalem: Magness Press, 1979.

Van Doren, Mark and Maurice Samuel. *Book of Praise Dialogues on the Psalms*. Edited and annotated by Edith Samuel. New York: John Day Company, 1975.

Weisel, Elie. *German Church Struggle and the Holocaust*. Edited by Franklin H. Little and Hubert F. Locke. Detroit: Wayne University Press, 1974, pp. 269–277.

———. *Jewish Digest*, 1972.

———. *One Generation After*. New York: Random House, 1965.

Weiss, Isaac Hirsch. *Dor Dor V'Dorshav*. Vol. 3. Berlin, 1924.

Welpton, Douglas E. "Confrontation in the Therapeutic Process" in *Confrontation in Psychotherapy*. Edited by Gerald Adler and Paul G. Meyerson. New York: Science Hall, year, pp. 251–267.

Wiggins, Renner, Clore, and Rose. *The Psychology of Personality*. Philippines: Addison-Wesley Publishing Company Inc., 1971.

Wrightsman, Lawrence S. and Kay Deaux. *Social Psychology in the 80'S*, third edition. Monterey, CA: Brooks Cole Publishing Company, 1977.

Zeire, Mordecai. *Lasheket Yesh Kol*. Tel Aviv: Education and Culture Centre of the General Federation of Labor Histadruth, 1966.

Zlotnick, Dov, trans. *The Tractate Mourning*. New Haven: Yale University Press, 1966.

Zohar, Vilna Edition, 1882.

INDEX

About the Author

Rabbi Sholom Stern, spiritual leader of Temple Beth El in Cedarhurst, NY, was ordained at the Jewish Theological Seminary in June 1966. A graduate of Yeshiva University, he is a trained pastoral counselor, having received a doctorate in pastoral counseling from the Hebrew Theological College in Skokie, Ill., in 1985. Currently he serves as honorary president of the Rabbi Isaac Trainin Coordinating Council of Bikur Cholim of Greater New York after having served as president for four years. The council promotes compassionate care for the sick, frail, and homebound, and serves as a national clearing house and resource center for the American Jewish Community in the area of *bikur cholim* (visiting the sick). Rabbi Stern is married to the former Batya Rabinowitz and they have two children, Eliyahu Etan and Danya Ronit.